SACRAMENTO ~ ~ ~ BRARY

4

D1031157

WITHDRAWN FROM COLLECTION
OF SACRAMENTO PUBLIC LIBRARY

BRITANNIA

PETER MILLIGAN | JUAN JOSÉ RYP | RAÚL ALLÉN | JORDIE BELLAIRE

CONTENTS

Collection Cover Art: Cary Nord

Assistant Editor: Lauren Hitzhusen
Editor-in-Chief: Warren Simons

VALIANT®

Peter Cuneo
Chairman

Dinesh Shamdasani
CEO & Chief Creative Officer

Gavin Cuneo
Chief Operating Officer & CFO

Fred Pierce
Publisher

Warren Simons
Editor-in-Chief

Walter Black
VP Operations

Hunter Gorinson
VP Marketing & Communications

Atom! Freeman
Director of Sales

Andy Liegl
Alex Rae
Sales Managers

Annie Rosa
Sales Coordinator

Josh Johns
Director of Digital Media and Development

Travis Escarfullery
Jeff Walker
Production & Design Managers

Kyle Andrukiewicz
Editor and Creative Executive

Robert Meyers
Managing Editor

Peter Stern
Publishing & Operations Manager

Andrew Steinbeiser
Marketing & Communications Manager

Danny Khazem
Associate Editor

Lauren Hitzhusen
Assistant Editor

Ivan Cohen
Collection Editor

Steve Blackwell
Collection Designer

Rian Hughes/Device
Trade Dress & Book Design

Russell Brown
President, Consumer Products,
Promotions and Ad Sales

Caritza Berlioz
Licensing Coodinator

Britannia™. Published by Valiant Entertainment LLC. Office of
Publication: 350 Seventh Avenue, New York, NY 10001. Compilation
copyright © 2017 Valiant Entertainment LLC. All rights reserved.
Contains materials originally published in single magazine form
as Britannia #1-4. Copyright © 2016 Valiant Entertainment LLC.
All rights reserved. All characters, their distinctive likeness
and related indicia featured in this publication are trademarks
of Valiant Entertainment LLC. The stories, characters, and
incidents featured in this publication are entirely fictional. Valiant
Entertainment does not read or accept unsolicited submissions of
ideas, stories, or artwork. Printed in the U.S.A. First Printing.
ISBN: 9781682151853.

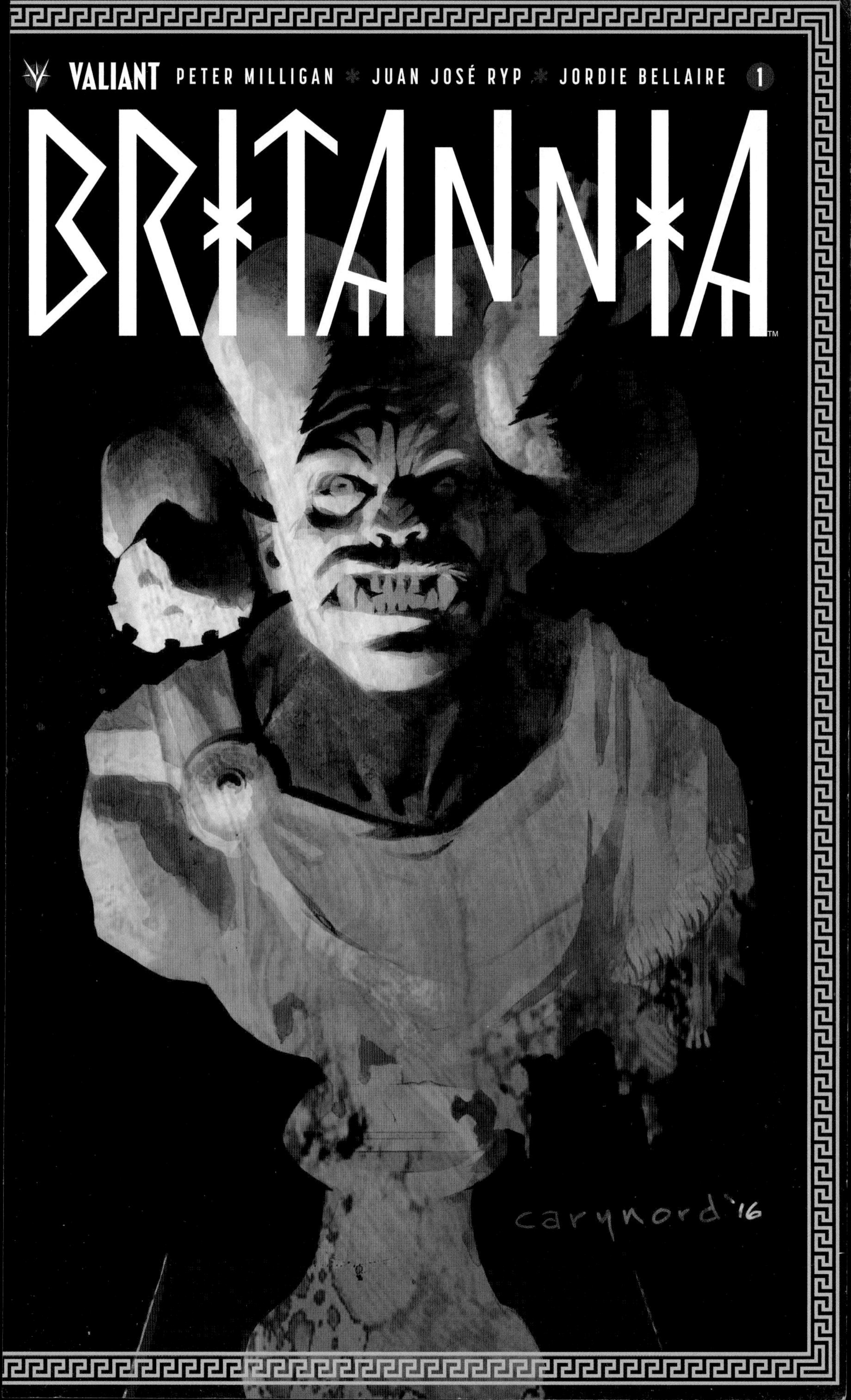
VALIANT
PETER MILLIGAN * JUAN JOSÉ RYP * JORDIE BELLAIRE
1
BRITANNIA™
carynord '16

BOOK I

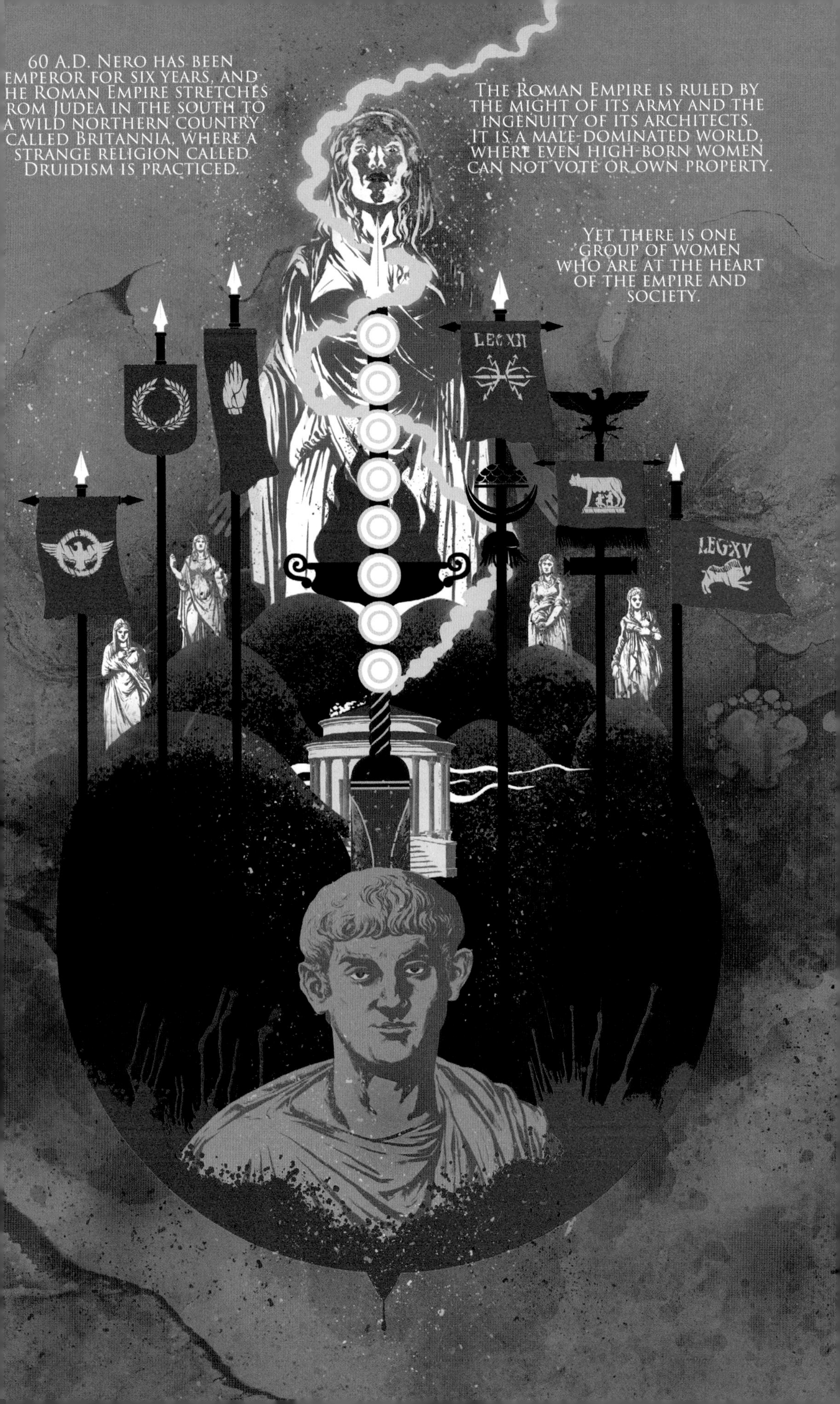
60 A.D. Nero has been emperor for six years, and he Roman Empire stretches rom Judea in the south to a wild northern country called Britannia, where a strange religion called Druidism is practiced.
The Roman Empire is ruled by the might of its army and the ingenuity of its architects. It is a male-dominated world, where even high-born women can not vote or own property.
Yet there is one group of women who are at the heart of the empire and society.
LEG XII
LEG·XV

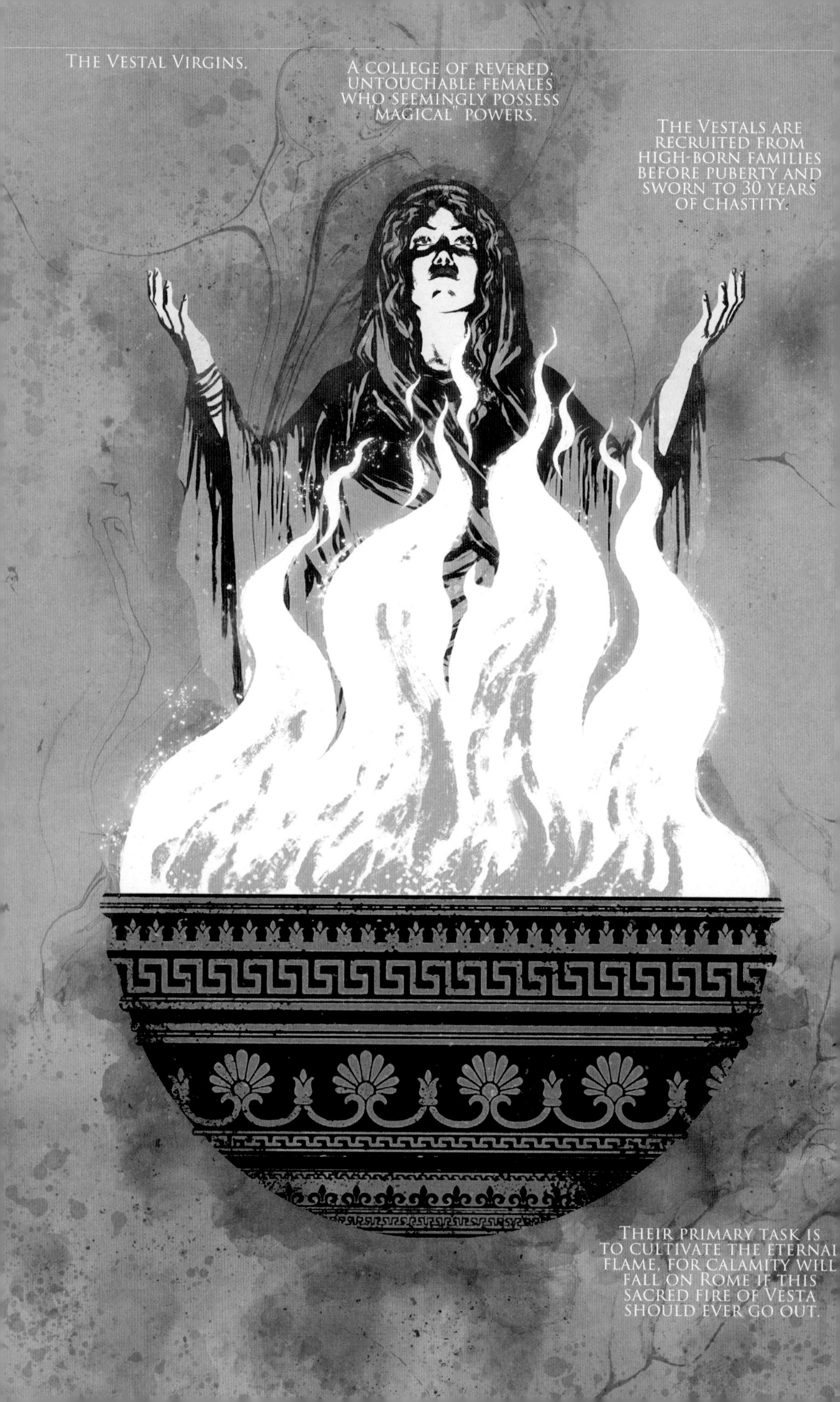

THE VESTAL VIRGINS.
A COLLEGE OF REVERED, UNTOUCHABLE FEMALES WHO SEEMINGLY POSSESS "MAGICAL" POWERS.
THE VESTALS ARE RECRUITED FROM HIGH-BORN FAMILIES BEFORE PUBERTY AND SWORN TO 30 YEARS OF CHASTITY.
THEIR PRIMARY TASK IS TO CULTIVATE THE ETERNAL FLAME, FOR CALAMITY WILL FALL ON ROME IF THIS SACRED FIRE OF VESTA SHOULD EVER GO OUT.

But they do a lot more than tend the sacred fire of Rome: being pure and incorruptible, they are put in charge of important wills and testaments, and guard sacred objects.

Their power is such that they can pardon a convicted slave simply by touching him. They are at the heart of religious life.

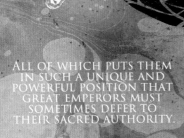

All of which puts them in such a unique and powerful position that great emperors must sometimes defer to their sacred authority.

The head of this powerful organization is Rubria, the Vestalis Maxima, or Chief Vestal...

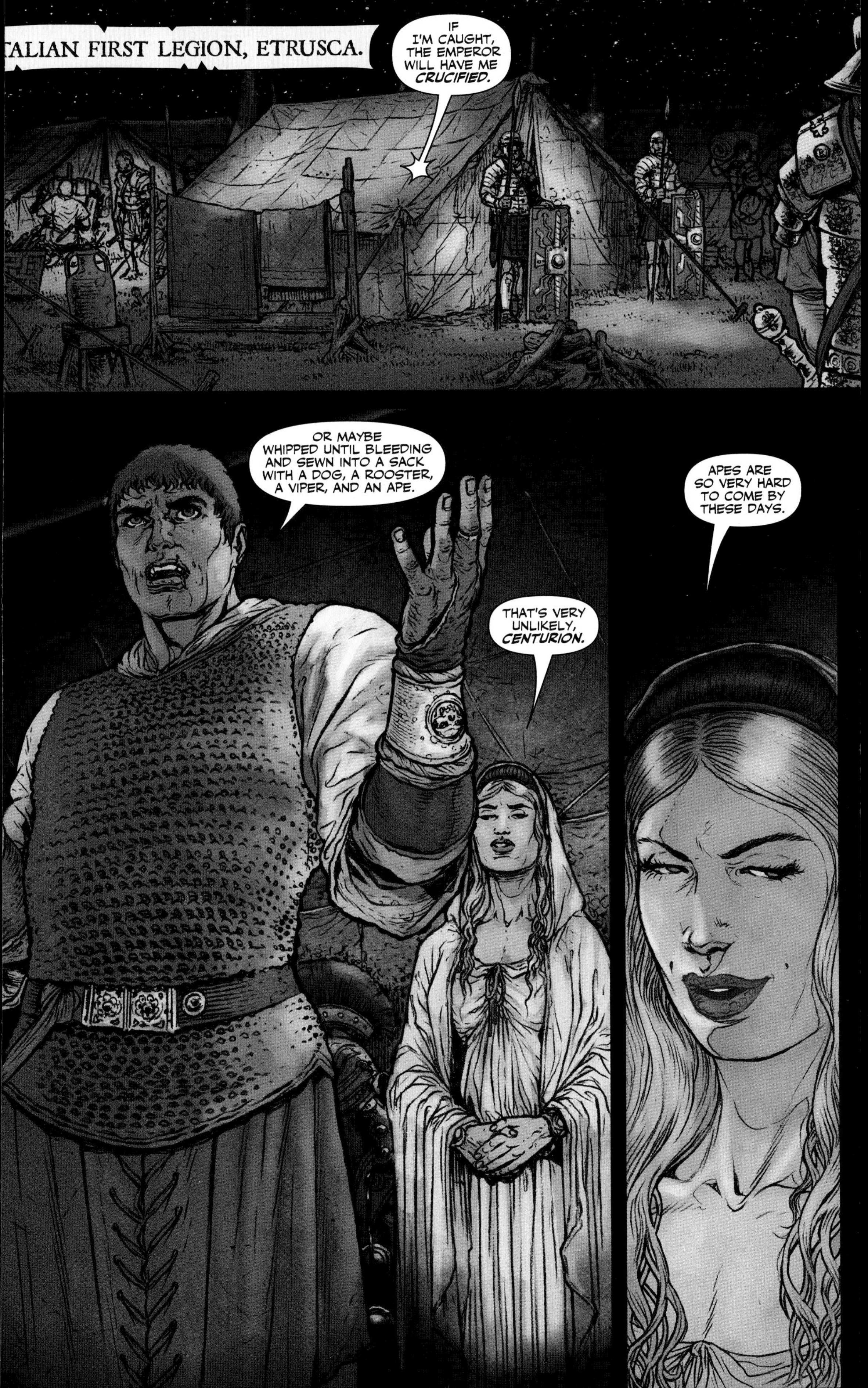

ITALIAN FIRST LEGION, ETRUSCA.
IF I'M CAUGHT, THE EMPEROR WILL HAVE ME CRUCIFIED.
OR MAYBE WHIPPED UNTIL BLEEDING AND SEWN INTO A SACK WITH A DOG, A ROOSTER, A VIPER, AND AN APE.
THAT'S VERY UNLIKELY, CENTURION.
APES ARE SO VERY HARD TO COME BY THESE DAYS.

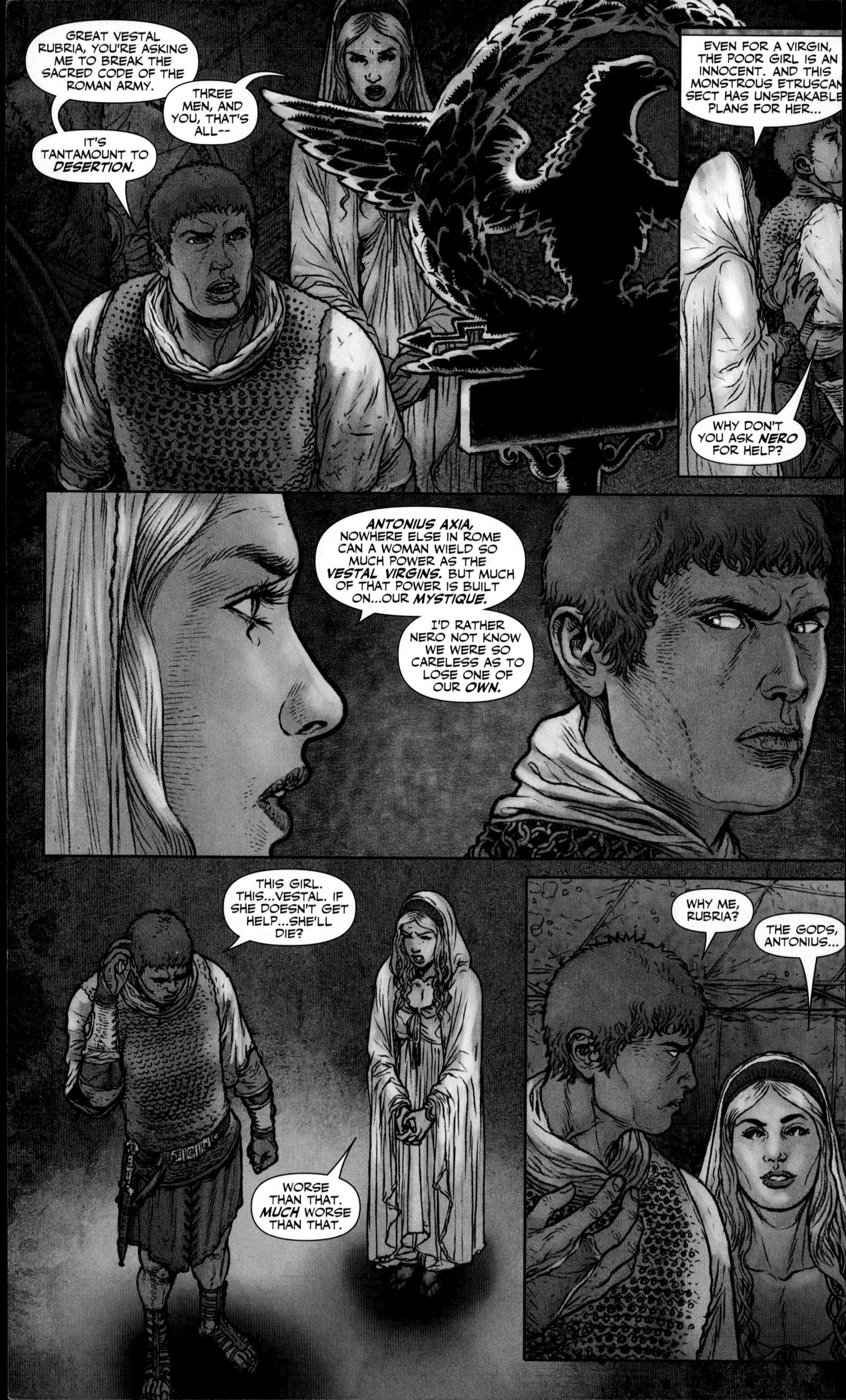
GREAT VESTAL RUBRIA, YOU'RE ASKING ME TO BREAK THE SACRED CODE OF THE ROMAN ARMY.
IT'S TANTAMOUNT TO DESERTION.
THREE MEN, AND YOU, THAT'S ALL--
EVEN FOR A VIRGIN, THE POOR GIRL IS AN INNOCENT. AND THIS MONSTROUS ETRUSCAN SECT HAS UNSPEAKABLE PLANS FOR HER...
WHY DON'T YOU ASK NERO FOR HELP?
ANTONIUS AXIA, NOWHERE ELSE IN ROME CAN A WOMAN WIELD SO MUCH POWER AS THE VESTAL VIRGINS. BUT MUCH OF THAT POWER IS BUILT ON...OUR MYSTIQUE.
I'D RATHER NERO NOT KNOW WE WERE SO CARELESS AS TO LOSE ONE OF OUR OWN.
THIS GIRL. THIS...VESTAL. IF SHE DOESN'T GET HELP...SHE'LL DIE?
WORSE THAN THAT. MUCH WORSE THAN THAT.
WHY ME, RUBRIA?
THE GODS, ANTONIUS...

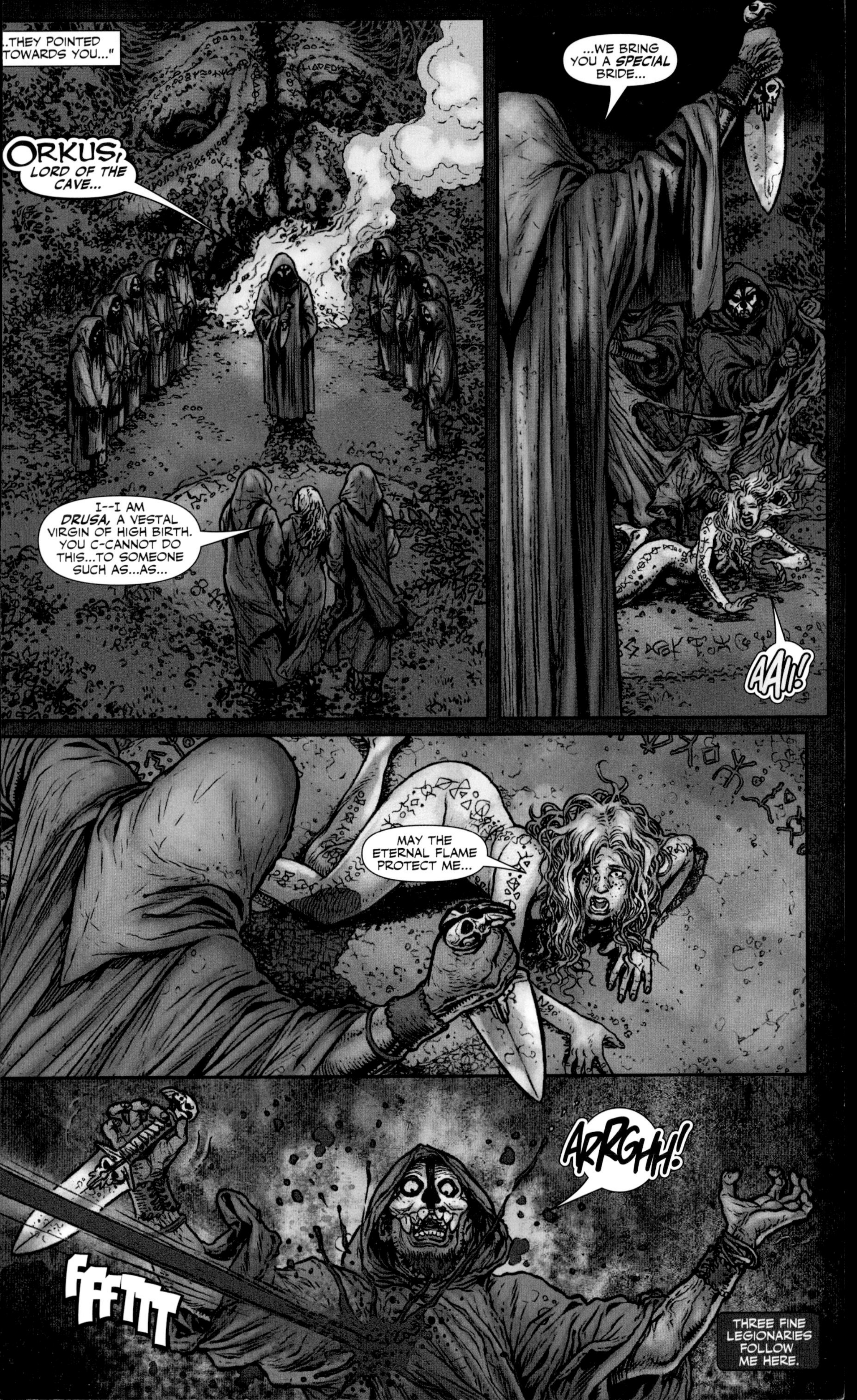

...THEY POINTED TOWARDS YOU..."
ORKUS, LORD OF THE CAVE...
I--I AM DRUSA, A VESTAL VIRGIN OF HIGH BIRTH. YOU C-CANNOT DO THIS...TO SOMEONE SUCH AS...AS...
...WE BRING YOU A SPECIAL BRIDE...
AAII!
MAY THE ETERNAL FLAME PROTECT ME...
ARRGHH!
FFFTTT
THREE FINE LEGIONARIES FOLLOW ME HERE.

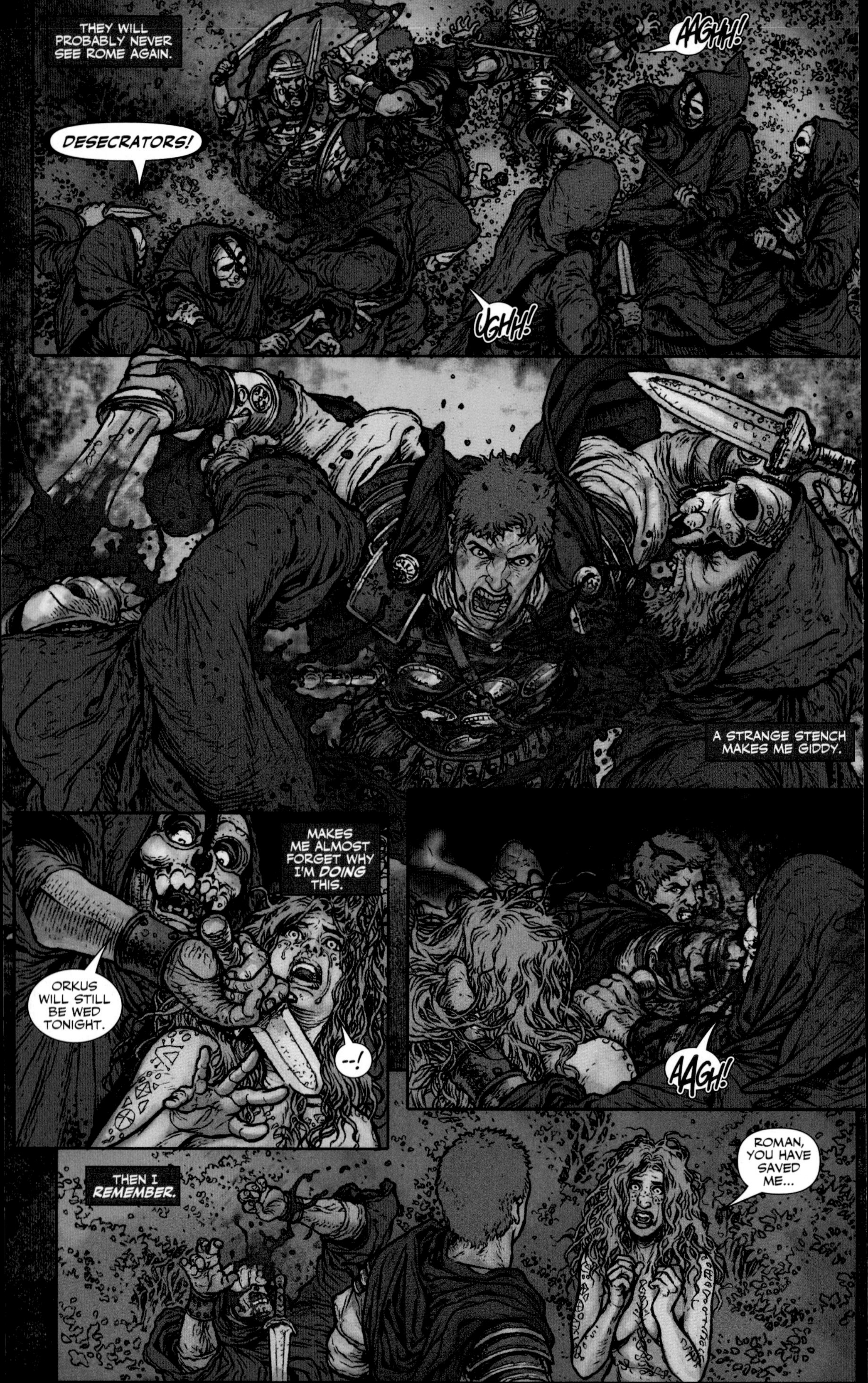
THEY WILL PROBABLY NEVER SEE ROME AGAIN.
AAGHH!
DESECRATORS!
UGHH!
A STRANGE STENCH MAKES ME GIDDY.
MAKES ME ALMOST FORGET WHY I'M *DOING* THIS.
ORKUS WILL STILL BE WED TONIGHT.
--!
AAGH!
THEN I *REMEMBER*.
ROMAN, YOU HAVE SAVED ME...

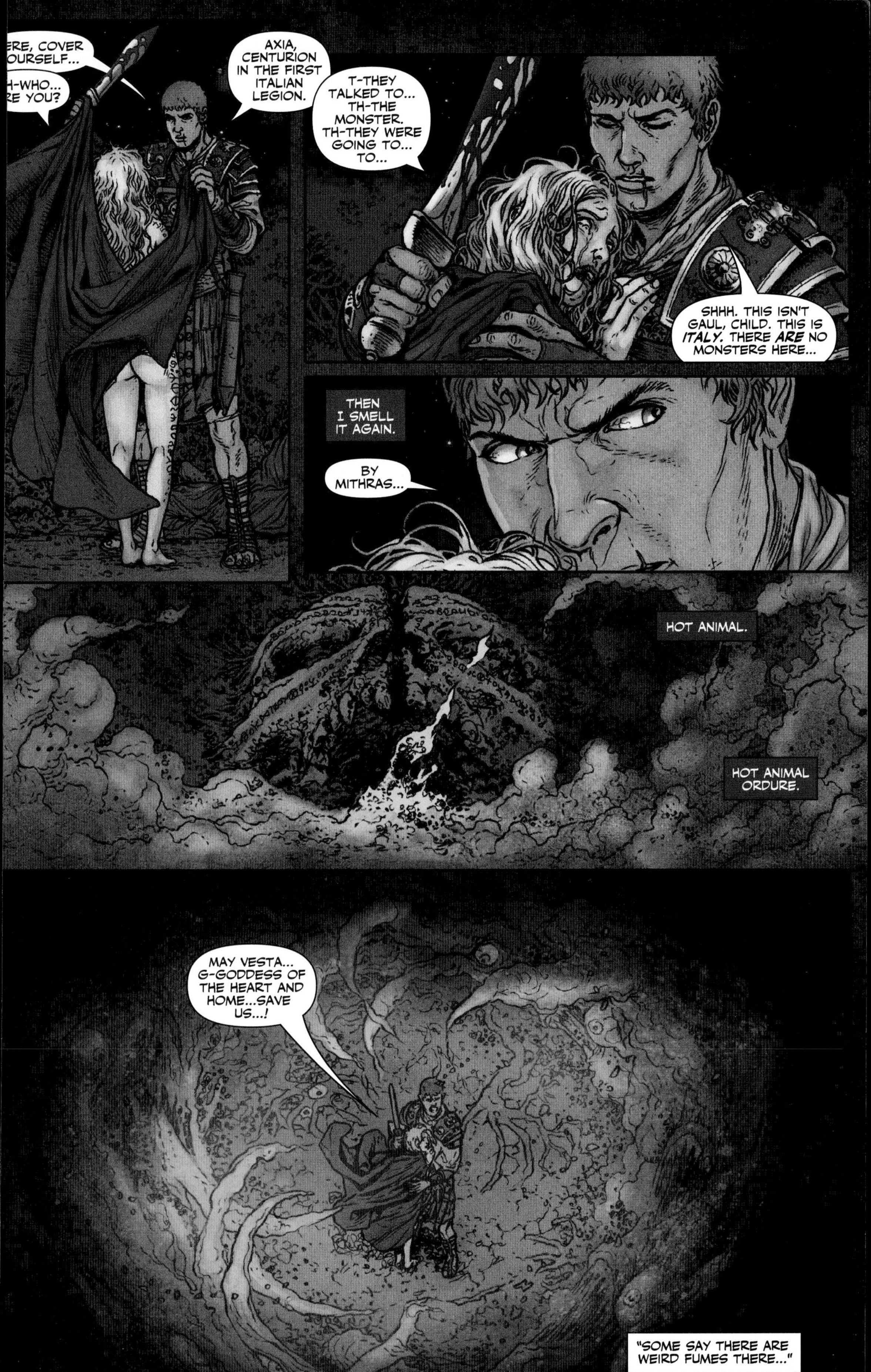
ERE, COVER OURSELF...
H-WHO... RE YOU?
AXIA, CENTURION IN THE FIRST ITALIAN LEGION.
T-THEY TALKED TO... TH-THE MONSTER. TH-THEY WERE GOING TO... TO...
SHHH. THIS ISN'T GAUL, CHILD. THIS IS ITALY. THERE ARE NO MONSTERS HERE...
THEN I SMELL IT AGAIN.
BY MITHRAS...
HOT ANIMAL.
HOT ANIMAL ORDURE.
MAY VESTA... G-GODDESS OF THE HEART AND HOME...SAVE US...!
"SOME SAY THERE ARE WEIRD FUMES THERE..."

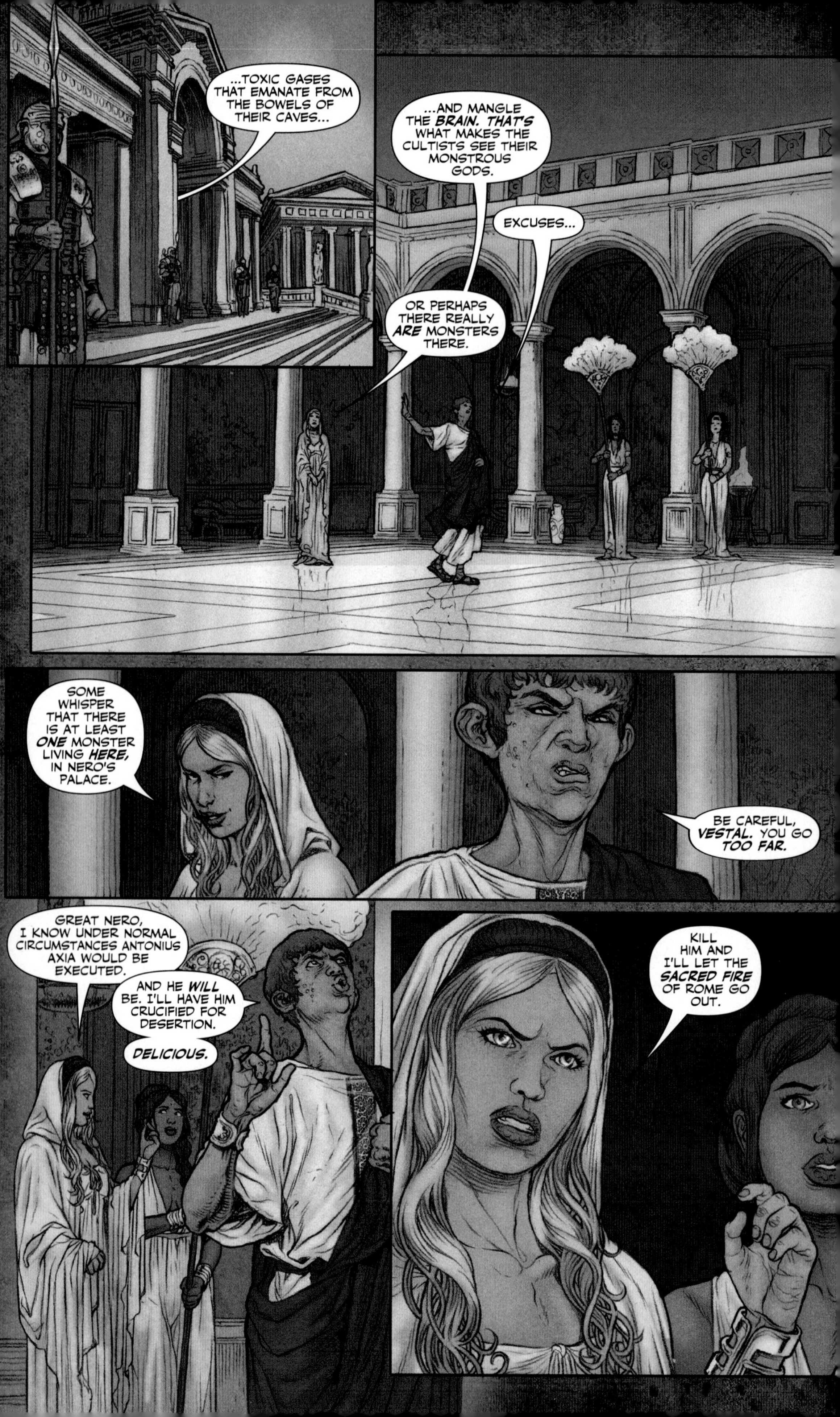
...TOXIC GASES THAT EMANATE FROM THE BOWELS OF THEIR CAVES...
...AND MANGLE THE BRAIN. THAT'S WHAT MAKES THE CULTISTS SEE THEIR MONSTROUS GODS.
EXCUSES...
OR PERHAPS THERE REALLY ARE MONSTERS THERE.
SOME WHISPER THAT THERE IS AT LEAST ONE MONSTER LIVING HERE, IN NERO'S PALACE.
BE CAREFUL, VESTAL. YOU GO TOO FAR.
GREAT NERO, I KNOW UNDER NORMAL CIRCUMSTANCES ANTONIUS AXIA WOULD BE EXECUTED.
AND HE WILL BE. I'LL HAVE HIM CRUCIFIED FOR DESERTION.
DELICIOUS.
KILL HIM AND I'LL LET THE SACRED FIRE OF ROME GO OUT.

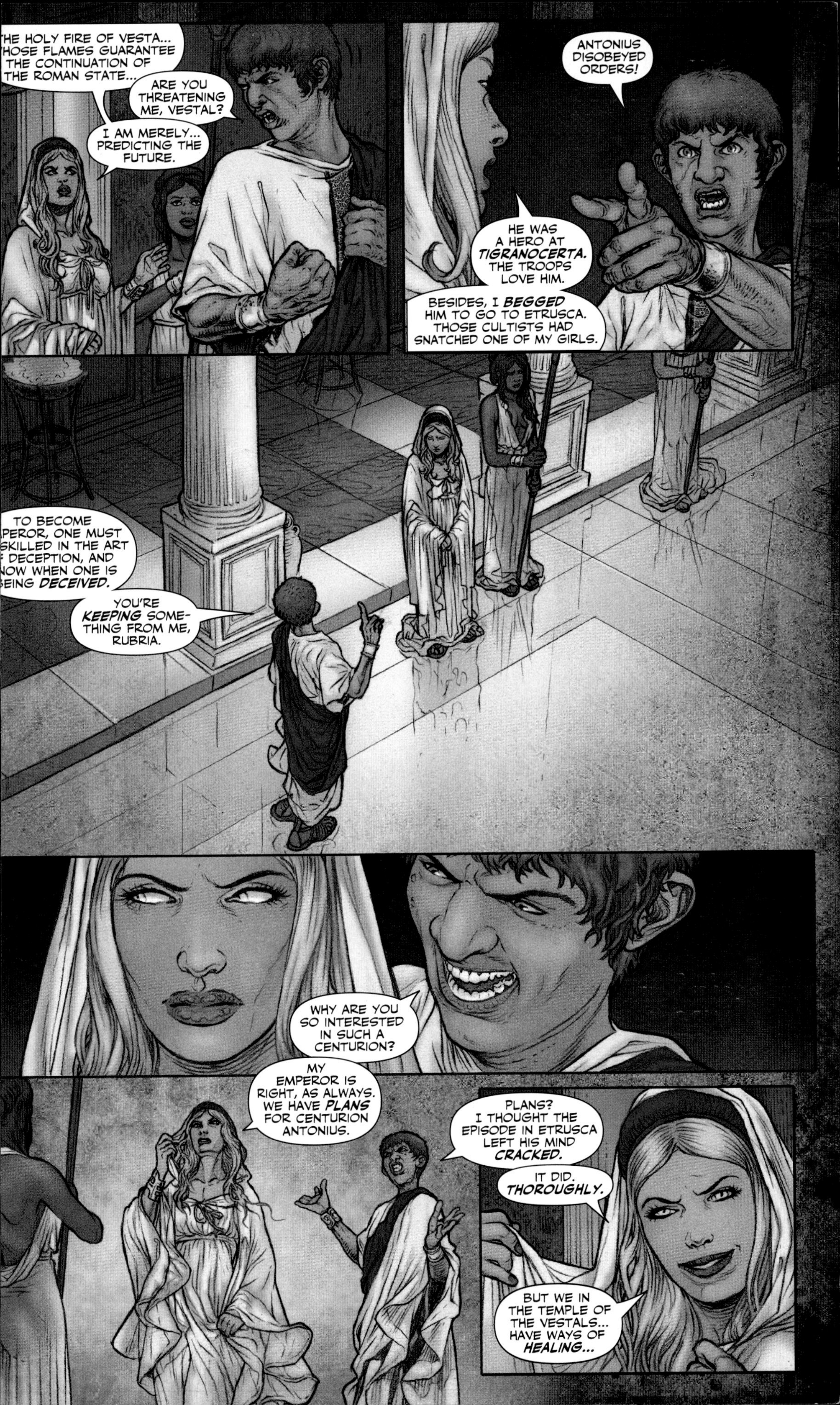
THE HOLY FIRE OF VESTA... THOSE FLAMES GUARANTEE THE CONTINUATION OF THE ROMAN STATE...
ARE YOU THREATENING ME, VESTAL?
I AM MERELY... PREDICTING THE FUTURE.
ANTONIUS DISOBEYED ORDERS!
HE WAS A HERO AT TIGRANOCERTA. THE TROOPS LOVE HIM.
BESIDES, I BEGGED HIM TO GO TO ETRUSCA. THOSE CULTISTS HAD SNATCHED ONE OF MY GIRLS.
TO BECOME EMPEROR, ONE MUST SKILLED IN THE ART OF DECEPTION, AND KNOW WHEN ONE IS BEING DECEIVED.
YOU'RE KEEPING SOMETHING FROM ME, RUBRIA.
WHY ARE YOU SO INTERESTED IN SUCH A CENTURION?
MY EMPEROR IS RIGHT, AS ALWAYS. WE HAVE PLANS FOR CENTURION ANTONIUS.
PLANS? I THOUGHT THE EPISODE IN ETRUSCA LEFT HIS MIND CRACKED.
IT DID. THOROUGHLY.
BUT WE IN THE TEMPLE OF THE VESTALS... HAVE WAYS OF HEALING...

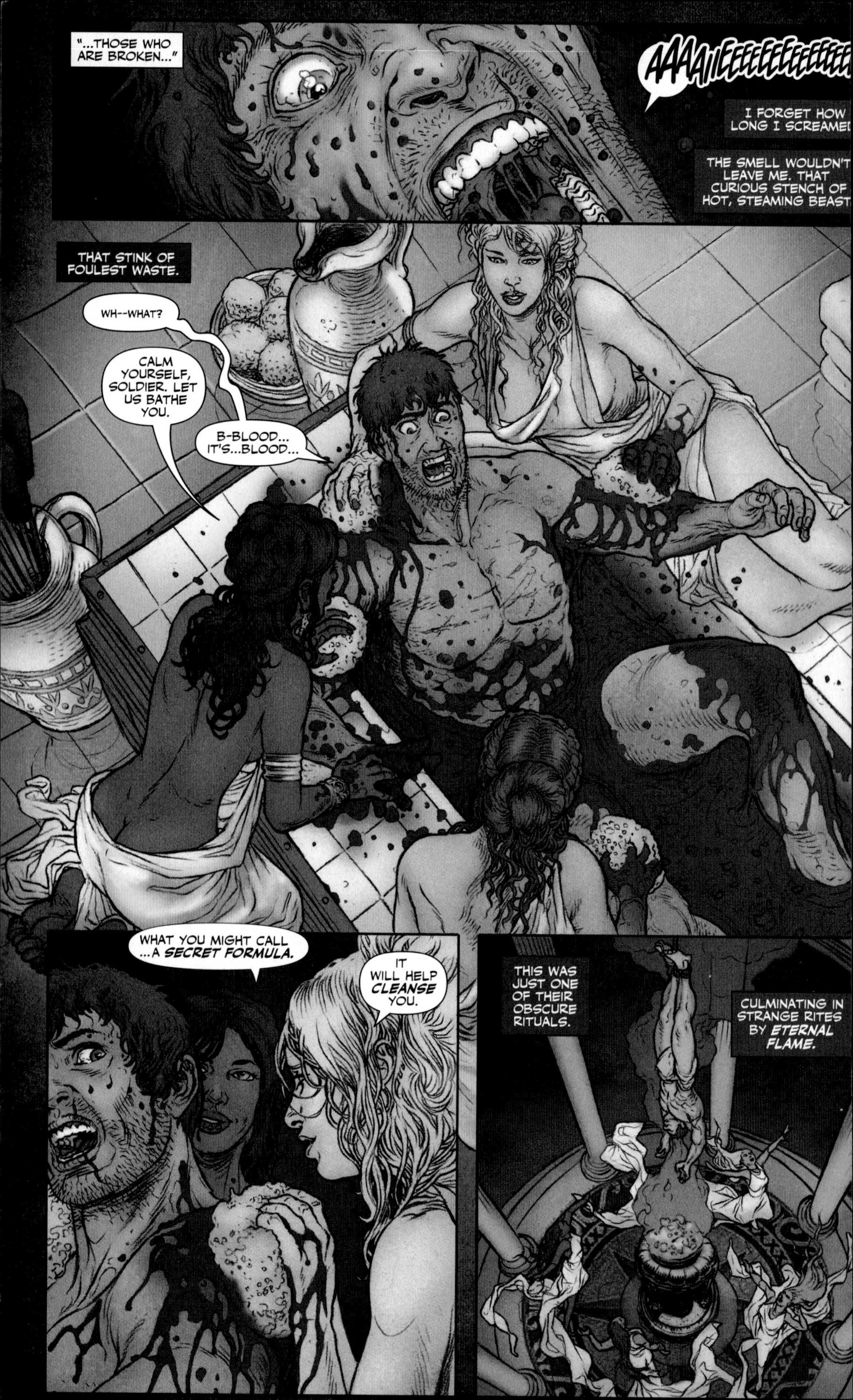
"...THOSE WHO ARE BROKEN..."
AAAAIIIEEEEEEEEEEEE
I FORGET HOW LONG I SCREAMED
THE SMELL WOULDN'T LEAVE ME. THAT CURIOUS STENCH OF HOT, STEAMING BEAST.
THAT STINK OF FOULEST WASTE.
WH--WHAT?
CALM YOURSELF, SOLDIER. LET US BATHE YOU.
B-BLOOD... IT'S...BLOOD...
WHAT YOU MIGHT CALL ...A *SECRET FORMULA.*
IT WILL HELP *CLEANSE* YOU.
THIS WAS JUST ONE OF THEIR OBSCURE RITUALS.
CULMINATING IN STRANGE RITES BY *ETERNAL FLAME.*

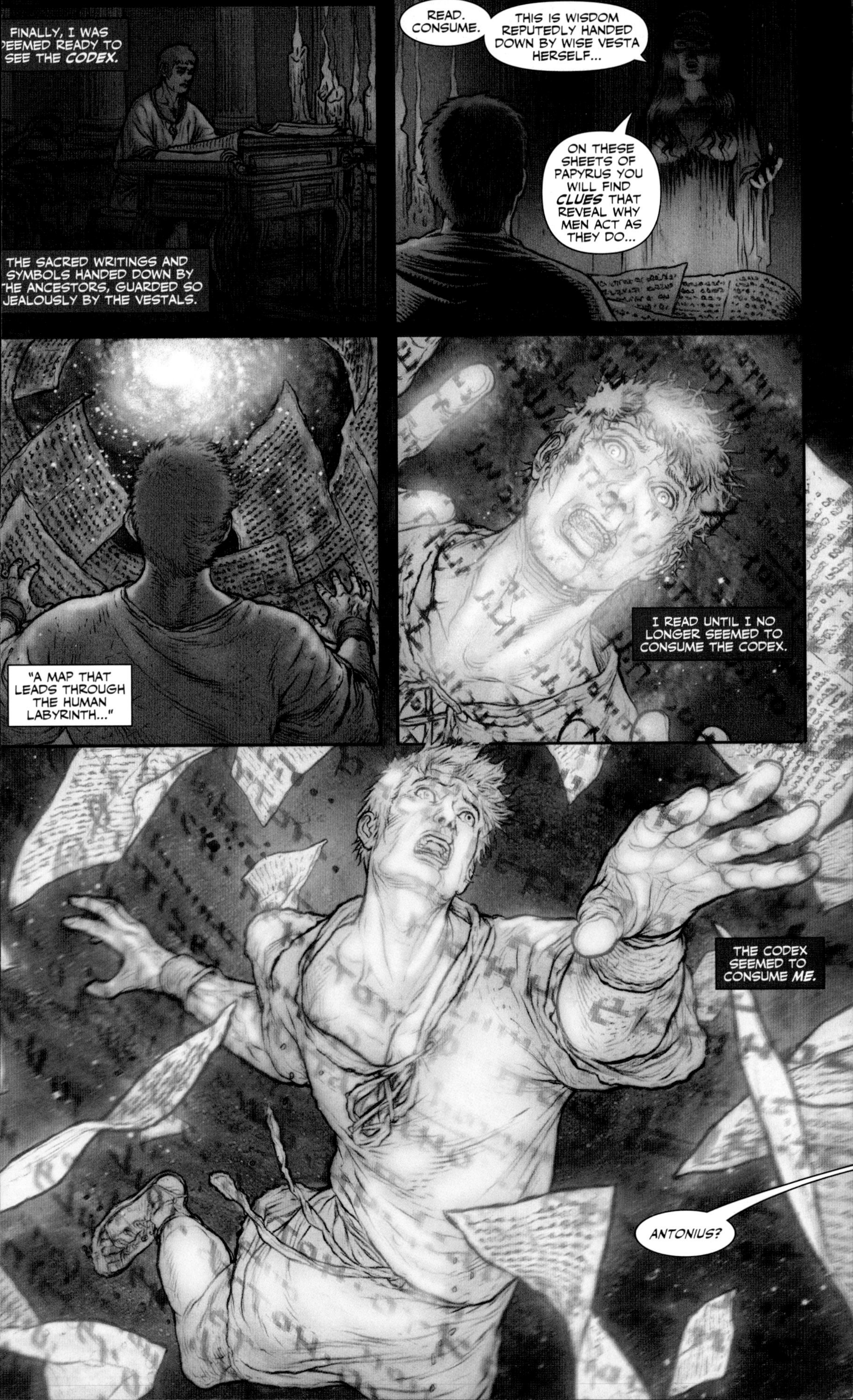

FINALLY, I WAS DEEMED READY TO SEE THE *CODEX.*
THE SACRED WRITINGS AND SYMBOLS HANDED DOWN BY THE ANCESTORS, GUARDED SO JEALOUSLY BY THE VESTALS.
READ. CONSUME.
THIS IS WISDOM REPUTEDLY HANDED DOWN BY WISE VESTA HERSELF...
ON THESE SHEETS OF PAPYRUS YOU WILL FIND ***CLUES*** THAT REVEAL WHY MEN ACT AS THEY DO...
"A MAP THAT LEADS THROUGH THE HUMAN LABYRINTH..."
I READ UNTIL I NO LONGER SEEMED TO CONSUME THE CODEX.
THE CODEX SEEMED TO CONSUME ***ME.***
ANTONIUS?

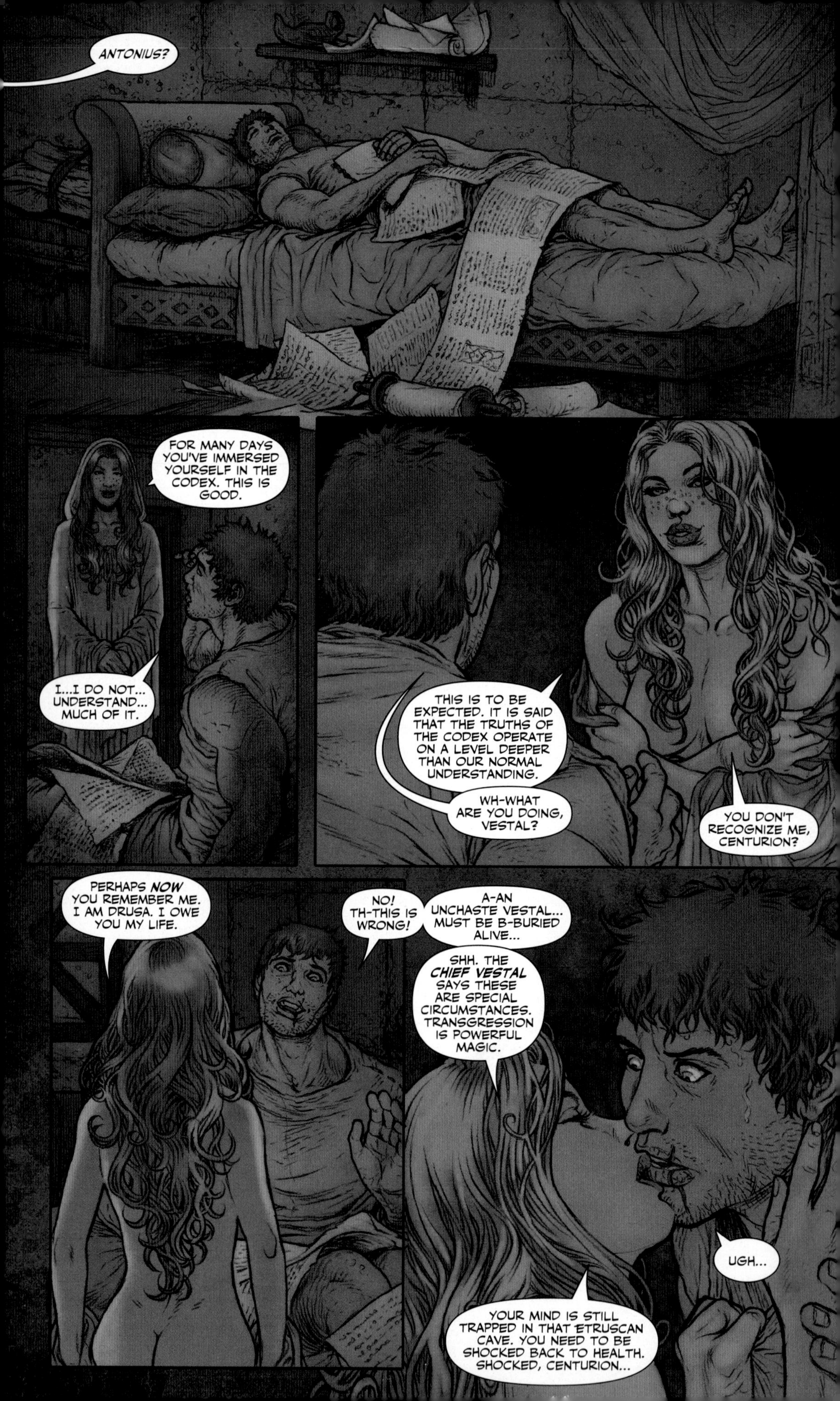
ANTONIUS?
FOR MANY DAYS YOU'VE IMMERSED YOURSELF IN THE CODEX. THIS IS GOOD.
I...I DO NOT... UNDERSTAND... MUCH OF IT.
THIS IS TO BE EXPECTED. IT IS SAID THAT THE TRUTHS OF THE CODEX OPERATE ON A LEVEL DEEPER THAN OUR NORMAL UNDERSTANDING.
WH-WHAT ARE YOU DOING, VESTAL?
YOU DON'T RECOGNIZE ME, CENTURION?
PERHAPS NOW YOU REMEMBER ME. I AM DRUSA. I OWE YOU MY LIFE.
NO! TH-THIS IS WRONG!
A-AN UNCHASTE VESTAL... MUST BE B-BURIED ALIVE...
SHH. THE CHIEF VESTAL SAYS THESE ARE SPECIAL CIRCUMSTANCES. TRANSGRESSION IS POWERFUL MAGIC.
UGH...
YOUR MIND IS STILL TRAPPED IN THAT ETRUSCAN CAVE. YOU NEED TO BE SHOCKED BACK TO HEALTH. SHOCKED, CENTURION...

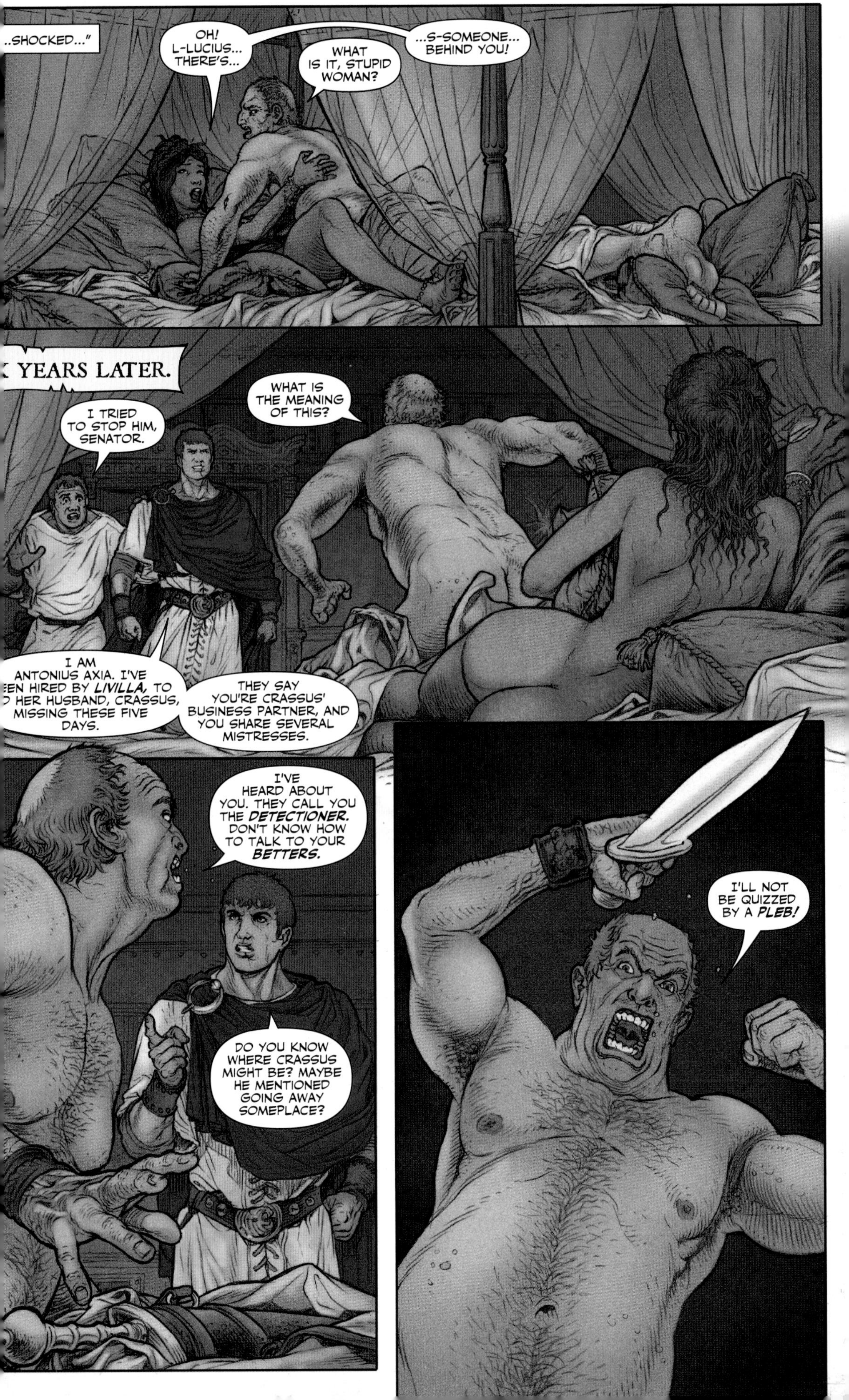
..SHOCKED..."
OH! L-LUCIUS... THERE'S...
WHAT IS IT, STUPID WOMAN?
...S-SOMEONE... BEHIND YOU!
YEARS LATER.
I TRIED TO STOP HIM, SENATOR.
WHAT IS THE MEANING OF THIS?
I AM ANTONIUS AXIA. I'VE EEN HIRED BY LIVILLA, TO D HER HUSBAND, CRASSUS, MISSING THESE FIVE DAYS.
THEY SAY YOU'RE CRASSUS' BUSINESS PARTNER, AND YOU SHARE SEVERAL MISTRESSES.
I'VE HEARD ABOUT YOU. THEY CALL YOU THE DETECTIONER. DON'T KNOW HOW TO TALK TO YOUR BETTERS.
DO YOU KNOW WHERE CRASSUS MIGHT BE? MAYBE HE MENTIONED GOING AWAY SOMEPLACE?
I'LL NOT BE QUIZZED BY A PLEB!

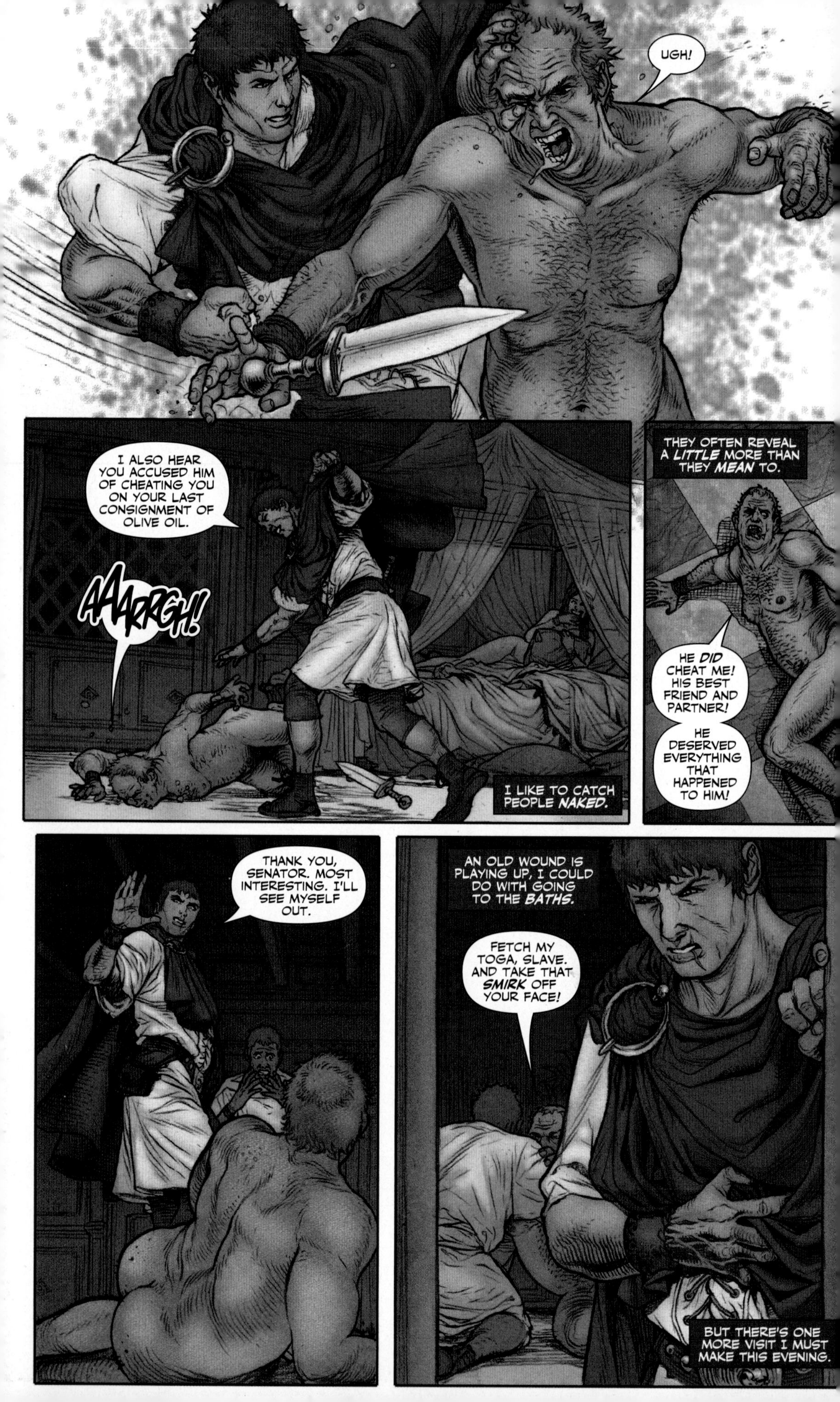
UGH!
I ALSO HEAR YOU ACCUSED HIM OF CHEATING YOU ON YOUR LAST CONSIGNMENT OF OLIVE OIL.
AAARRGH!
I LIKE TO CATCH PEOPLE NAKED.
THEY OFTEN REVEAL A LITTLE MORE THAN THEY MEAN TO.
HE DID CHEAT ME! HIS BEST FRIEND AND PARTNER!
HE DESERVED EVERYTHING THAT HAPPENED TO HIM!
THANK YOU, SENATOR. MOST INTERESTING. I'LL SEE MYSELF OUT.
AN OLD WOUND IS PLAYING UP, I COULD DO WITH GOING TO THE BATHS.
FETCH MY TOGA, SLAVE. AND TAKE THAT SMIRK OFF YOUR FACE!
BUT THERE'S ONE MORE VISIT I MUST MAKE THIS EVENING.

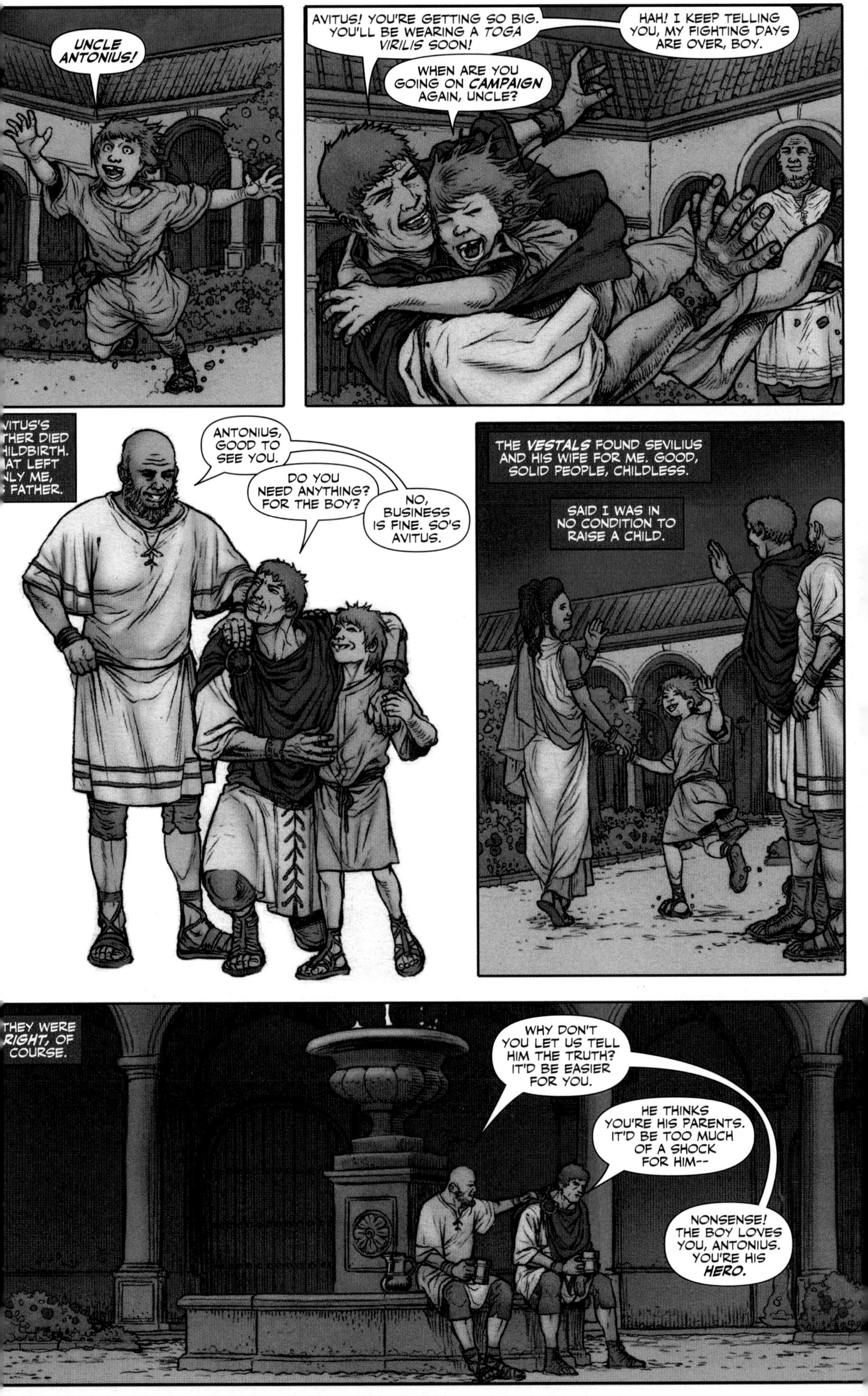

UNCLE ANTONIUS!
AVITUS! YOU'RE GETTING SO BIG. YOU'LL BE WEARING A *TOGA VIRILIS* SOON!
WHEN ARE YOU GOING ON *CAMPAIGN* AGAIN, UNCLE?
HAH! I KEEP TELLING YOU, MY FIGHTING DAYS ARE OVER, BOY.
VITUS'S THER DIED HILDBIRTH. AT LEFT NLY ME, FATHER.
ANTONIUS, GOOD TO SEE YOU.
DO YOU NEED ANYTHING? FOR THE BOY?
NO, BUSINESS IS FINE. SO'S AVITUS.
THE *VESTALS* FOUND SEVILIUS AND HIS WIFE FOR ME. GOOD, SOLID PEOPLE, CHILDLESS.
SAID I WAS IN NO CONDITION TO RAISE A CHILD.
THEY WERE *RIGHT,* OF COURSE.
WHY DON'T YOU LET US TELL HIM THE TRUTH? IT'D BE EASIER FOR YOU.
HE THINKS YOU'RE HIS PARENTS. IT'D BE TOO MUCH OF A SHOCK FOR HIM--
NONSENSE! THE BOY LOVES YOU, ANTONIUS. YOU'RE HIS *HERO.*

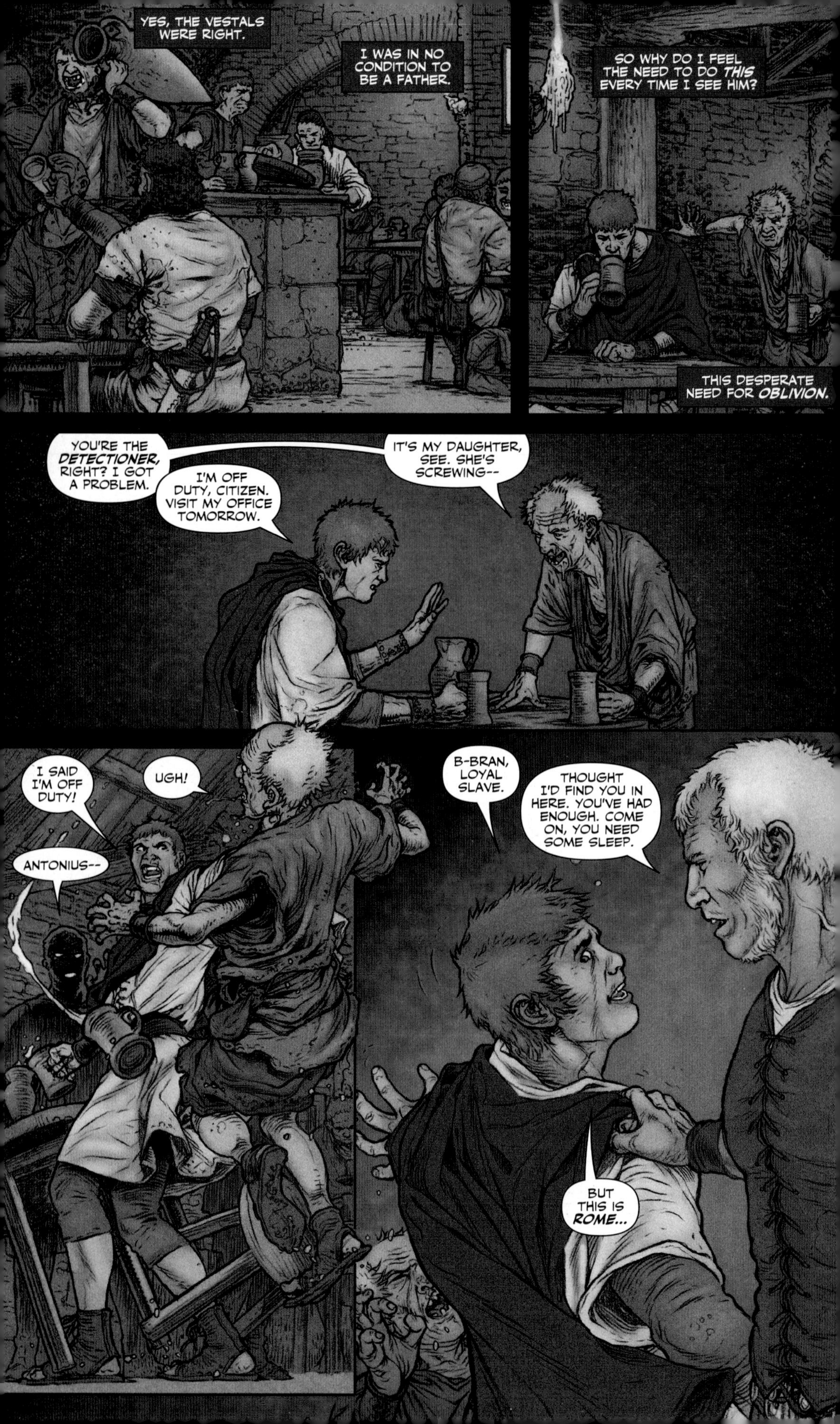
YES, THE VESTALS WERE RIGHT.
I WAS IN NO CONDITION TO BE A FATHER.
SO WHY DO I FEEL THE NEED TO DO *THIS* EVERY TIME I SEE HIM?
THIS DESPERATE NEED FOR *OBLIVION.*
YOU'RE THE *DETECTIONER,* RIGHT? I GOT A PROBLEM.
I'M OFF DUTY, CITIZEN. VISIT MY OFFICE TOMORROW.
IT'S MY DAUGHTER, SEE. SHE'S SCREWING--
I SAID I'M OFF DUTY!
UGH!
ANTONIUS--
B-BRAN, LOYAL SLAVE.
THOUGHT I'D FIND YOU IN HERE. YOU'VE HAD ENOUGH. COME ON, YOU NEED SOME SLEEP.
BUT THIS IS *ROME...*

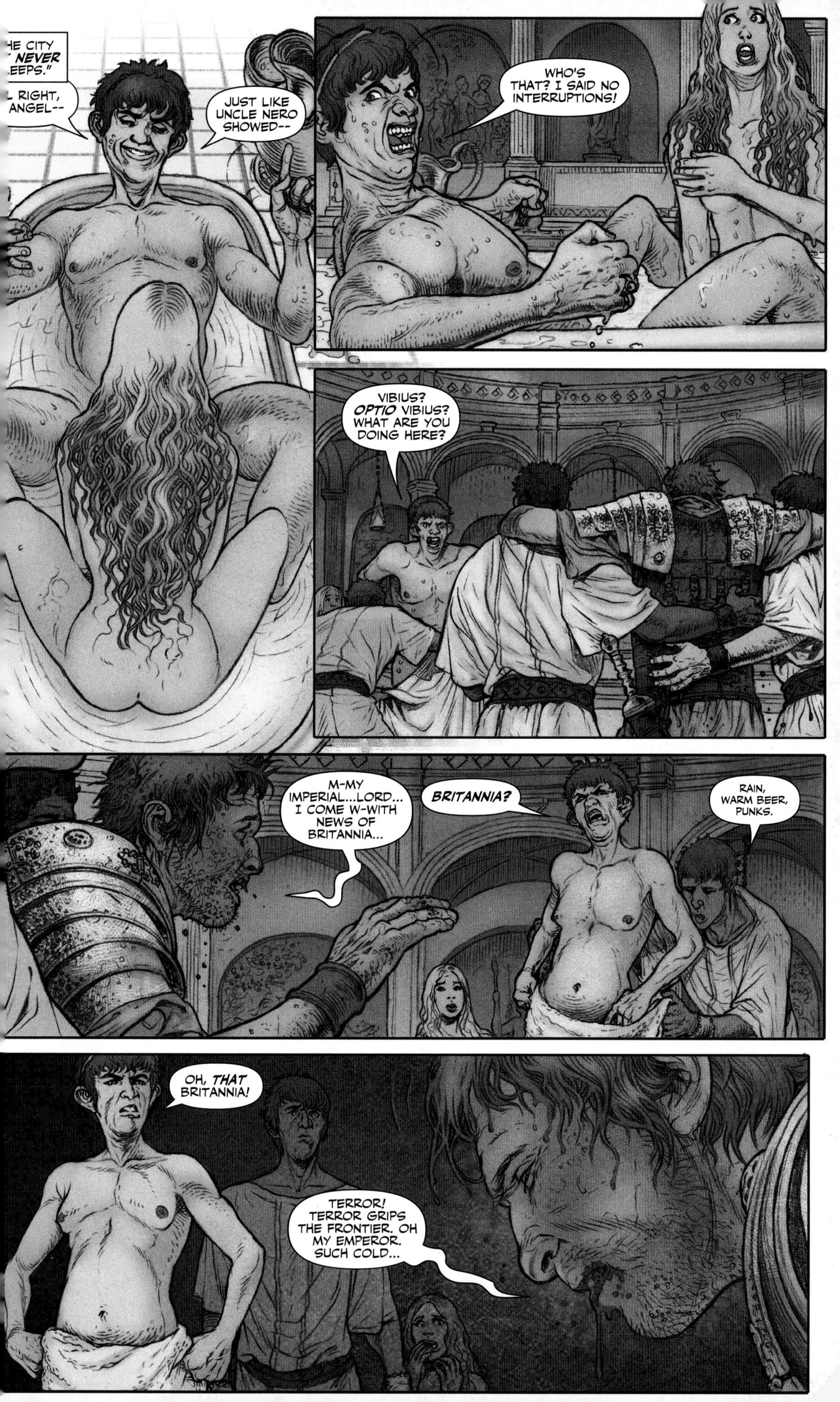

HE CITY
NEVER
EEPS."
L RIGHT,
ANGEL--
JUST LIKE UNCLE NERO SHOWED--
WHO'S THAT? I SAID NO INTERRUPTIONS!
VIBIUS? *OPTIO* VIBIUS? WHAT ARE YOU DOING HERE?
M-MY IMPERIAL...LORD... I COME W-WITH NEWS OF BRITANNIA...
BRITANNIA?
RAIN, WARM BEER, PUNKS.
OH, *THAT* BRITANNIA!
TERROR! TERROR GRIPS THE FRONTIER. OH MY EMPEROR. SUCH COLD...

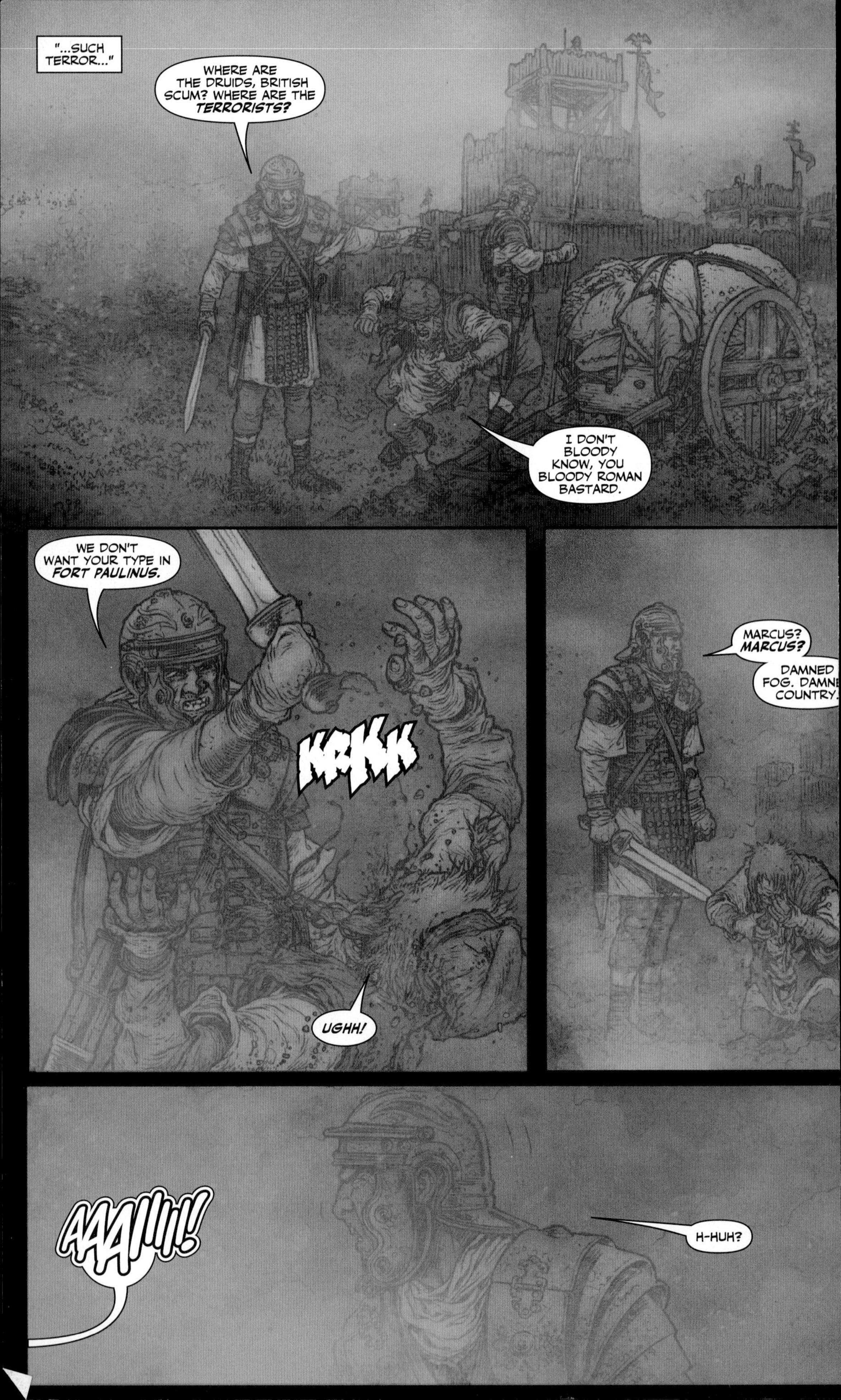
"...SUCH TERROR..."
WHERE ARE THE DRUIDS, BRITISH SCUM? WHERE ARE THE TERRORISTS?
I DON'T BLOODY KNOW, YOU BLOODY ROMAN BASTARD.
WE DON'T WANT YOUR TYPE IN FORT PAULINUS.
KRKK
UGHH!
MARCUS? MARCUS?
DAMNED FOG. DAMNE COUNTRY.
AAAIIIII!
H-HUH?

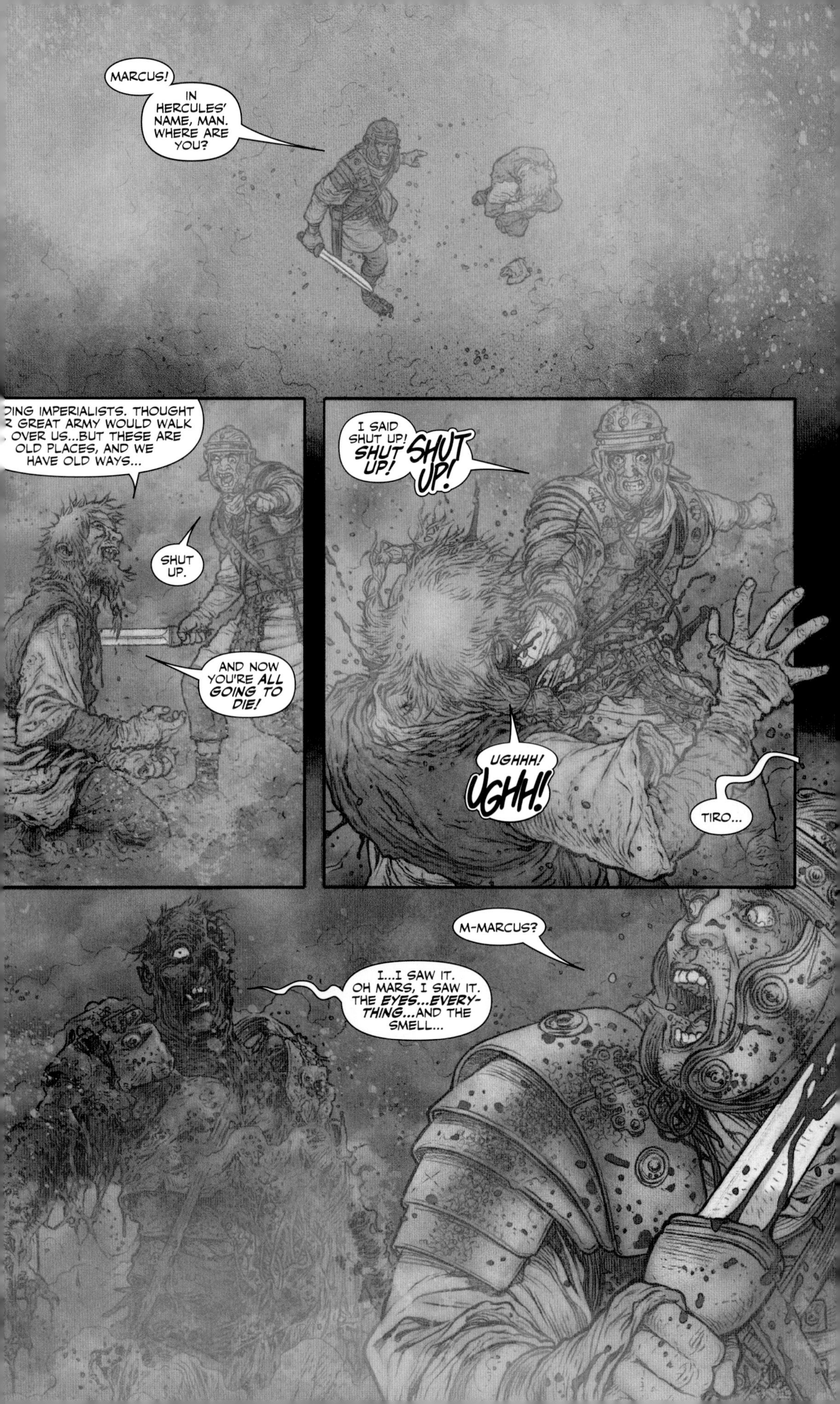
MARCUS!
IN HERCULES' NAME, MAN. WHERE ARE YOU?
DING IMPERIALISTS. THOUGHT R GREAT ARMY WOULD WALK OVER US...BUT THESE ARE OLD PLACES, AND WE HAVE OLD WAYS...
SHUT UP.
AND NOW YOU'RE ALL GOING TO DIE!
I SAID SHUT UP! SHUT UP! SHUT UP!
UGHHH! UGHH!
TIRO...
M-MARCUS?
I...I SAW IT. OH MARS, I SAW IT. THE EYES...EVERYTHING...AND THE SMELL...

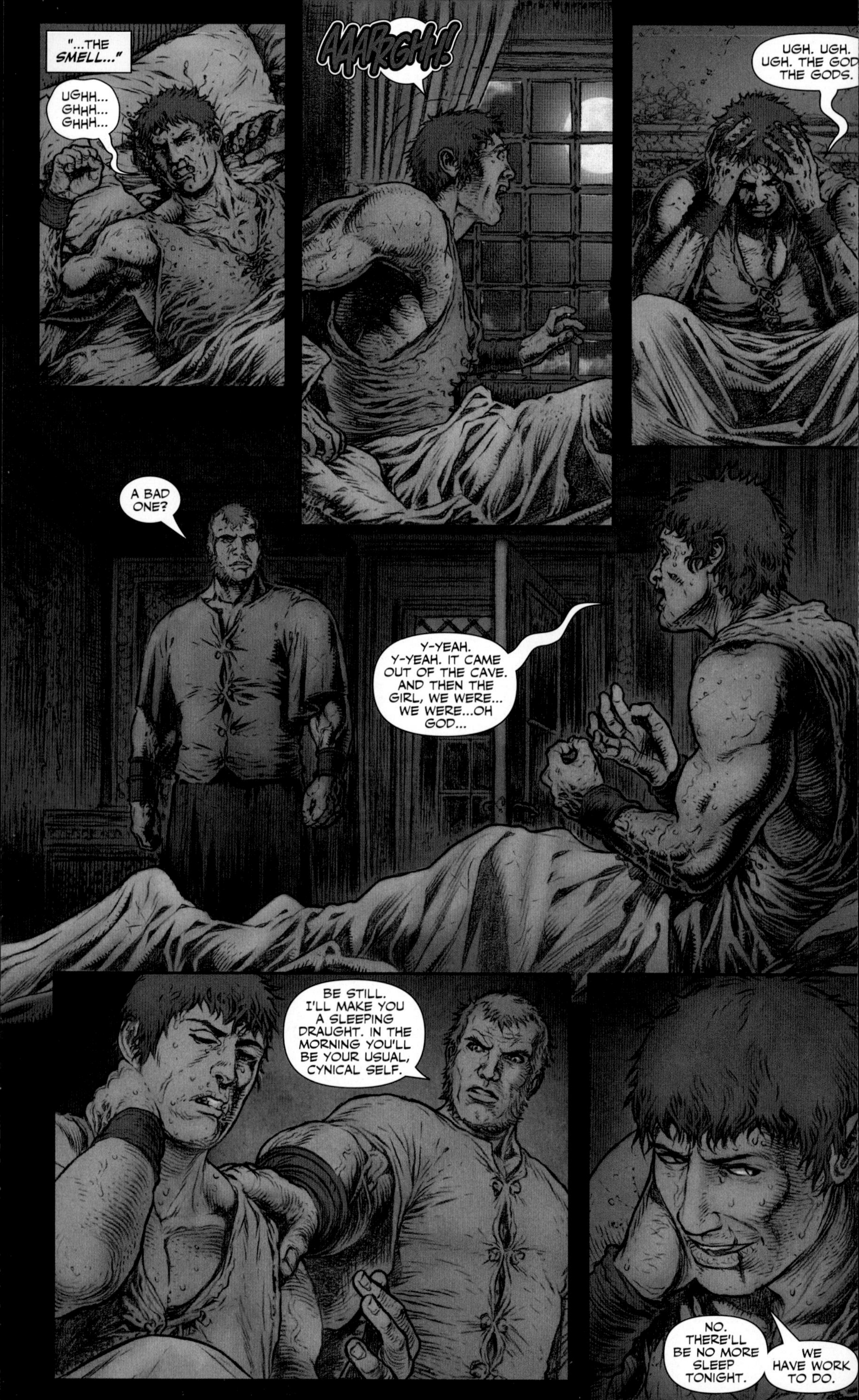
"...THE SMELL..."
UGHH... GHHH... GHHH...
AAARRGHH!
UGH. UGH. UGH. THE GOD THE GODS.
A BAD ONE?
Y-YEAH. Y-YEAH. IT CAME OUT OF THE CAVE. AND THEN THE GIRL, WE WERE... WE WERE...OH GOD...
BE STILL. I'LL MAKE YOU A SLEEPING DRAUGHT. IN THE MORNING YOU'LL BE YOUR USUAL, CYNICAL SELF.
NO. THERE'LL BE NO MORE SLEEP TONIGHT.
WE HAVE WORK TO DO.

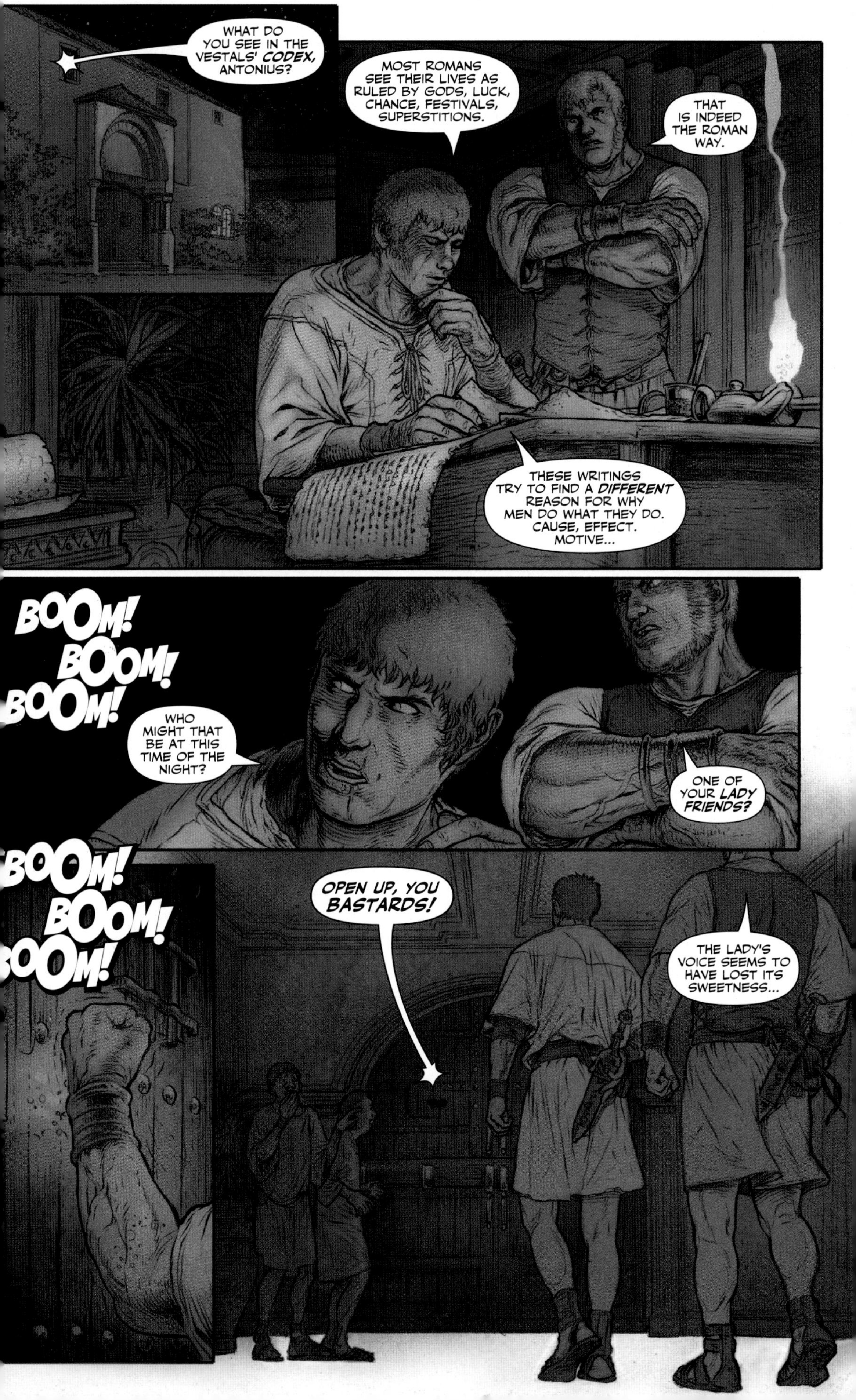

WHAT DO YOU SEE IN THE VESTALS' *CODEX,* ANTONIUS?
MOST ROMANS SEE THEIR LIVES AS RULED BY GODS, LUCK, CHANCE, FESTIVALS, SUPERSTITIONS.
THAT IS INDEED THE ROMAN WAY.
THESE WRITINGS TRY TO FIND A *DIFFERENT* REASON FOR WHY MEN DO WHAT THEY DO. CAUSE, EFFECT. MOTIVE...
BOOM! BOOM! BOOM!
WHO MIGHT THAT BE AT THIS TIME OF THE NIGHT?
ONE OF YOUR *LADY FRIENDS?*
BOOM! BOOM! BOOM!
OPEN UP, YOU BASTARDS!
THE LADY'S VOICE SEEMS TO HAVE LOST ITS SWEETNESS...

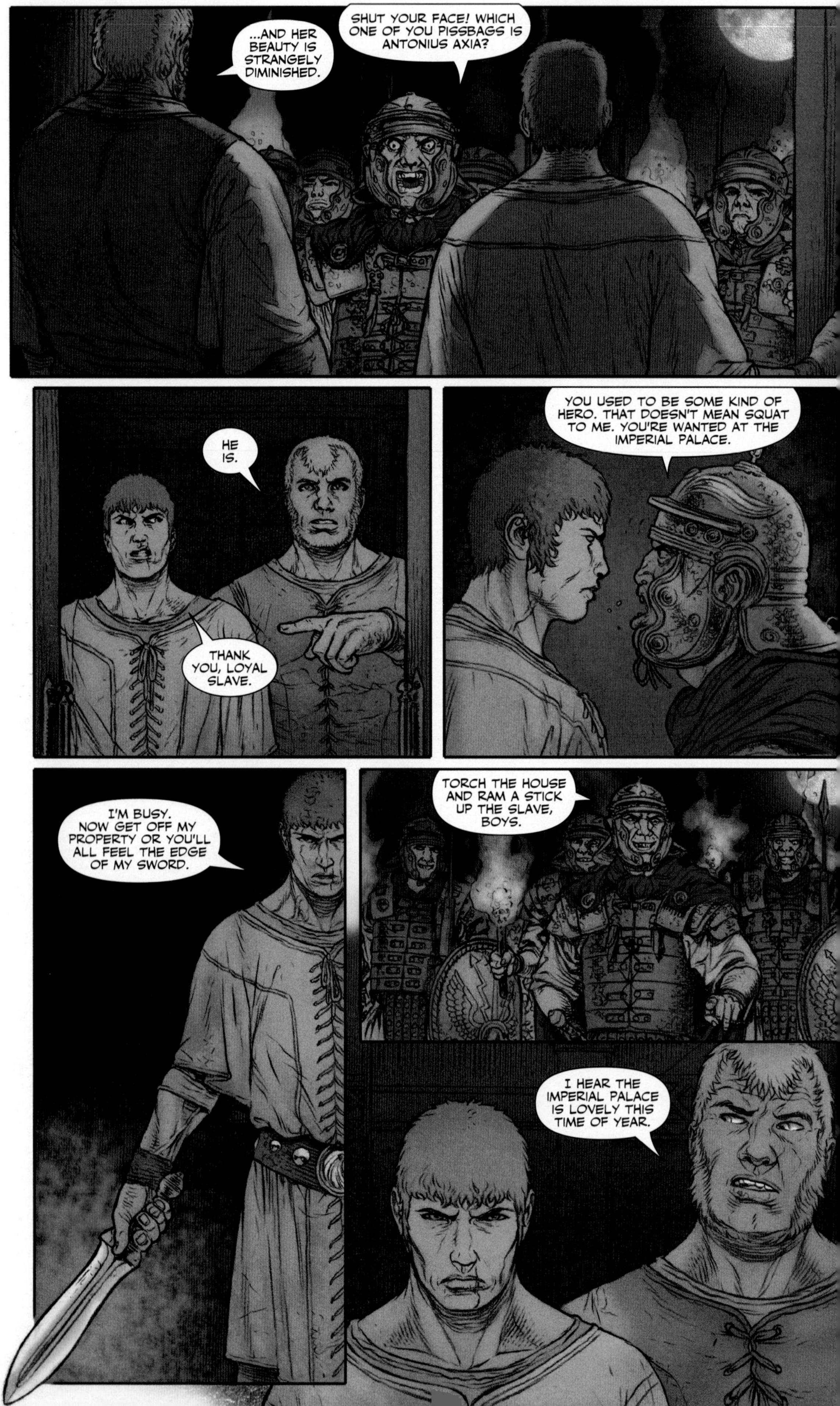

...AND HER BEAUTY IS STRANGELY DIMINISHED.
SHUT YOUR FACE! WHICH ONE OF YOU PISSBAGS IS ANTONIUS AXIA?
HE IS.
THANK YOU, LOYAL SLAVE.
YOU USED TO BE SOME KIND OF HERO. THAT DOESN'T MEAN SQUAT TO ME. YOU'RE WANTED AT THE IMPERIAL PALACE.
I'M BUSY. NOW GET OFF MY PROPERTY OR YOU'LL ALL FEEL THE EDGE OF MY SWORD.
TORCH THE HOUSE AND RAM A STICK UP THE SLAVE, BOYS.
I HEAR THE IMPERIAL PALACE IS LOVELY THIS TIME OF YEAR.

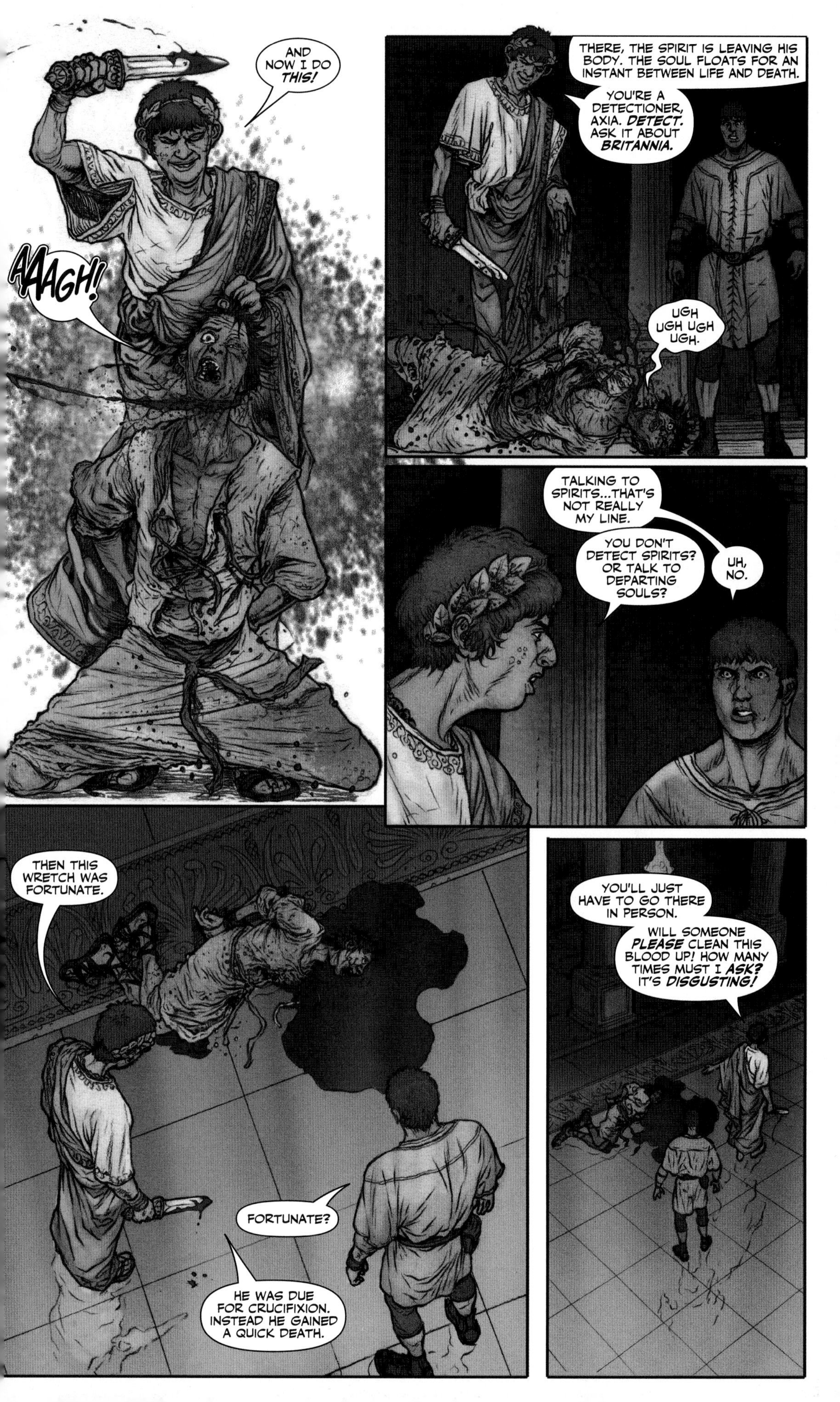

AND NOW I DO *THIS!*
AAAGH!
THERE, THE SPIRIT IS LEAVING HIS BODY. THE SOUL FLOATS FOR AN INSTANT BETWEEN LIFE AND DEATH.
YOU'RE A DETECTIONER, AXIA. ***DETECT.*** ASK IT ABOUT ***BRITANNIA.***
UGH UGH UGH UGH.
TALKING TO SPIRITS...THAT'S NOT REALLY MY LINE.
YOU DON'T DETECT SPIRITS? OR TALK TO DEPARTING SOULS?
UH, NO.
THEN THIS WRETCH WAS FORTUNATE.
FORTUNATE?
HE WAS DUE FOR CRUCIFIXION. INSTEAD HE GAINED A QUICK DEATH.
YOU'LL JUST HAVE TO GO THERE IN PERSON.
WILL SOMEONE ***PLEASE*** CLEAN THIS BLOOD UP! HOW MANY TIMES MUST I ***ASK?*** IT'S ***DISGUSTING!***

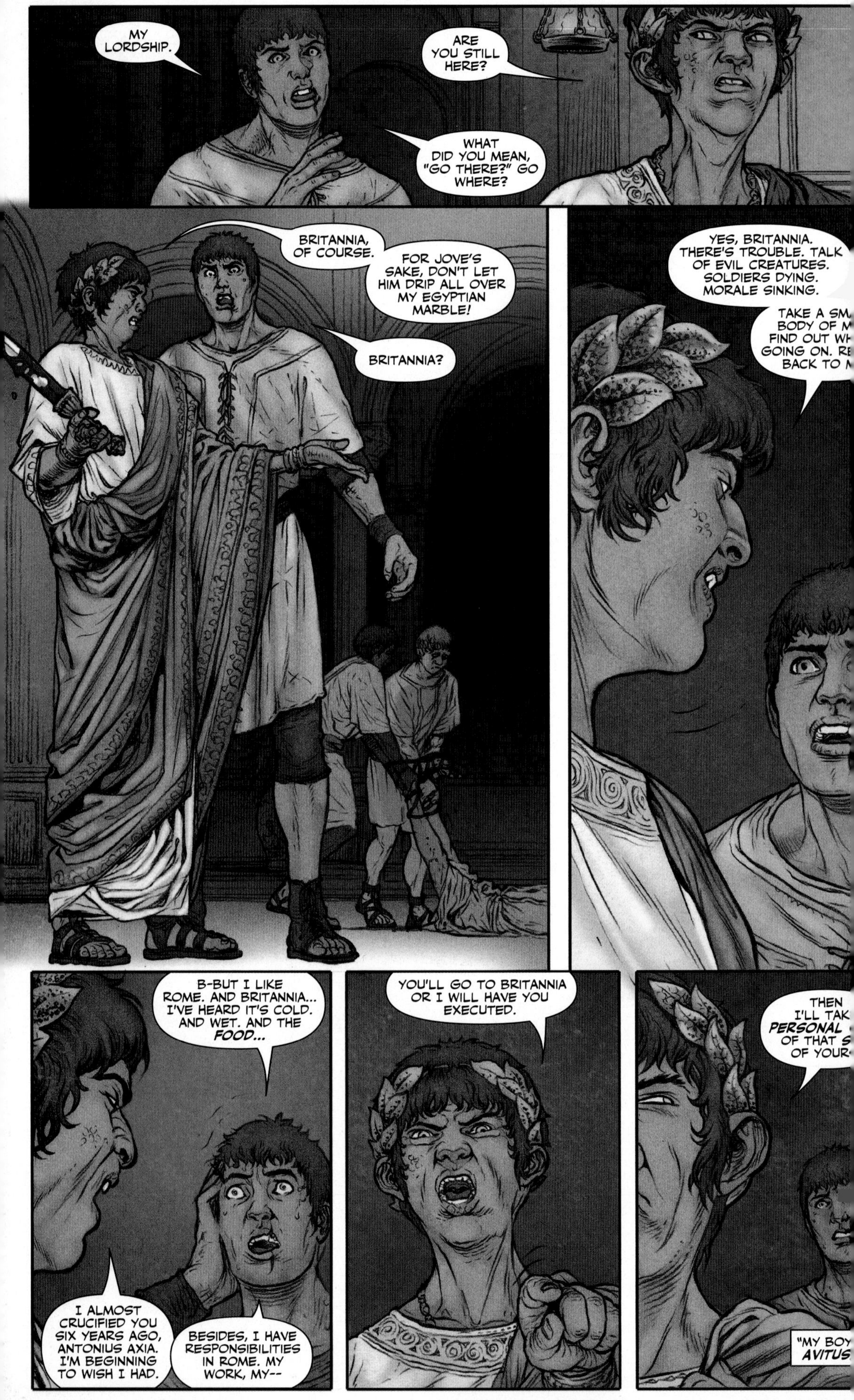
MY LORDSHIP.
ARE YOU STILL HERE?
WHAT DID YOU MEAN, "GO THERE?" GO WHERE?
BRITANNIA, OF COURSE.
FOR JOVE'S SAKE, DON'T LET HIM DRIP ALL OVER MY EGYPTIAN MARBLE!
BRITANNIA?
YES, BRITANNIA. THERE'S TROUBLE. TALK OF EVIL CREATURES. SOLDIERS DYING. MORALE SINKING.
TAKE A SM BODY OF M FIND OUT WH GOING ON. RE BACK TO M
B-BUT I LIKE ROME. AND BRITANNIA... I'VE HEARD IT'S COLD. AND WET. AND THE *FOOD*...
BESIDES, I HAVE RESPONSIBILITIES IN ROME. MY WORK, MY--
I ALMOST CRUCIFIED YOU SIX YEARS AGO, ANTONIUS AXIA. I'M BEGINNING TO WISH I HAD.
YOU'LL GO TO BRITANNIA OR I WILL HAVE YOU EXECUTED.
THEN I'LL TAK *PERSONAL* OF THAT S OF YOUR
"MY BOY *AVITUS*

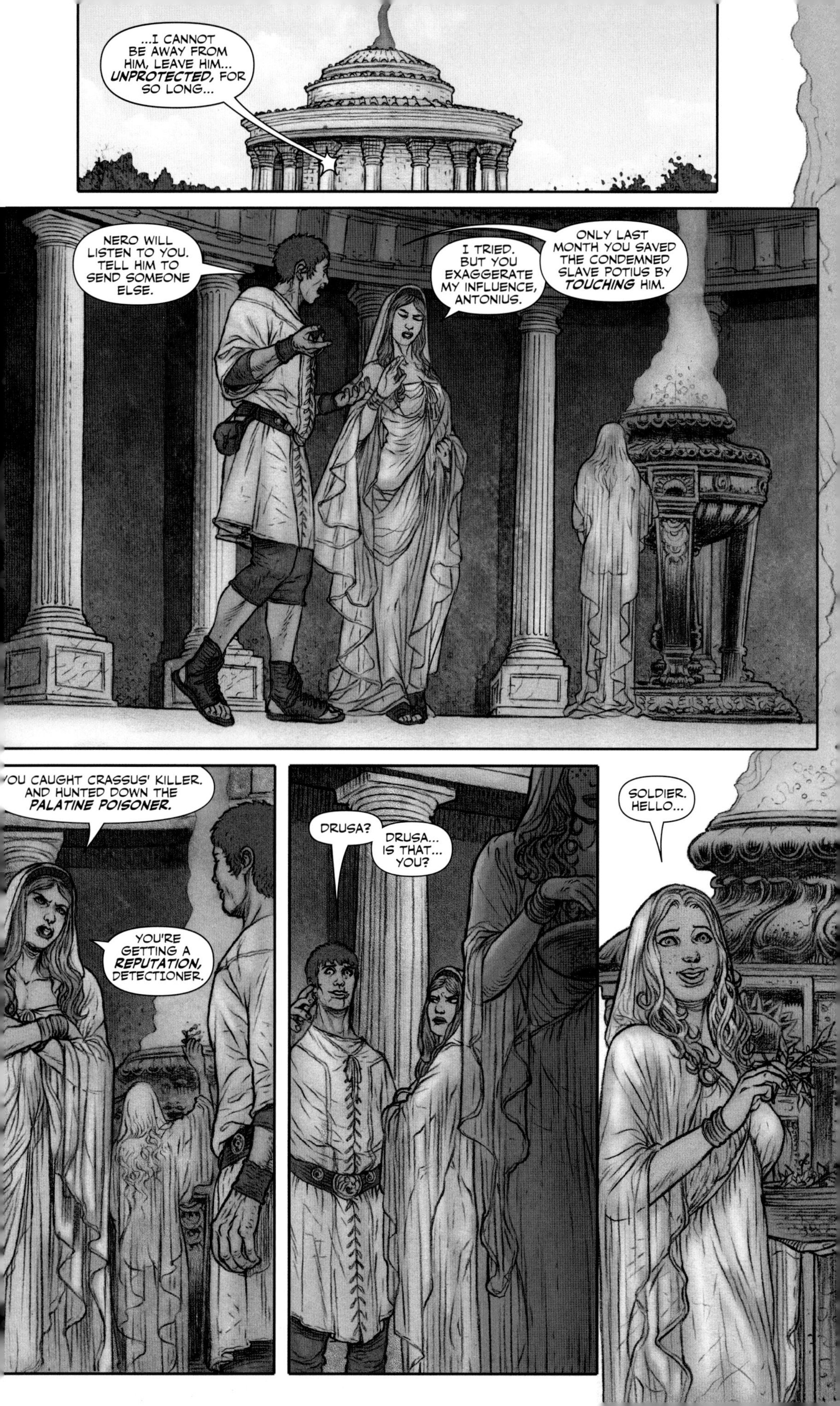
...I CANNOT BE AWAY FROM HIM, LEAVE HIM... *UNPROTECTED,* FOR SO LONG...
NERO WILL LISTEN TO YOU. TELL HIM TO SEND SOMEONE ELSE.
I TRIED. BUT YOU EXAGGERATE MY INFLUENCE, ANTONIUS.
ONLY LAST MONTH YOU SAVED THE CONDEMNED SLAVE POTIUS BY *TOUCHING* HIM.
YOU CAUGHT CRASSUS' KILLER. AND HUNTED DOWN THE *PALATINE POISONER.*
YOU'RE GETTING A *REPUTATION,* DETECTIONER.
DRUSA?
DRUSA... IS THAT... YOU?
SOLDIER. HELLO...

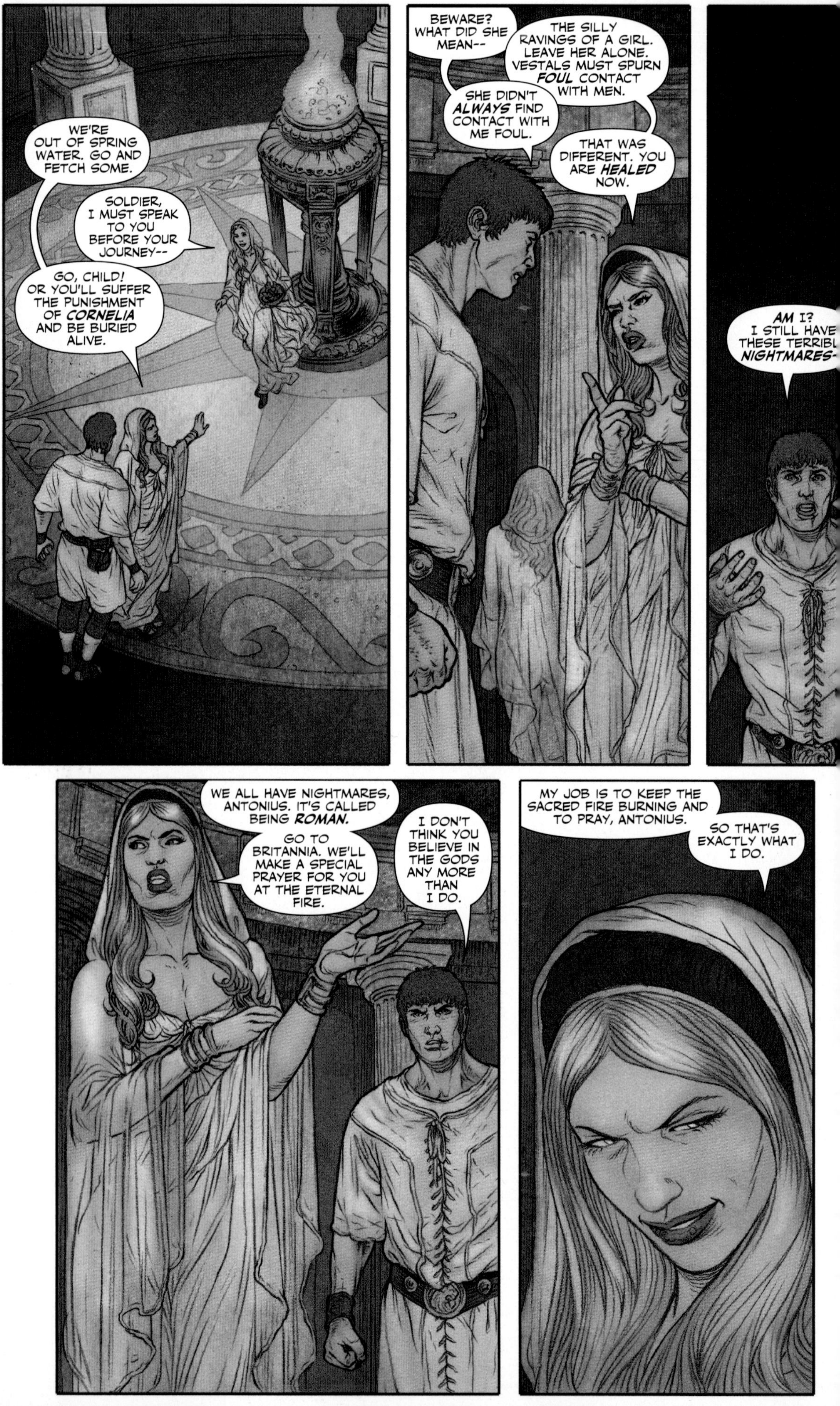
WE'RE OUT OF SPRING WATER. GO AND FETCH SOME.
SOLDIER, I MUST SPEAK TO YOU BEFORE YOUR JOURNEY--
GO, CHILD! OR YOU'LL SUFFER THE PUNISHMENT OF CORNELIA AND BE BURIED ALIVE.
BEWARE? WHAT DID SHE MEAN--
THE SILLY RAVINGS OF A GIRL. LEAVE HER ALONE. VESTALS MUST SPURN FOUL CONTACT WITH MEN.
SHE DIDN'T ALWAYS FIND CONTACT WITH ME FOUL.
THAT WAS DIFFERENT. YOU ARE HEALED NOW.
AM I? I STILL HAVE THESE TERRIBL NIGHTMARES-
WE ALL HAVE NIGHTMARES, ANTONIUS. IT'S CALLED BEING ROMAN.
GO TO BRITANNIA. WE'LL MAKE A SPECIAL PRAYER FOR YOU AT THE ETERNAL FIRE.
I DON'T THINK YOU BELIEVE IN THE GODS ANY MORE THAN I DO.
MY JOB IS TO KEEP THE SACRED FIRE BURNING AND TO PRAY, ANTONIUS.
SO THAT'S EXACTLY WHAT I DO.

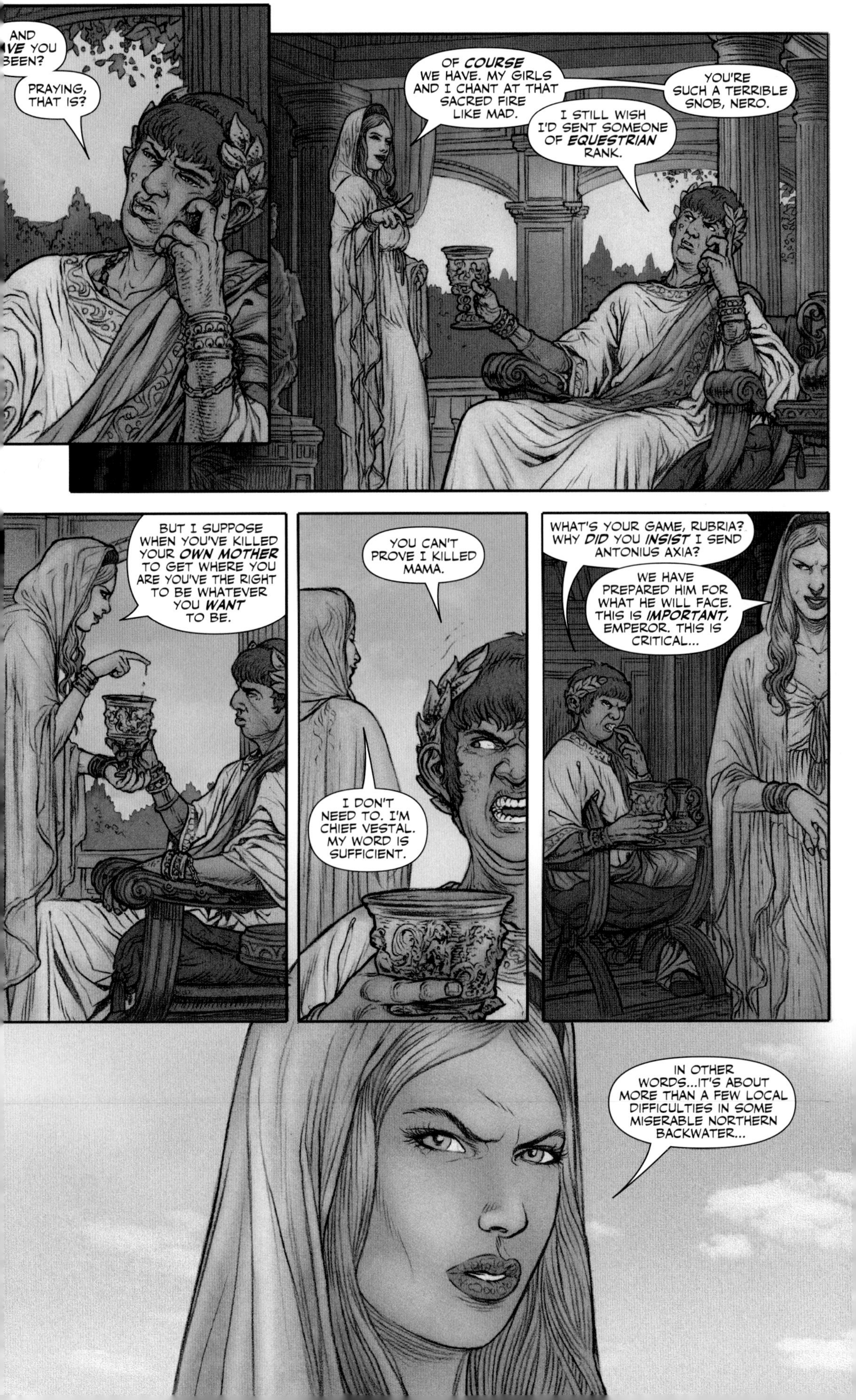

AND ...AVE YOU ...BEEN?
PRAYING, THAT IS?
OF COURSE WE HAVE. MY GIRLS AND I CHANT AT THAT SACRED FIRE LIKE MAD.
YOU'RE SUCH A TERRIBLE SNOB, NERO.
I STILL WISH I'D SENT SOMEONE OF EQUESTRIAN RANK.
BUT I SUPPOSE WHEN YOU'VE KILLED YOUR OWN MOTHER TO GET WHERE YOU ARE YOU'VE THE RIGHT TO BE WHATEVER YOU WANT TO BE.
YOU CAN'T PROVE I KILLED MAMA.
I DON'T NEED TO. I'M CHIEF VESTAL. MY WORD IS SUFFICIENT.
WHAT'S YOUR GAME, RUBRIA? WHY DID YOU INSIST I SEND ANTONIUS AXIA?
WE HAVE PREPARED HIM FOR WHAT HE WILL FACE. THIS IS IMPORTANT, EMPEROR. THIS IS CRITICAL...
IN OTHER WORDS...IT'S ABOUT MORE THAN A FEW LOCAL DIFFICULTIES IN SOME MISERABLE NORTHERN BACKWATER...

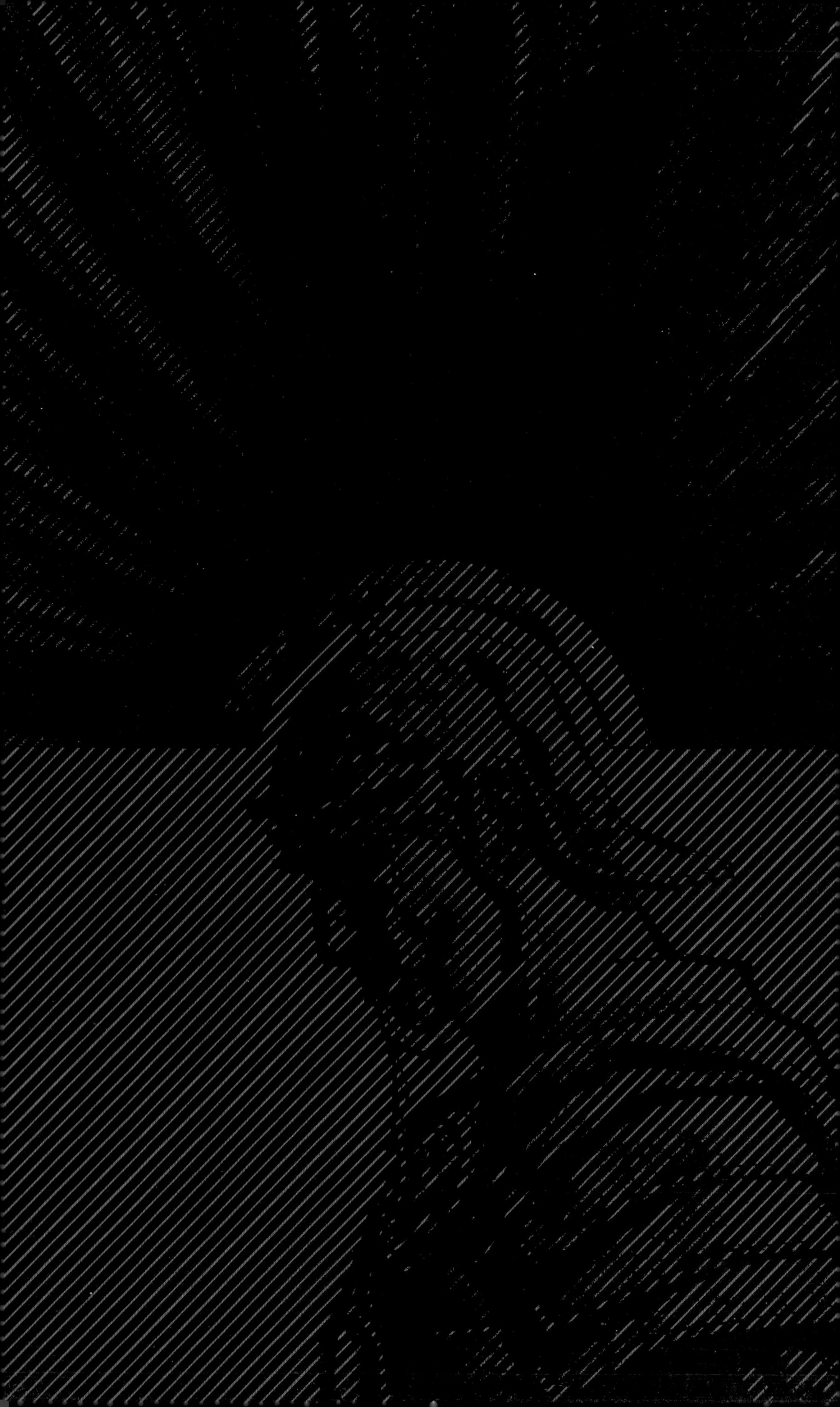

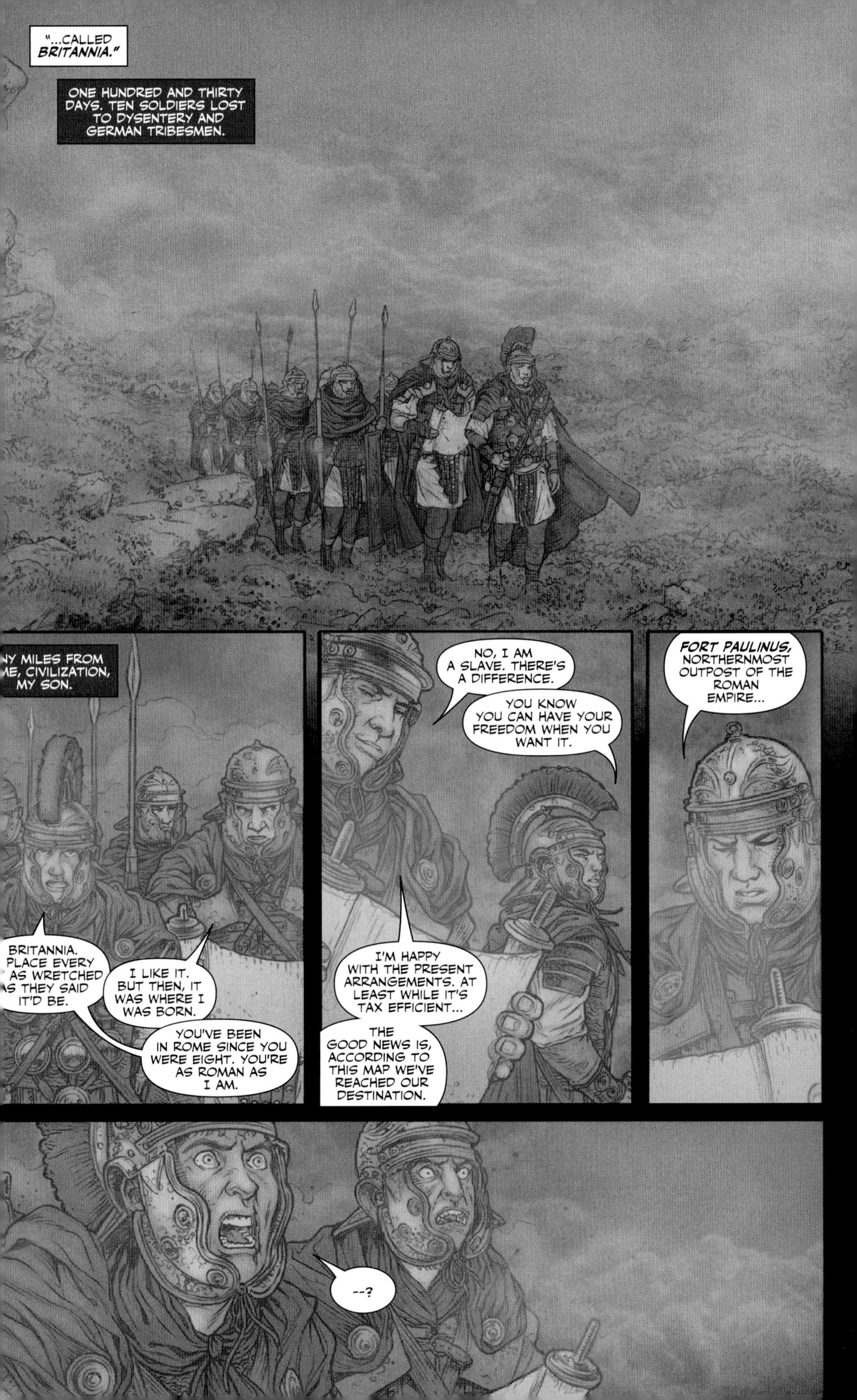
"...CALLED BRITANNIA."
ONE HUNDRED AND THIRTY DAYS. TEN SOLDIERS LOST TO DYSENTERY AND GERMAN TRIBESMEN.
NY MILES FROM ME, CIVILIZATION, MY SON.
BRITANNIA. PLACE EVERY AS WRETCHED S THEY SAID IT'D BE.
I LIKE IT. BUT THEN, IT WAS WHERE I WAS BORN.
YOU'VE BEEN IN ROME SINCE YOU WERE EIGHT. YOU'RE AS ROMAN AS I AM.
NO, I AM A SLAVE. THERE'S A DIFFERENCE.
YOU KNOW YOU CAN HAVE YOUR FREEDOM WHEN YOU WANT IT.
I'M HAPPY WITH THE PRESENT ARRANGEMENTS. AT LEAST WHILE IT'S TAX EFFICIENT...
THE GOOD NEWS IS, ACCORDING TO THIS MAP WE'VE REACHED OUR DESTINATION.
FORT PAULINUS, NORTHERNMOST OUTPOST OF THE ROMAN EMPIRE...
--?

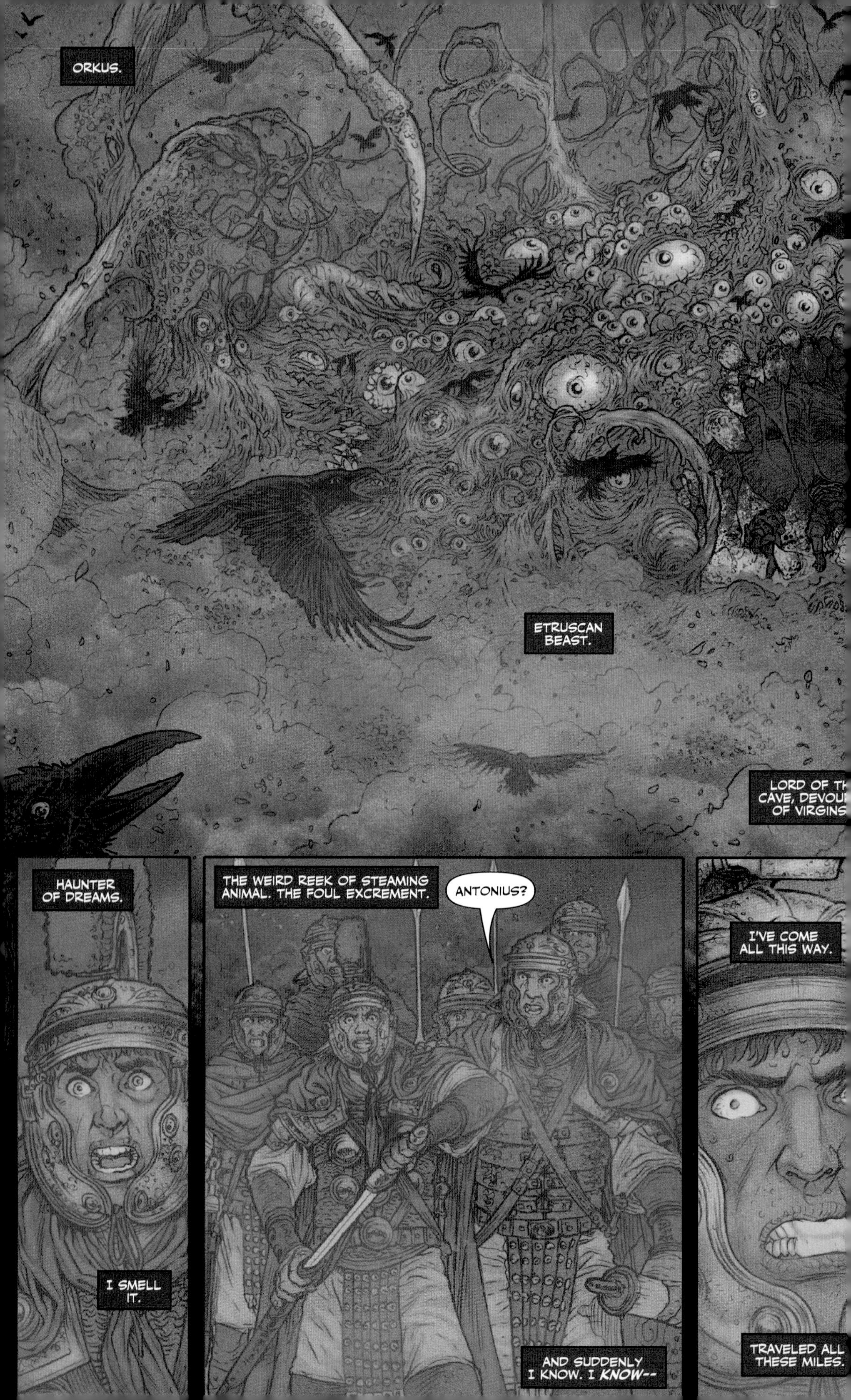
ORKUS.
ETRUSCAN BEAST.
LORD OF
CAVE,
OF VIRGINS
HAUNTER OF DREAMS.
I SMELL IT.
THE WEIRD REEK OF STEAMING ANIMAL. THE FOUL EXCREMENT.
ANTONIUS?
AND SUDDENLY I KNOW. I *KNOW--*
I'VE COME ALL THIS WAY.
TRAVELED ALL THESE MILES.

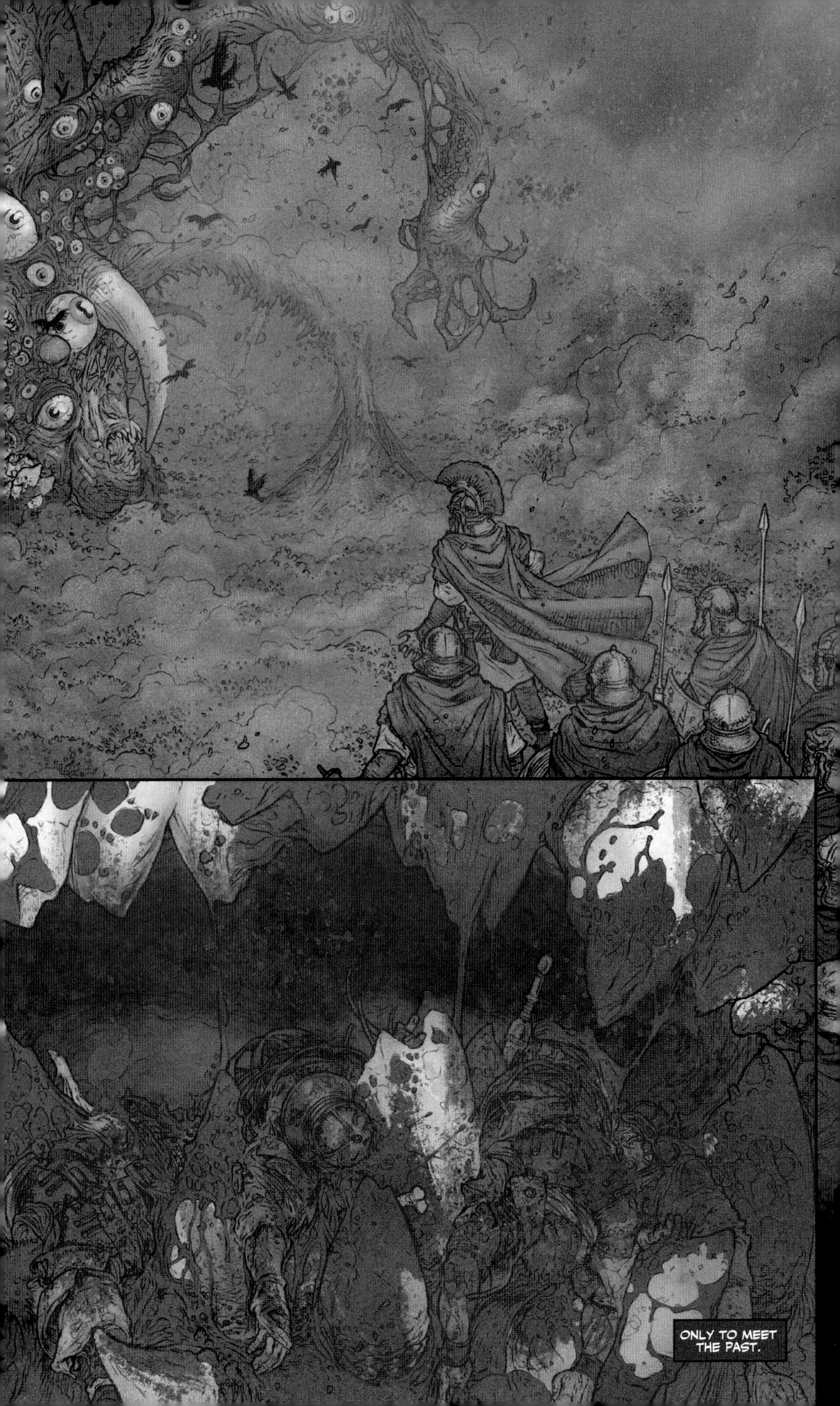
ONLY TO MEET THE PAST.

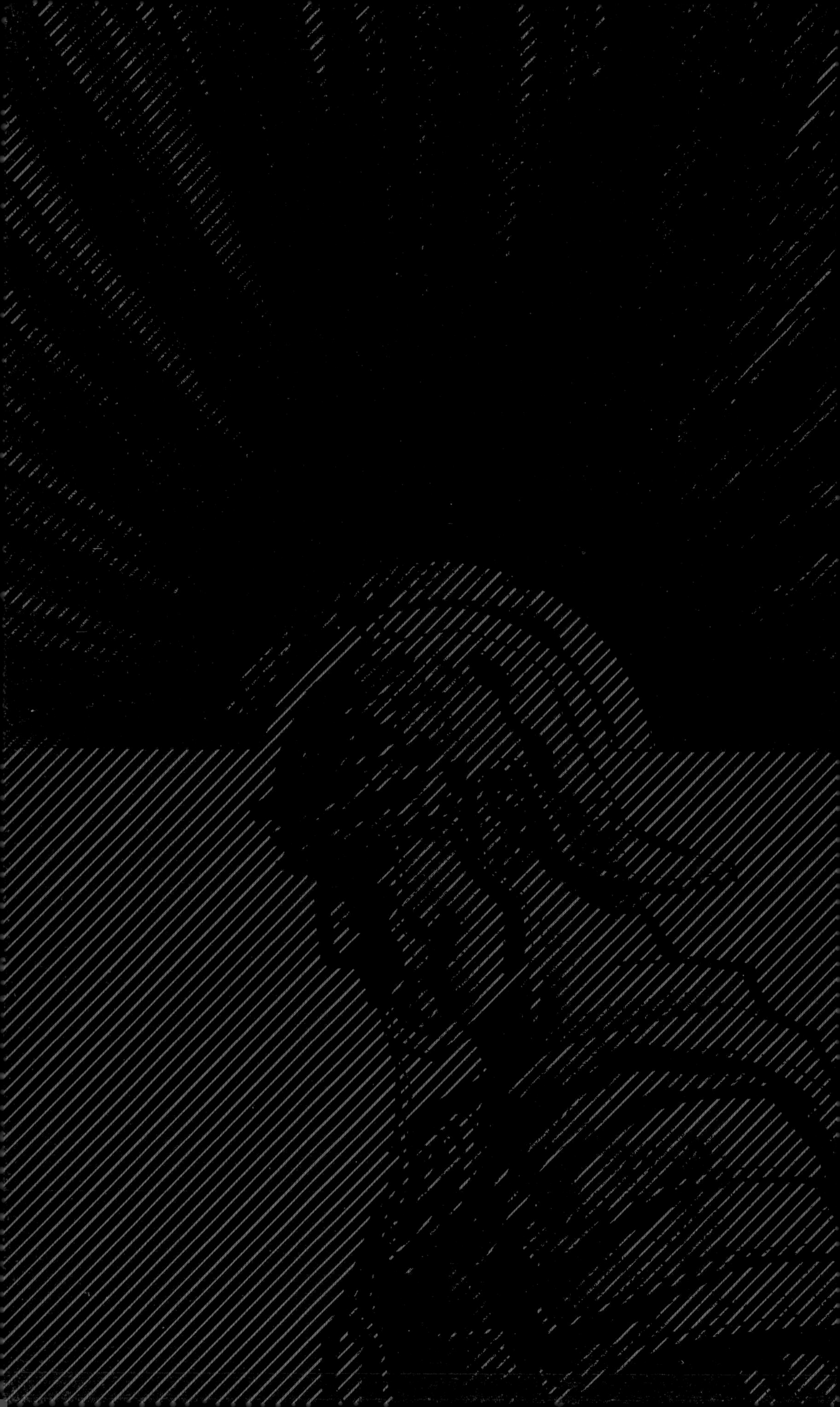

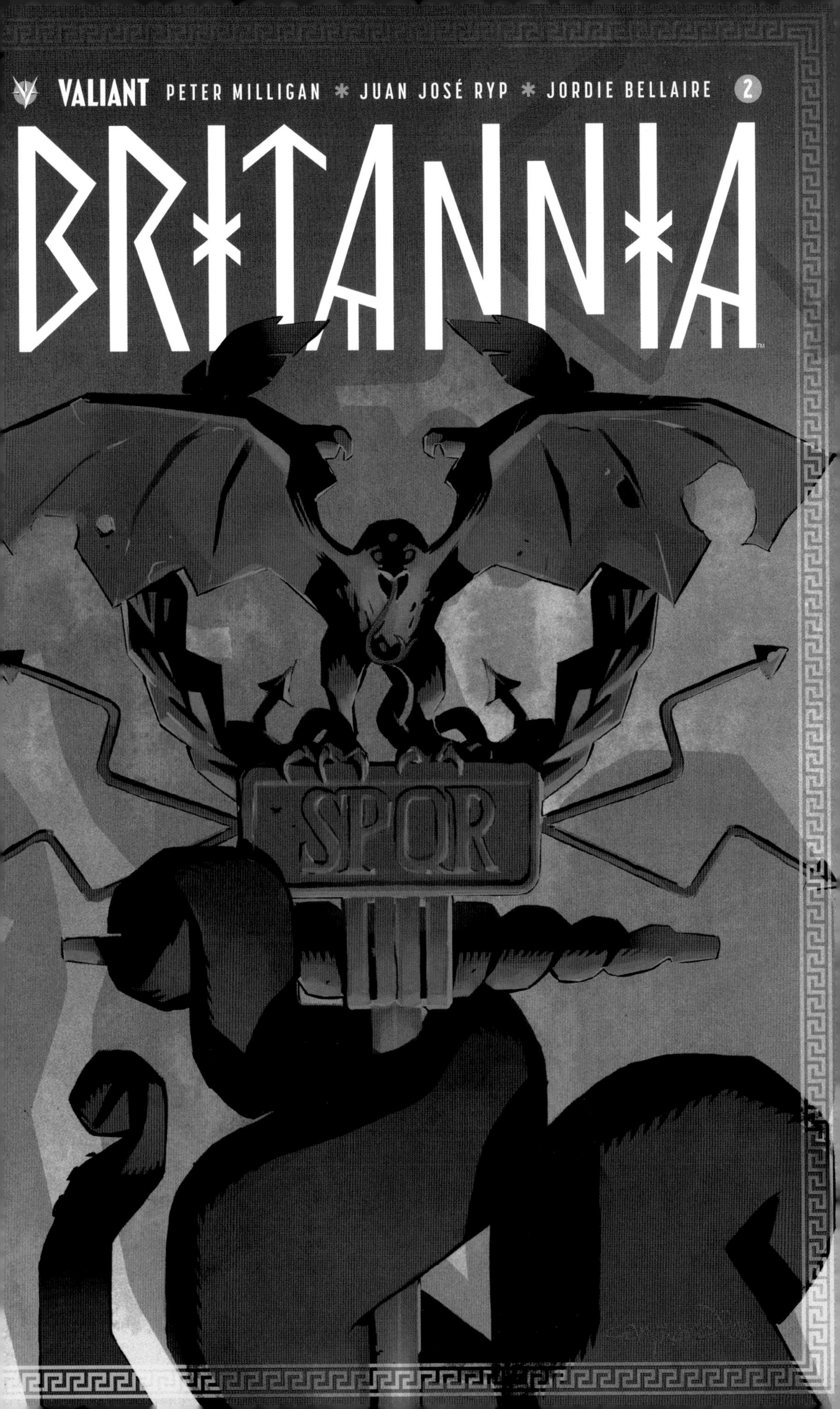
VALIANT
PETER MILLIGAN * JUAN JOSÉ RYP * JORDIE BELLAIRE
2
BRITANNIA
SPQR

BOOK II

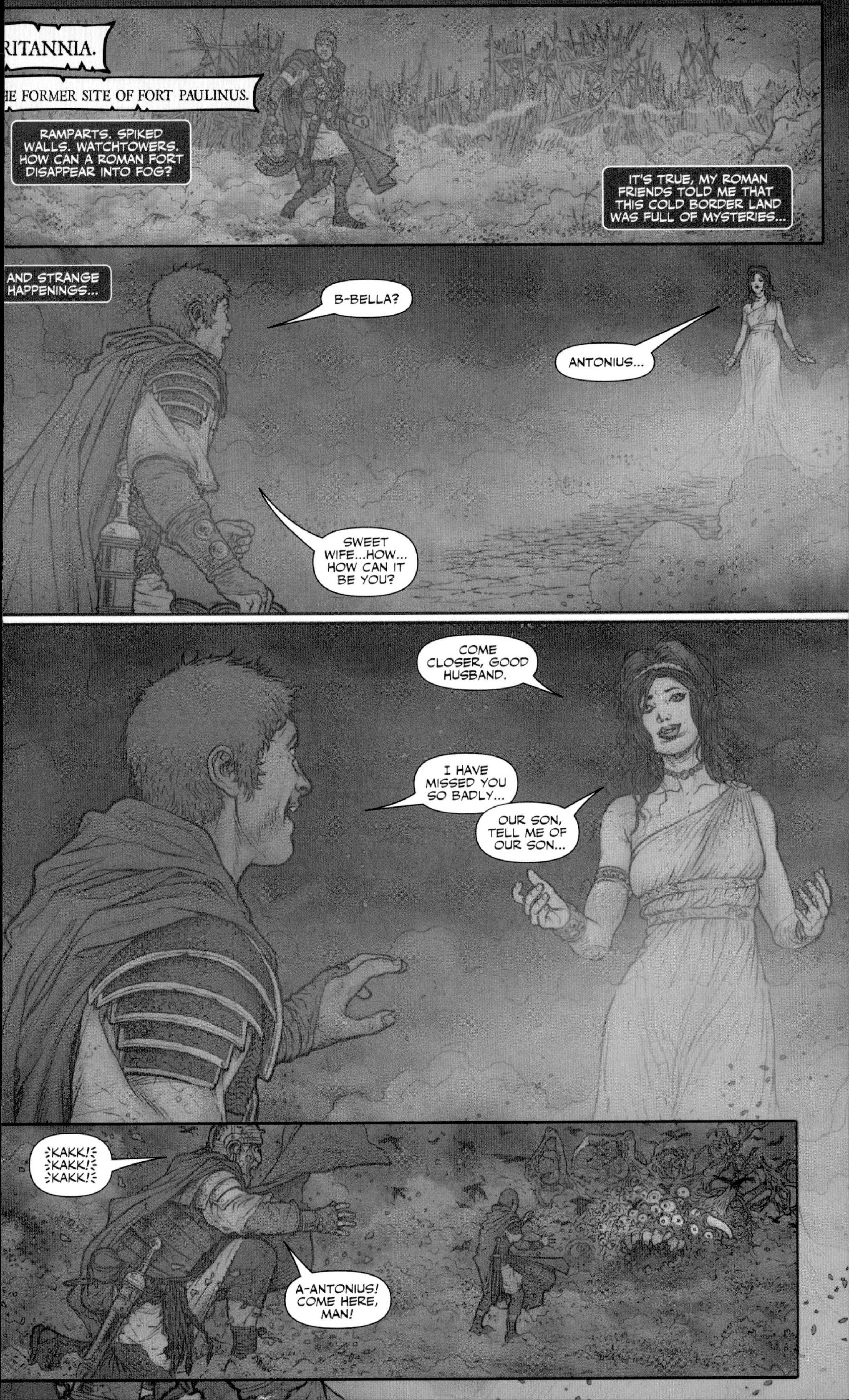
RITANNIA.
HE FORMER SITE OF FORT PAULINUS.
RAMPARTS. SPIKED WALLS. WATCHTOWERS. HOW CAN A ROMAN FORT DISAPPEAR INTO FOG?
IT'S TRUE, MY ROMAN FRIENDS TOLD ME THAT THIS COLD BORDER LAND WAS FULL OF MYSTERIES...
AND STRANGE HAPPENINGS...
B-BELLA?
ANTONIUS...
SWEET WIFE...HOW... HOW CAN IT BE YOU?
COME CLOSER, GOOD HUSBAND.
I HAVE MISSED YOU SO BADLY...
OUR SON, TELL ME OF OUR SON...
KAKK! KAKK! KAKK!
A-ANTONIUS! COME HERE, MAN!

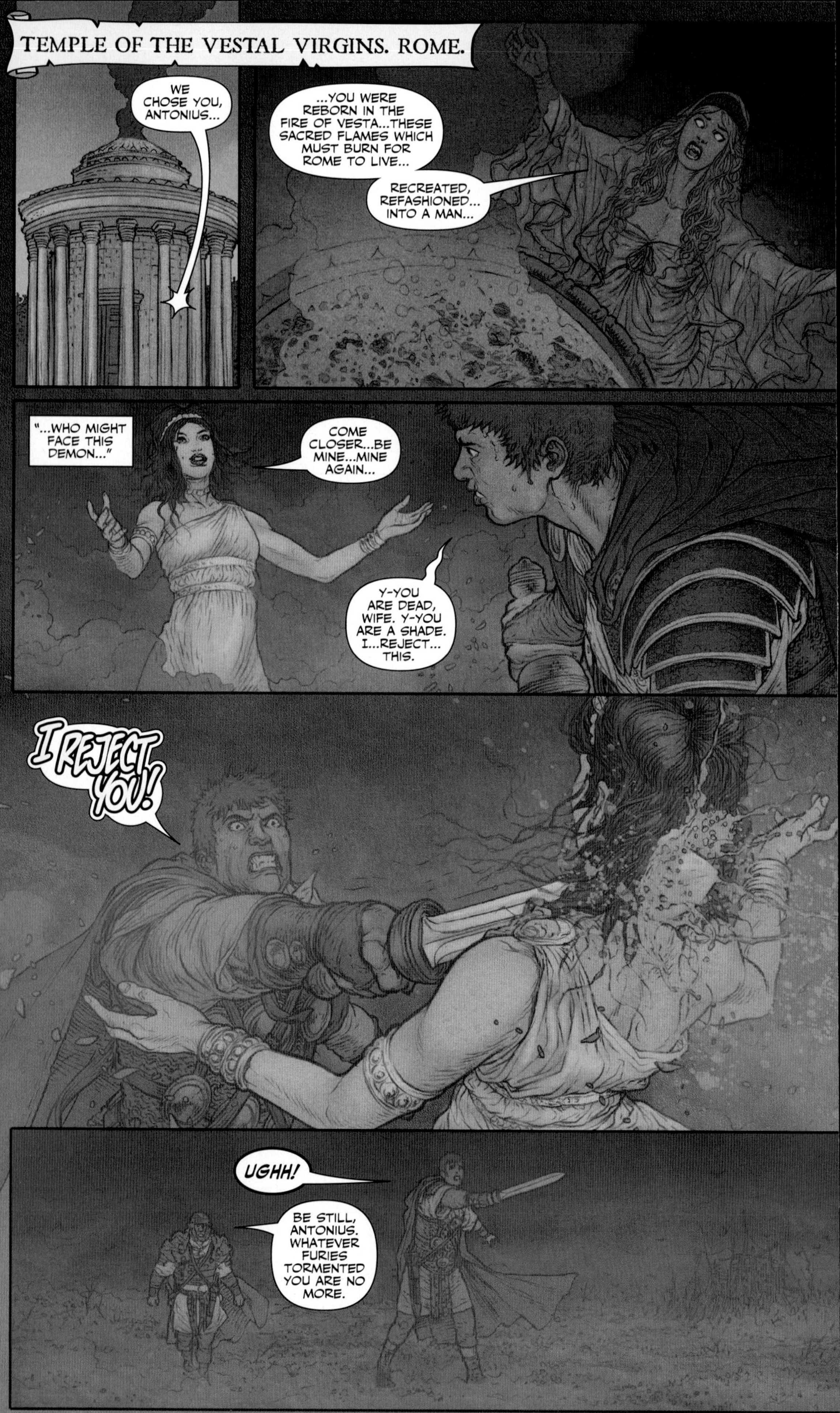
TEMPLE OF THE VESTAL VIRGINS. ROME.
WE CHOSE YOU, ANTONIUS...
...YOU WERE REBORN IN THE FIRE OF VESTA...THESE SACRED FLAMES WHICH MUST BURN FOR ROME TO LIVE...
RECREATED, REFASHIONED... INTO A MAN...
"...WHO MIGHT FACE THIS DEMON..."
COME CLOSER...BE MINE...MINE AGAIN...
Y-YOU ARE DEAD, WIFE. Y-YOU ARE A SHADE. I...REJECT... THIS.
I REJECT YOU!
UGHH!
BE STILL, ANTONIUS. WHATEVER FURIES TORMENTED YOU ARE NO MORE.

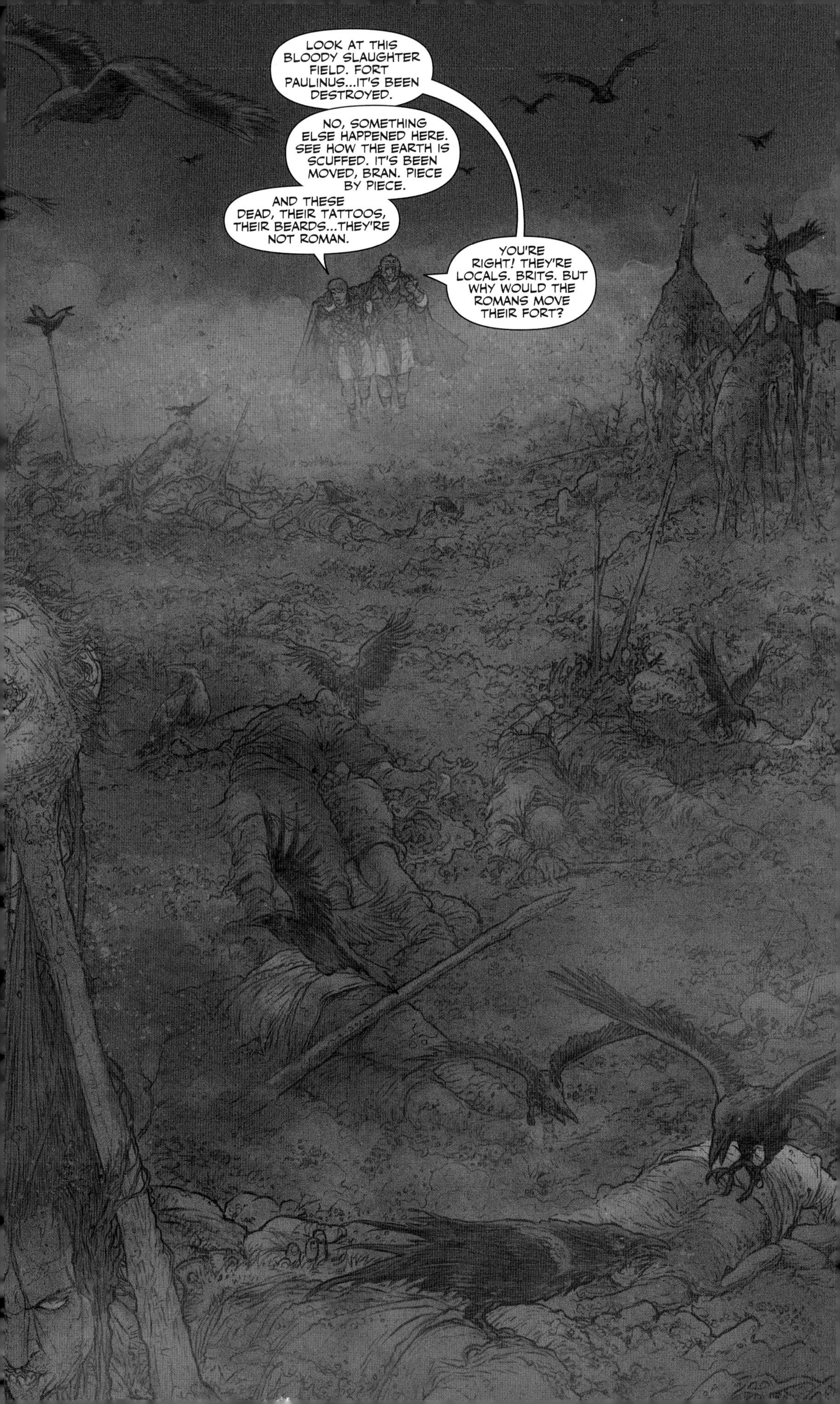
LOOK AT THIS BLOODY SLAUGHTER FIELD. FORT PAULINUS...IT'S BEEN DESTROYED.
NO, SOMETHING ELSE HAPPENED HERE. SEE HOW THE EARTH IS SCUFFED. IT'S BEEN MOVED, BRAN. PIECE BY PIECE.
AND THESE DEAD, THEIR TATTOOS, THEIR BEARDS...THEY'RE NOT ROMAN.
YOU'RE RIGHT! THEY'RE LOCALS. BRITS. BUT WHY WOULD THE ROMANS MOVE THEIR FORT?

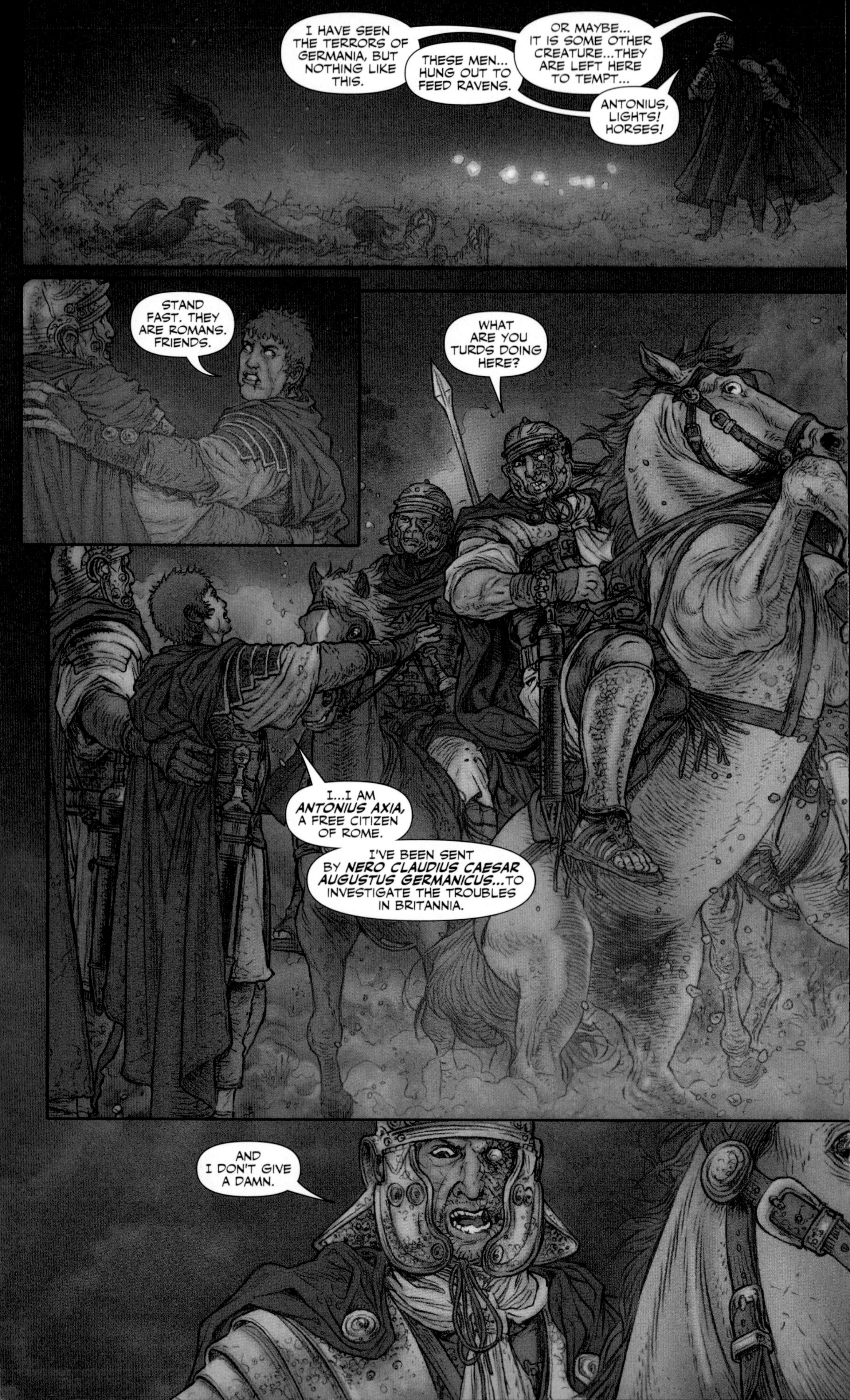
I HAVE SEEN THE TERRORS OF GERMANIA, BUT NOTHING LIKE THIS.
THESE MEN... HUNG OUT TO FEED RAVENS.
OR MAYBE... IT IS SOME OTHER CREATURE...THEY ARE LEFT HERE TO TEMPT...
ANTONIUS, LIGHTS! HORSES!
STAND FAST. THEY ARE ROMANS. FRIENDS.
WHAT ARE YOU TURDS DOING HERE?
I...I AM ANTONIUS AXIA, A FREE CITIZEN OF ROME.
I'VE BEEN SENT BY NERO CLAUDIUS CAESAR AUGUSTUS GERMANICUS...TO INVESTIGATE THE TROUBLES IN BRITANNIA.
AND I DON'T GIVE A DAMN.

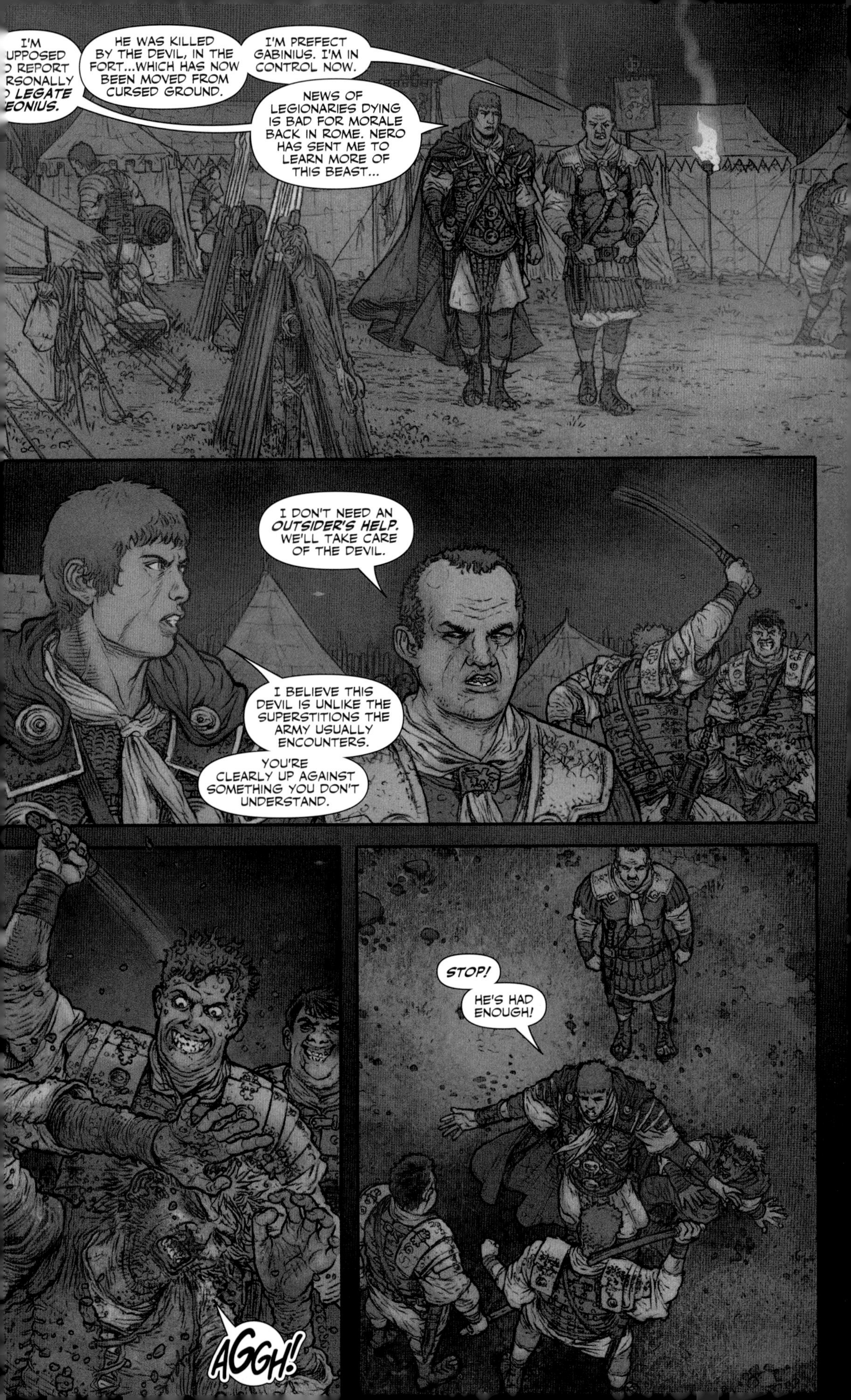
I'M
UPPOSED
O REPORT
RSONALLY
O LEGATE
EONIUS.
HE WAS KILLED
BY THE DEVIL, IN THE
FORT...WHICH HAS NOW
BEEN MOVED FROM
CURSED GROUND.
I'M PREFECT
GABINIUS. I'M IN
CONTROL NOW.
NEWS OF
LEGIONARIES DYING
IS BAD FOR MORALE
BACK IN ROME. NERO
HAS SENT ME TO
LEARN MORE OF
THIS BEAST...
I DON'T NEED AN
OUTSIDER'S HELP.
WE'LL TAKE CARE
OF THE DEVIL.
I BELIEVE THIS
DEVIL IS UNLIKE THE
SUPERSTITIONS THE
ARMY USUALLY
ENCOUNTERS.
YOU'RE
CLEARLY UP AGAINST
SOMETHING YOU DON'T
UNDERSTAND.
AGGH!
STOP!
HE'S HAD
ENOUGH!

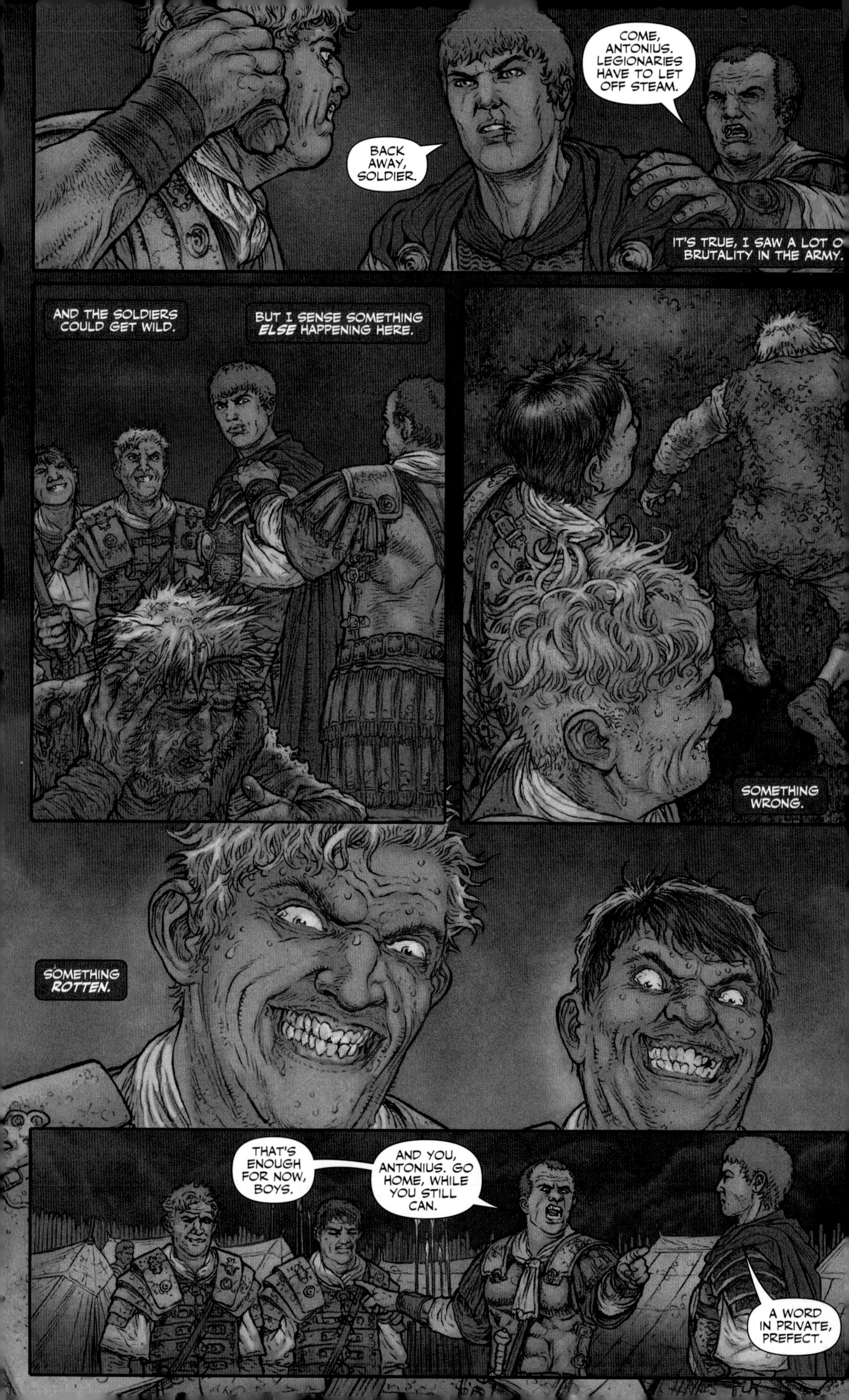
BACK AWAY, SOLDIER.
COME, ANTONIUS. LEGIONARIES HAVE TO LET OFF STEAM.
IT'S TRUE, I SAW A LOT OF BRUTALITY IN THE ARMY.
AND THE SOLDIERS COULD GET WILD.
BUT I SENSE SOMETHING *ELSE* HAPPENING HERE.
SOMETHING WRONG.
SOMETHING *ROTTEN.*
THAT'S ENOUGH FOR NOW, BOYS.
AND YOU, ANTONIUS. GO HOME, WHILE YOU STILL CAN.
A WORD IN PRIVATE, PREFECT.

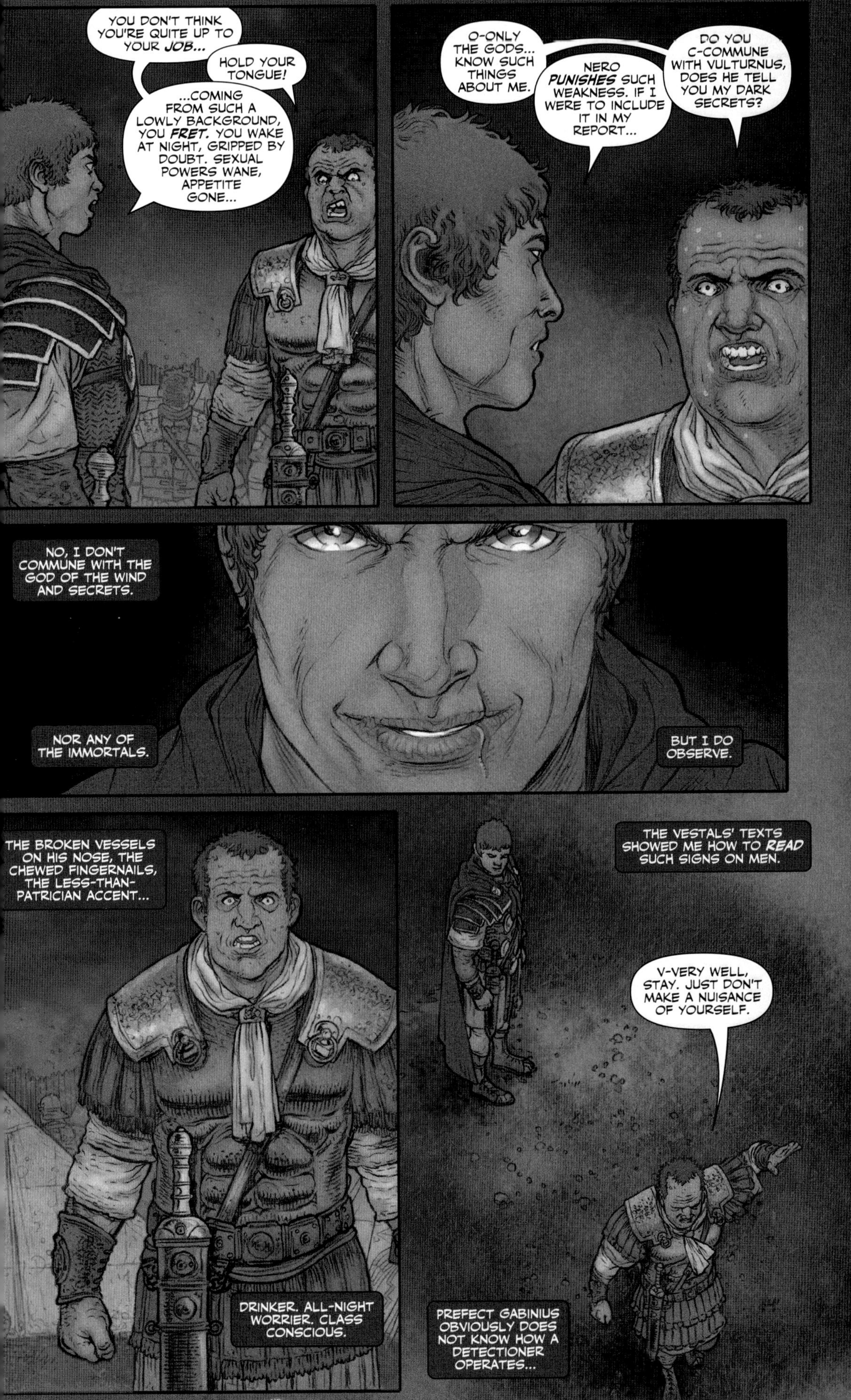
YOU DON'T THINK YOU'RE QUITE UP TO YOUR JOB...
HOLD YOUR TONGUE!
...COMING FROM SUCH A LOWLY BACKGROUND, YOU FRET. YOU WAKE AT NIGHT, GRIPPED BY DOUBT. SEXUAL POWERS WANE, APPETITE GONE...
DO YOU C-COMMUNE WITH VULTURNUS, DOES HE TELL YOU MY DARK SECRETS?
NERO PUNISHES SUCH WEAKNESS. IF I WERE TO INCLUDE IT IN MY REPORT...
O-ONLY THE GODS... KNOW SUCH THINGS ABOUT ME.
NO, I DON'T COMMUNE WITH THE GOD OF THE WIND AND SECRETS.
NOR ANY OF THE IMMORTALS.
BUT I DO OBSERVE.
THE BROKEN VESSELS ON HIS NOSE, THE CHEWED FINGERNAILS, THE LESS-THAN-PATRICIAN ACCENT...
DRINKER. ALL-NIGHT WORRIER. CLASS CONSCIOUS.
THE VESTALS' TEXTS SHOWED ME HOW TO READ SUCH SIGNS ON MEN.
V-VERY WELL, STAY. JUST DON'T MAKE A NUISANCE OF YOURSELF.
PREFECT GABINIUS OBVIOUSLY DOES NOT KNOW HOW A DETECTIONER OPERATES...

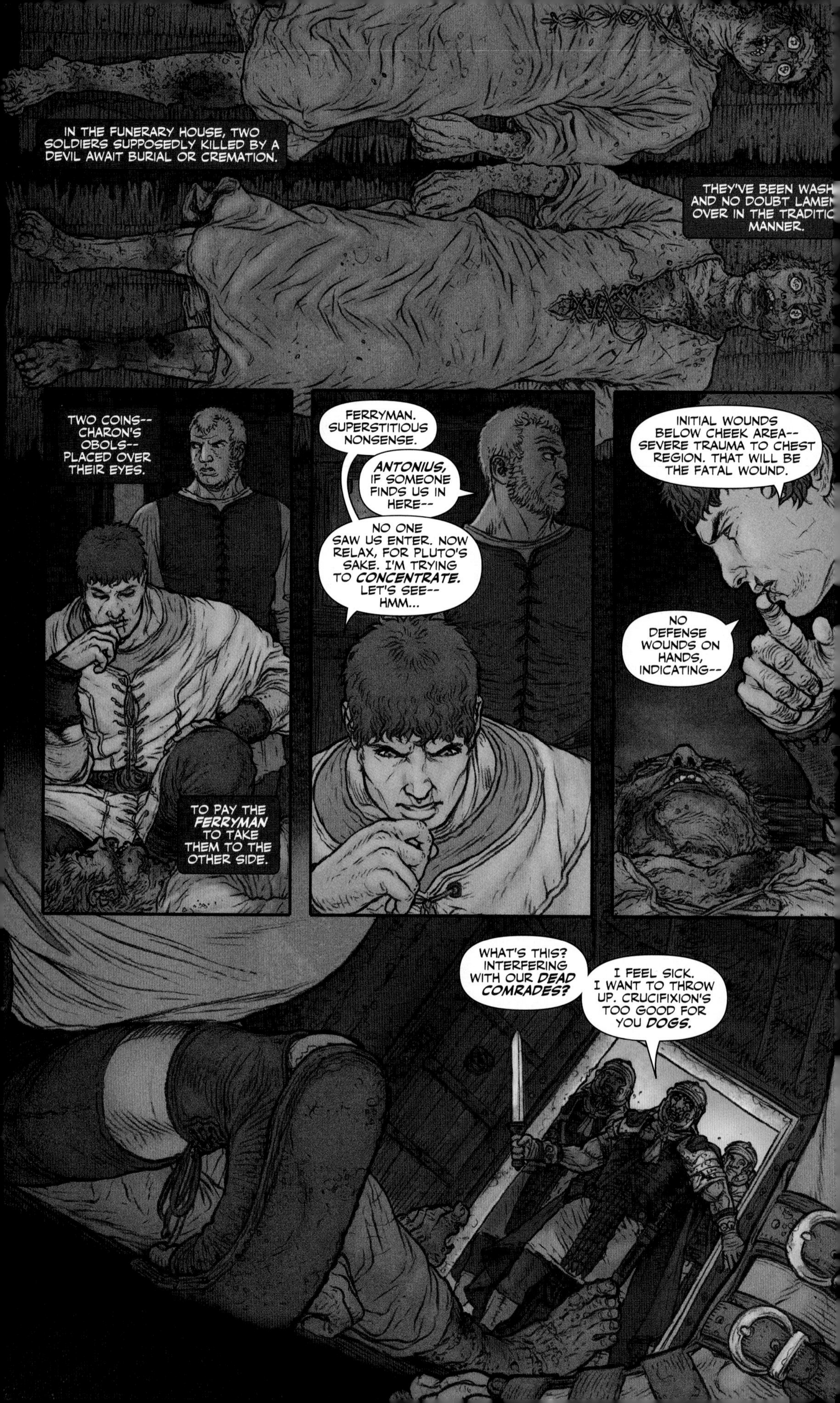
IN THE FUNERARY HOUSE, TWO SOLDIERS SUPPOSEDLY KILLED BY A DEVIL AWAIT BURIAL OR CREMATION.
THEY'VE BEEN WASH AND NO DOUBT LAMEN OVER IN THE TRADITIC MANNER.
TWO COINS-- CHARON'S OBOLS-- PLACED OVER THEIR EYES.
TO PAY THE FERRYMAN TO TAKE THEM TO THE OTHER SIDE.
FERRYMAN. SUPERSTITIOUS NONSENSE.
ANTONIUS, IF SOMEONE FINDS US IN HERE--
NO ONE SAW US ENTER. NOW RELAX, FOR PLUTO'S SAKE. I'M TRYING TO CONCENTRATE. LET'S SEE-- HMM...
INITIAL WOUNDS BELOW CHEEK AREA-- SEVERE TRAUMA TO CHEST REGION. THAT WILL BE THE FATAL WOUND.
NO DEFENSE WOUNDS ON HANDS, INDICATING--
WHAT'S THIS? INTERFERING WITH OUR DEAD COMRADES?
I FEEL SICK. I WANT TO THROW UP. CRUCIFIXION'S TOO GOOD FOR YOU DOGS.

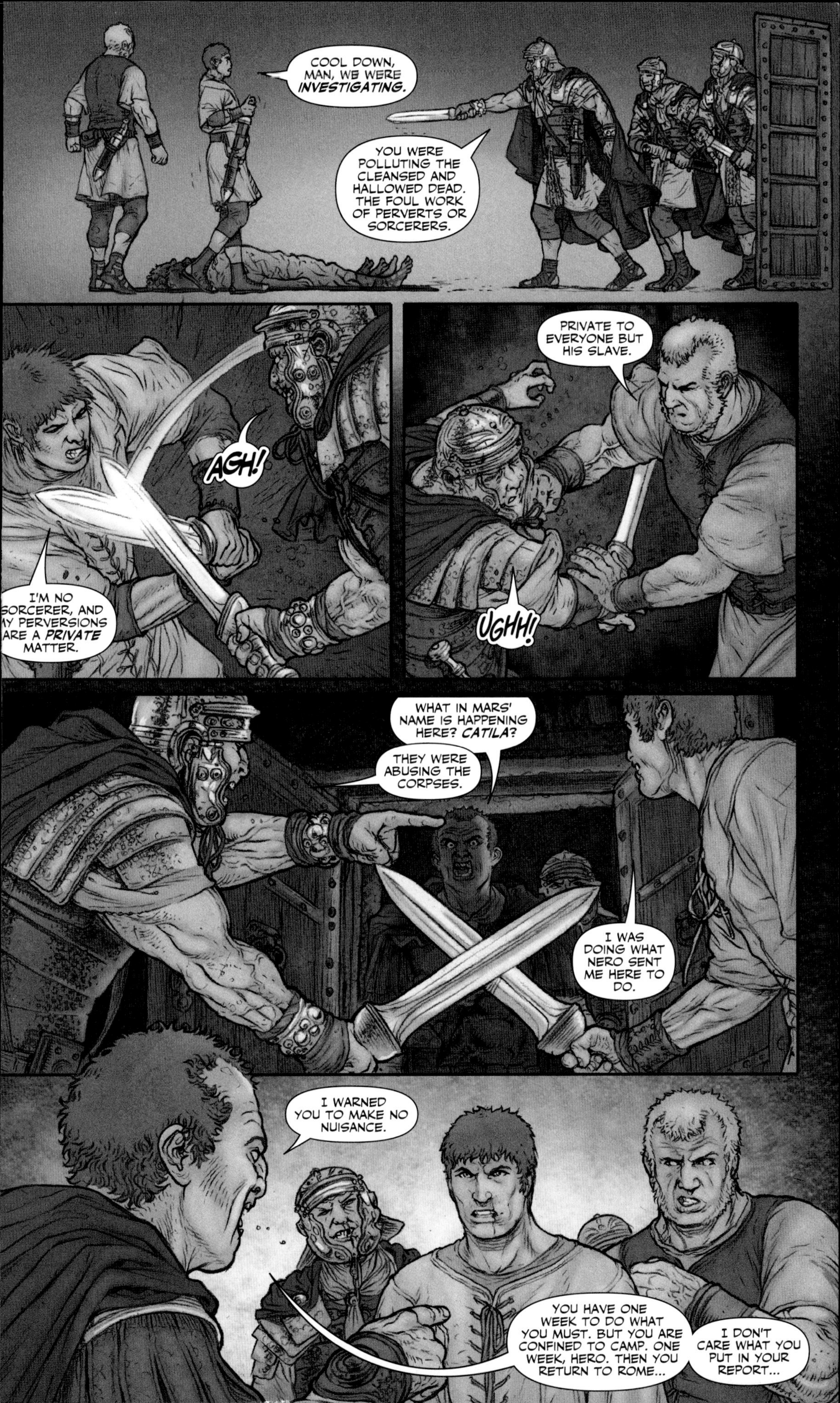
COOL DOWN, MAN, WE WERE *INVESTIGATING*.
YOU WERE POLLUTING THE CLEANSED AND HALLOWED DEAD. THE FOUL WORK OF PERVERTS OR SORCERERS.
AGH!
I'M NO SORCERER, AND MY PERVERSIONS ARE A *PRIVATE* MATTER.
PRIVATE TO EVERYONE BUT HIS SLAVE.
UGHH!
WHAT IN MARS' NAME IS HAPPENING HERE? *CATILA*?
THEY WERE ABUSING THE CORPSES.
I WAS DOING WHAT NERO SENT ME HERE TO DO.
I WARNED YOU TO MAKE NO NUISANCE.
YOU HAVE ONE WEEK TO DO WHAT YOU MUST. BUT YOU ARE CONFINED TO CAMP. ONE WEEK, HERO. THEN YOU RETURN TO ROME...
I DON'T CARE WHAT YOU PUT IN YOUR REPORT...

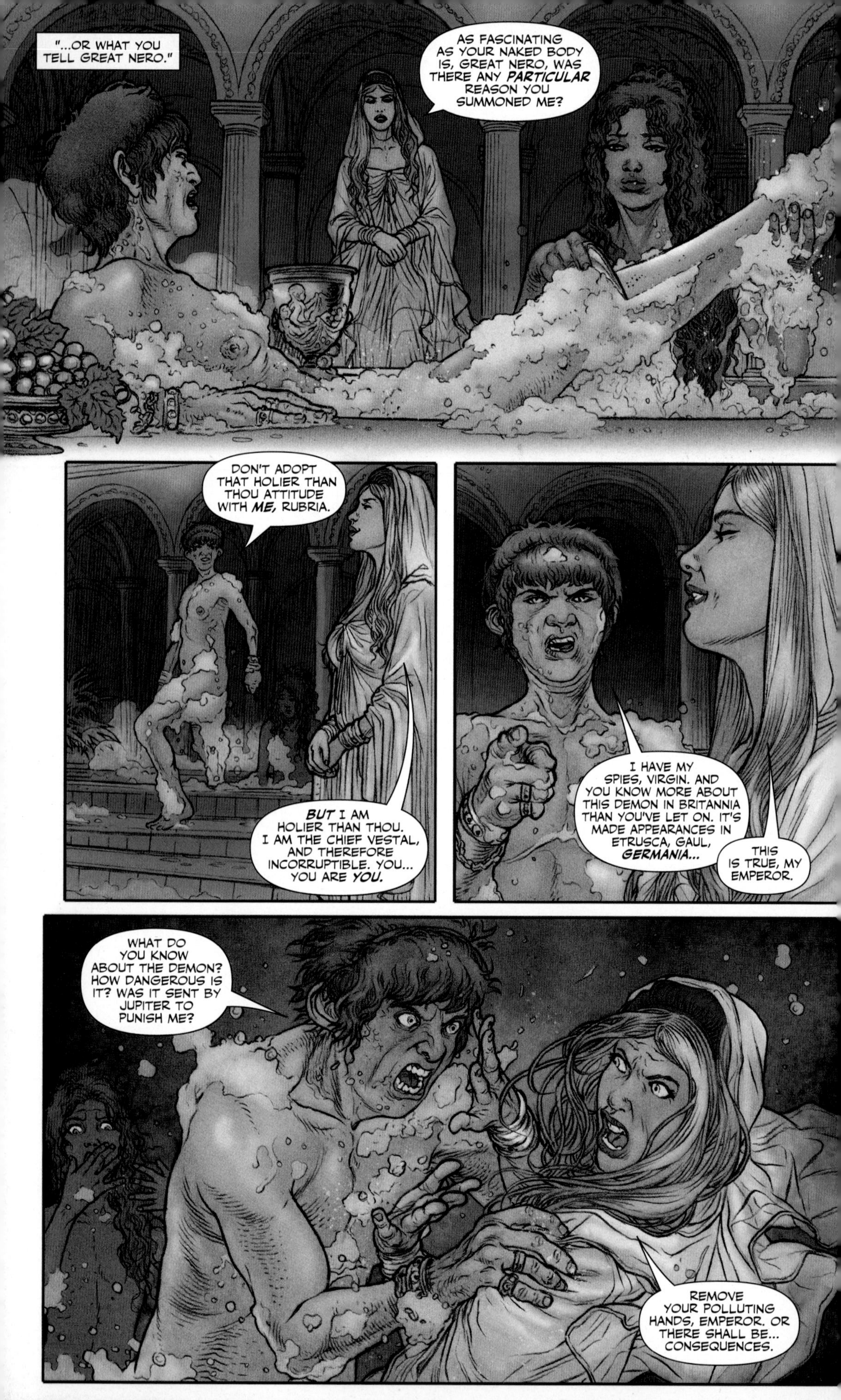
"...OR WHAT YOU TELL GREAT NERO."
AS FASCINATING AS YOUR NAKED BODY IS, GREAT NERO, WAS THERE ANY *PARTICULAR* REASON YOU SUMMONED ME?
DON'T ADOPT THAT HOLIER THAN THOU ATTITUDE WITH *ME,* RUBRIA.
BUT I AM HOLIER THAN THOU. I AM THE CHIEF VESTAL, AND THEREFORE INCORRUPTIBLE. YOU... YOU ARE *YOU.*
I HAVE MY SPIES, VIRGIN. AND YOU KNOW MORE ABOUT THIS DEMON IN BRITANNIA THAN YOU'VE LET ON. IT'S MADE APPEARANCES IN ETRUSCA, GAUL, *GERMANIA...*
THIS IS TRUE, MY EMPEROR.
WHAT DO YOU KNOW ABOUT THE DEMON? HOW DANGEROUS IS IT? WAS IT SENT BY JUPITER TO PUNISH ME?
REMOVE YOUR POLLUTING HANDS, EMPEROR. OR THERE SHALL BE... CONSEQUENCES.

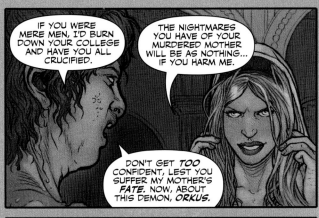

CONSEQUENCES, EH? SOMETIMES I THINK THE POWER OF THE VESTALS IS TOO GREAT. WOMEN, OWNING PROPERTY...IT'S NOT NATURAL!

IF YOU WERE MERE MEN, I'D BURN DOWN YOUR COLLEGE AND HAVE YOU ALL CRUCIFIED.

THE NIGHTMARES YOU HAVE OF YOUR MURDERED MOTHER WILL BE AS NOTHING... IF YOU HARM ME.

DON'T GET *TOO* CONFIDENT, LEST YOU SUFFER MY MOTHER'S *FATE*. NOW, ABOUT THIS DEMON, *ORKUS*.

I FEAR IT IS ANCIENT. A RARE SUMMONING...

A THREAT TO ROME?

POSSIBLY. WHICH IS WHY WE FOUND THIS LOW-BORN SOLDIER, ANTONIUS. HE WAS AN EMOTIONAL WRECK, BUT WE SHAPED HIM INTO A *WEAPON*.

HE SOUNDS DANGEROUS. I MIGHT HAVE USE FOR HIM WHEN HE RETURNS.

OH, I DOUBT HE'LL RETURN. HE MIGHT KILL ORKUS, BUT HE'LL PROBABLY PERISH IN THE PROCESS.

THESE BURNT OUT SOLDIERS ARE SO EASY TO MANIPULATE.

YOU'RE AS CALLOUS AS I AM, VIRGIN. WHAT A COUPLING WE'D MAKE. HOW ABOUT...A SECRET LIAISON SOME EVENING?

BE CAREFUL, NERO...OR YOU'LL RUIN *BOTH* OF OUR REPUTATIONS...

JUST PRAY THAT WE HAVE CHOSEN WELL IN ANTONIUS AXIA...

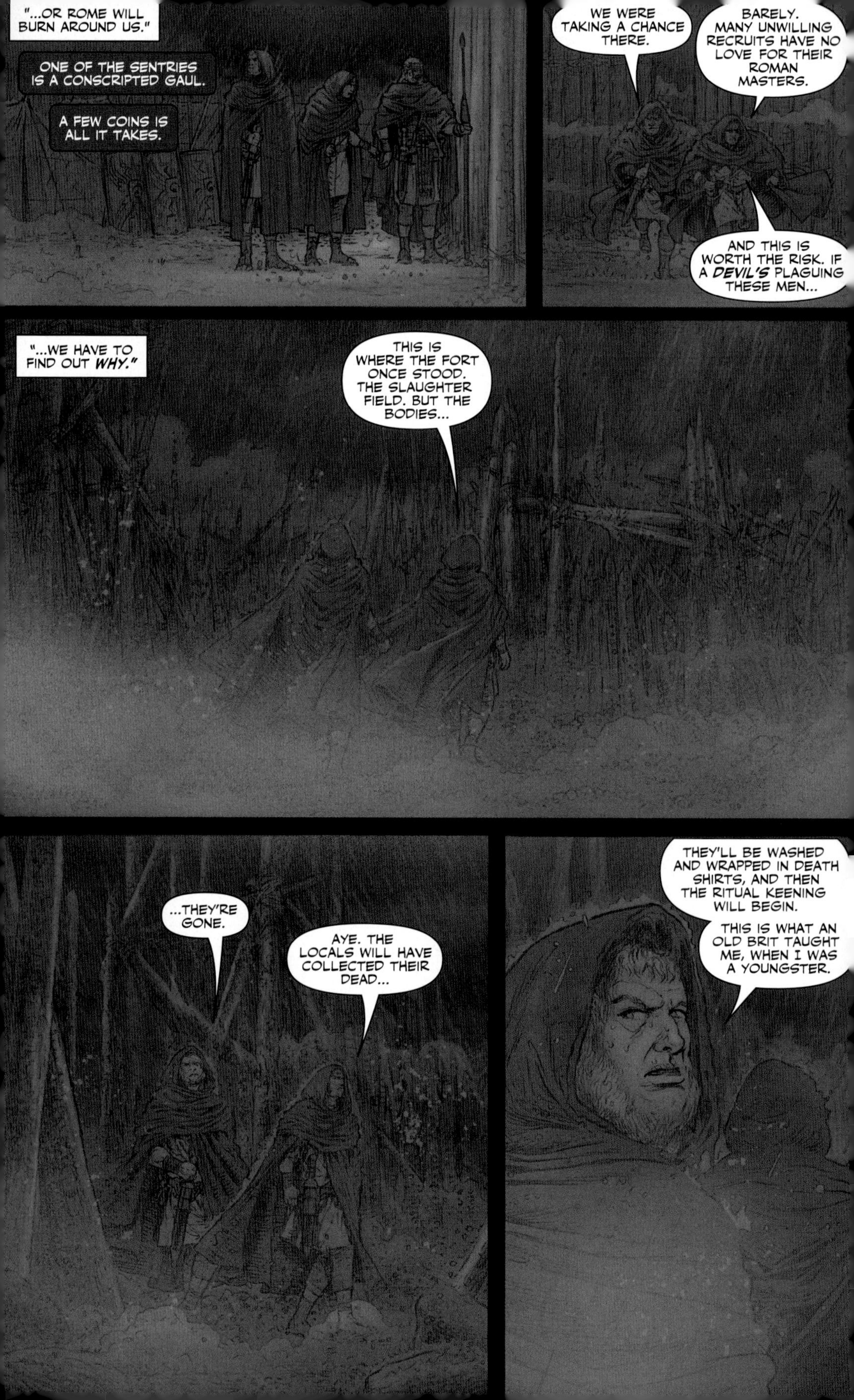
"...OR ROME WILL BURN AROUND US."
ONE OF THE SENTRIES IS A CONSCRIPTED GAUL.
A FEW COINS IS ALL IT TAKES.
WE WERE TAKING A CHANCE THERE.
BARELY. MANY UNWILLING RECRUITS HAVE NO LOVE FOR THEIR ROMAN MASTERS.
AND THIS IS WORTH THE RISK. IF A *DEVIL'S* PLAGUING THESE MEN...
"...WE HAVE TO FIND OUT *WHY.*"
THIS IS WHERE THE FORT ONCE STOOD. THE SLAUGHTER FIELD. BUT THE BODIES...
...THEY'RE GONE.
AYE. THE LOCALS WILL HAVE COLLECTED THEIR DEAD...
THEY'LL BE WASHED AND WRAPPED IN DEATH SHIRTS, AND THEN THE RITUAL KEENING WILL BEGIN.
THIS IS WHAT AN OLD BRIT TAUGHT ME, WHEN I WAS A YOUNGSTER.

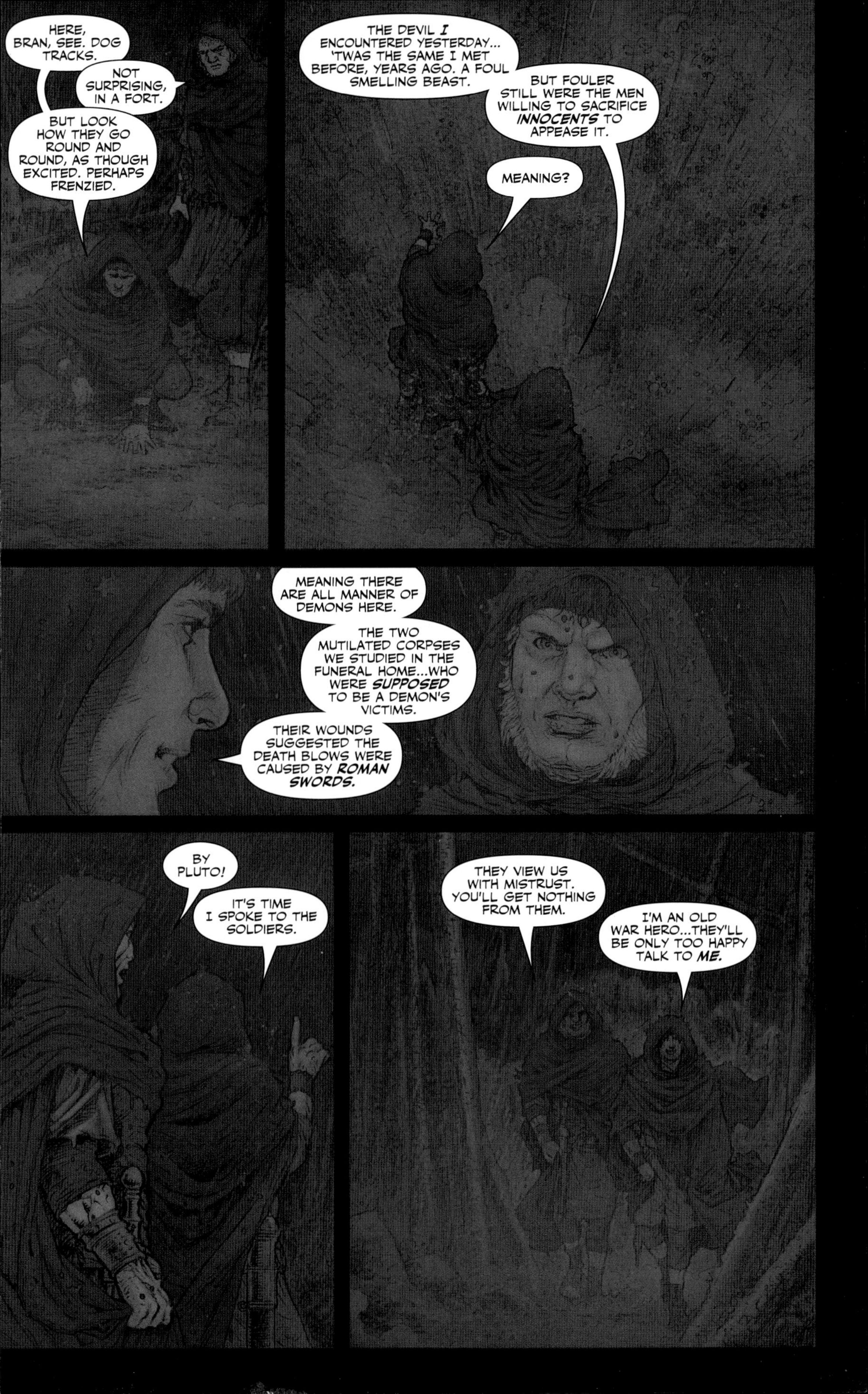
HERE, BRAN, SEE. DOG TRACKS.
NOT SURPRISING, IN A FORT.
BUT LOOK HOW THEY GO ROUND AND ROUND, AS THOUGH EXCITED. PERHAPS FRENZIED.
THE DEVIL *I* ENCOUNTERED YESTERDAY... 'TWAS THE SAME I MET BEFORE, YEARS AGO. A FOUL SMELLING BEAST.
BUT FOULER STILL WERE THE MEN WILLING TO SACRIFICE ***INNOCENTS*** TO APPEASE IT.
MEANING?
MEANING THERE ARE ALL MANNER OF DEMONS HERE.
THE TWO MUTILATED CORPSES WE STUDIED IN THE FUNERAL HOME...WHO WERE ***SUPPOSED*** TO BE A DEMON'S VICTIMS.
THEIR WOUNDS SUGGESTED THE DEATH BLOWS WERE CAUSED BY ***ROMAN SWORDS.***
BY PLUTO!
IT'S TIME I SPOKE TO THE SOLDIERS.
THEY VIEW US WITH MISTRUST. YOU'LL GET NOTHING FROM THEM.
I'M AN OLD WAR HERO...THEY'LL BE ONLY TOO HAPPY TALK TO ***ME.***

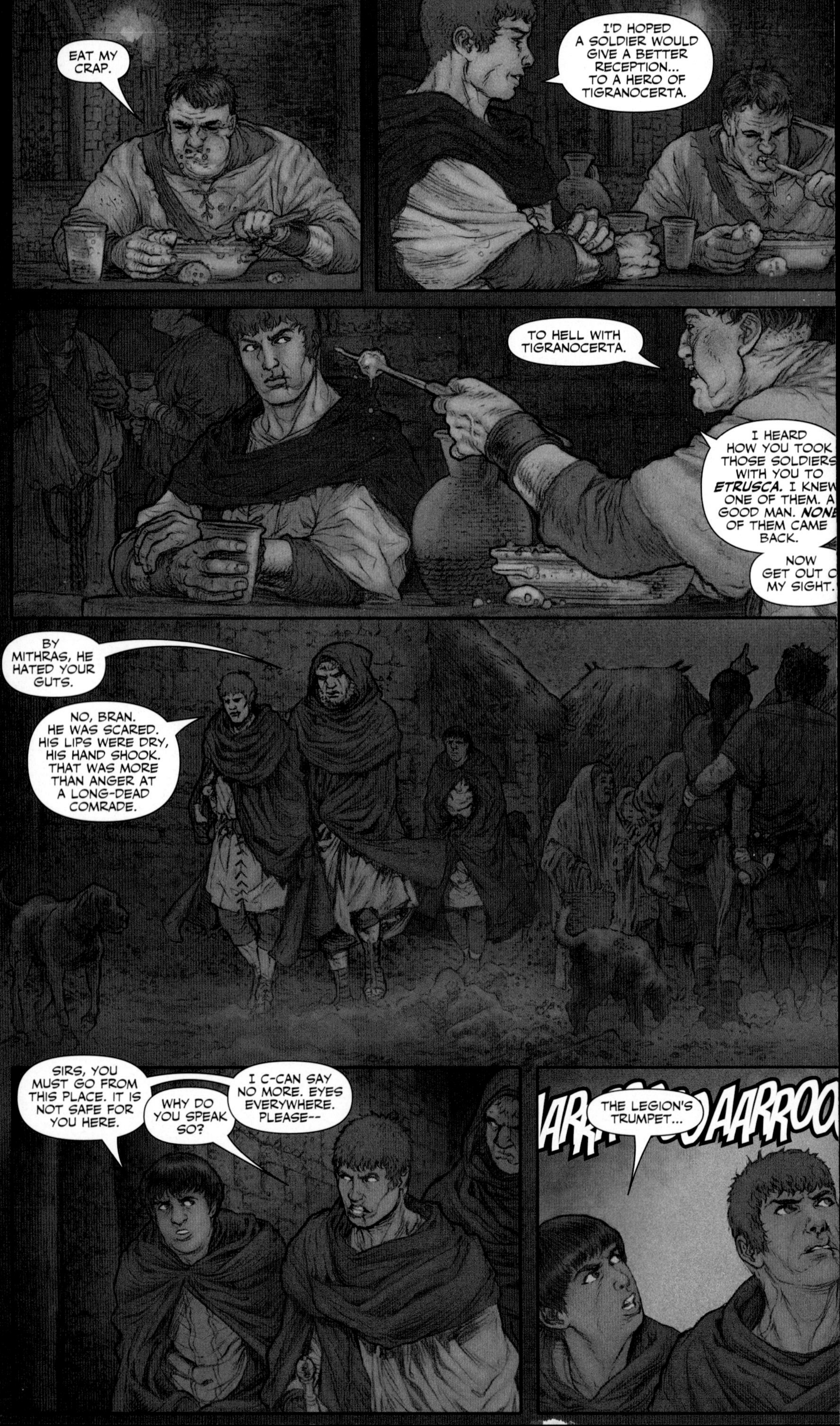
EAT MY CRAP.
I'D HOPED A SOLDIER WOULD GIVE A BETTER RECEPTION... TO A HERO OF TIGRANOCERTA.
TO HELL WITH TIGRANOCERTA.
I HEARD HOW YOU TOOK THOSE SOLDIERS WITH YOU TO ETRUSCA. I KNEW ONE OF THEM. A GOOD MAN. NONE OF THEM CAME BACK.
NOW GET OUT OF MY SIGHT.
BY MITHRAS, HE HATED YOUR GUTS.
NO, BRAN. HE WAS SCARED. HIS LIPS WERE DRY, HIS HAND SHOOK. THAT WAS MORE THAN ANGER AT A LONG-DEAD COMRADE.
SIRS, YOU MUST GO FROM THIS PLACE. IT IS NOT SAFE FOR YOU HERE.
WHY DO YOU SPEAK SO?
I C-CAN SAY NO MORE. EYES EVERYWHERE. PLEASE--
THE LEGION'S TRUMPET...

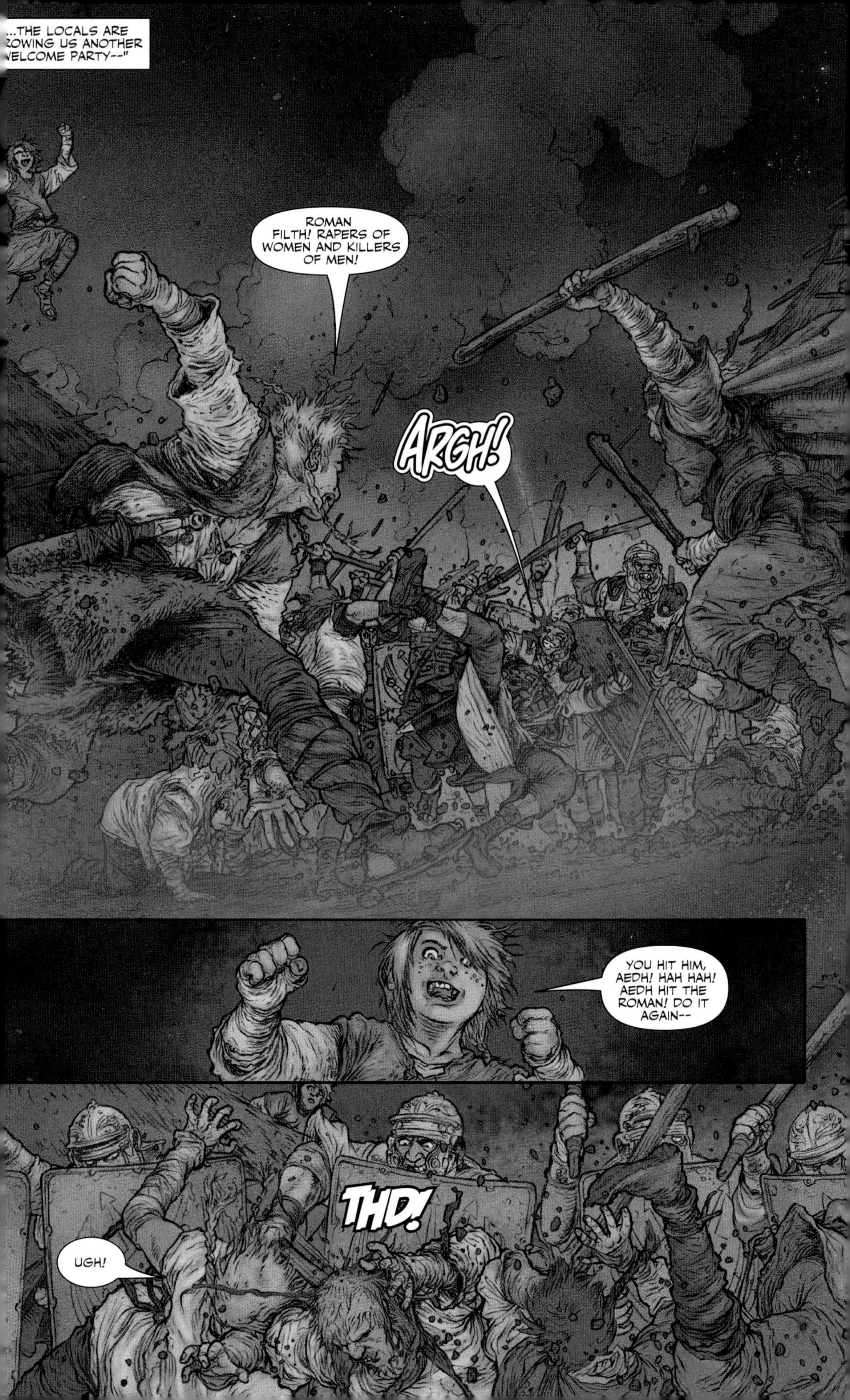
...THE LOCALS ARE
ROWING US ANOTHER
WELCOME PARTY--"
ROMAN FILTH! RAPERS OF WOMEN AND KILLERS OF MEN!
ARGH!
YOU HIT HIM, AEDH! HAH HAH! AEDH HIT THE ROMAN! DO IT AGAIN--
THD!
UGH!

WHAT'S GOING ON, SOLDIER?

SOME LOCAL *THUGS* STARTED THROWING STONES AT OUR BOYS. THEY'RE ALWAYS MAKING TROUBLE FOR US.

VERY UNGRATEFUL OF THEM.

I WANTED TO COME ALONG.

SEE MY COMPATRIOTS-- THESE ROUGH BORDER SOLDIERS--IN ACTION.

IT'S NOTHING LESS THAN I'D EXPECTED.

MURDERING ROMAN BASTARD!

BRITISH WITCH.

I'LL PUT A WYRD ON YOU!

WH-WHO'S SHE?

THAT'S BODMALL. ONE OF THEIR *WYRD WOMEN.*

WYRD IS THEIR DRUIDS' MAGIC.

STAY WELL CLEAR OF *THAT* ONE. SHE'S *TROUBLE.*

THEY SAY SHE DROVE A LOCAL CRAZY HE CARVED NAME ON HIS PRIV PARTS. BLED T DEATH SINGING THE MOON.

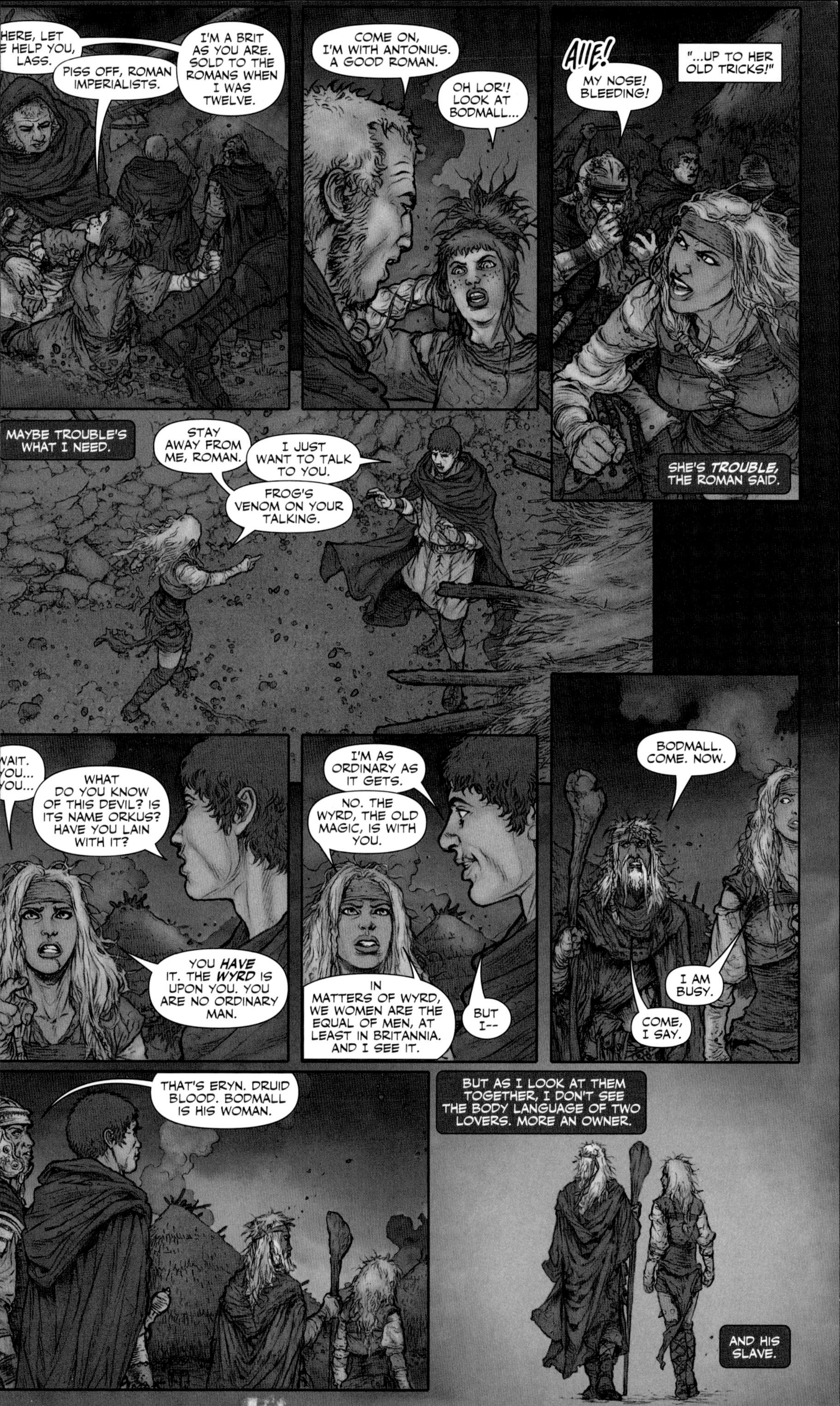
HERE, LET
E HELP YOU,
LASS.
PISS OFF, ROMAN IMPERIALISTS.
I'M A BRIT AS YOU ARE. SOLD TO THE ROMANS WHEN I WAS TWELVE.
COME ON, I'M WITH ANTONIUS. A GOOD ROMAN.
OH LOR'! LOOK AT BODMALL...
AIIE!
MY NOSE! BLEEDING!
"...UP TO HER OLD TRICKS!"
SHE'S TROUBLE, THE ROMAN SAID.
MAYBE TROUBLE'S WHAT I NEED.
STAY AWAY FROM ME, ROMAN.
I JUST WANT TO TALK TO YOU.
FROG'S VENOM ON YOUR TALKING.
AIT. OU... OU...
WHAT DO YOU KNOW OF THIS DEVIL? IS ITS NAME ORKUS? HAVE YOU LAIN WITH IT?
YOU HAVE IT. THE WYRD IS UPON YOU. YOU ARE NO ORDINARY MAN.
I'M AS ORDINARY AS IT GETS.
NO. THE WYRD, THE OLD MAGIC, IS WITH YOU.
IN MATTERS OF WYRD, WE WOMEN ARE THE EQUAL OF MEN, AT LEAST IN BRITANNIA. AND I SEE IT.
BUT I--
BODMALL. COME. NOW.
I AM BUSY.
COME, I SAY.
THAT'S ERYN. DRUID BLOOD. BODMALL IS HIS WOMAN.
BUT AS I LOOK AT THEM TOGETHER, I DON'T SEE THE BODY LANGUAGE OF TWO LOVERS. MORE AN OWNER.
AND HIS SLAVE.

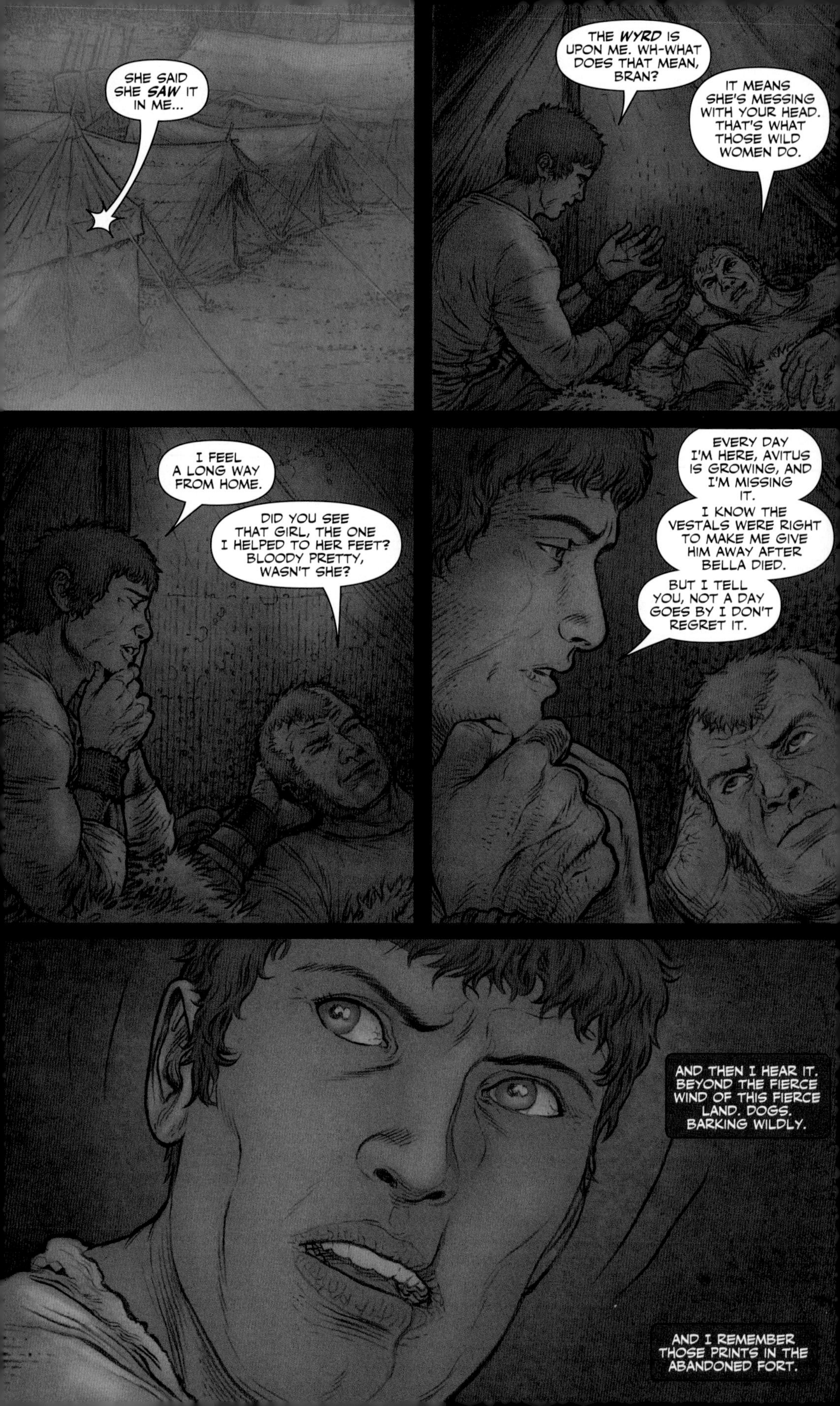
SHE SAID SHE SAW IT IN ME...
THE WYRD IS UPON ME. WH-WHAT DOES THAT MEAN, BRAN?
IT MEANS SHE'S MESSING WITH YOUR HEAD. THAT'S WHAT THOSE WILD WOMEN DO.
I FEEL A LONG WAY FROM HOME.
DID YOU SEE THAT GIRL, THE ONE I HELPED TO HER FEET? BLOODY PRETTY, WASN'T SHE?
EVERY DAY I'M HERE, AVITUS IS GROWING, AND I'M MISSING IT.
I KNOW THE VESTALS WERE RIGHT TO MAKE ME GIVE HIM AWAY AFTER BELLA DIED.
BUT I TELL YOU, NOT A DAY GOES BY I DON'T REGRET IT.
AND THEN I HEAR IT. BEYOND THE FIERCE WIND OF THIS FIERCE LAND. DOGS. BARKING WILDLY.
AND I REMEMBER THOSE PRINTS IN THE ABANDONED FORT.

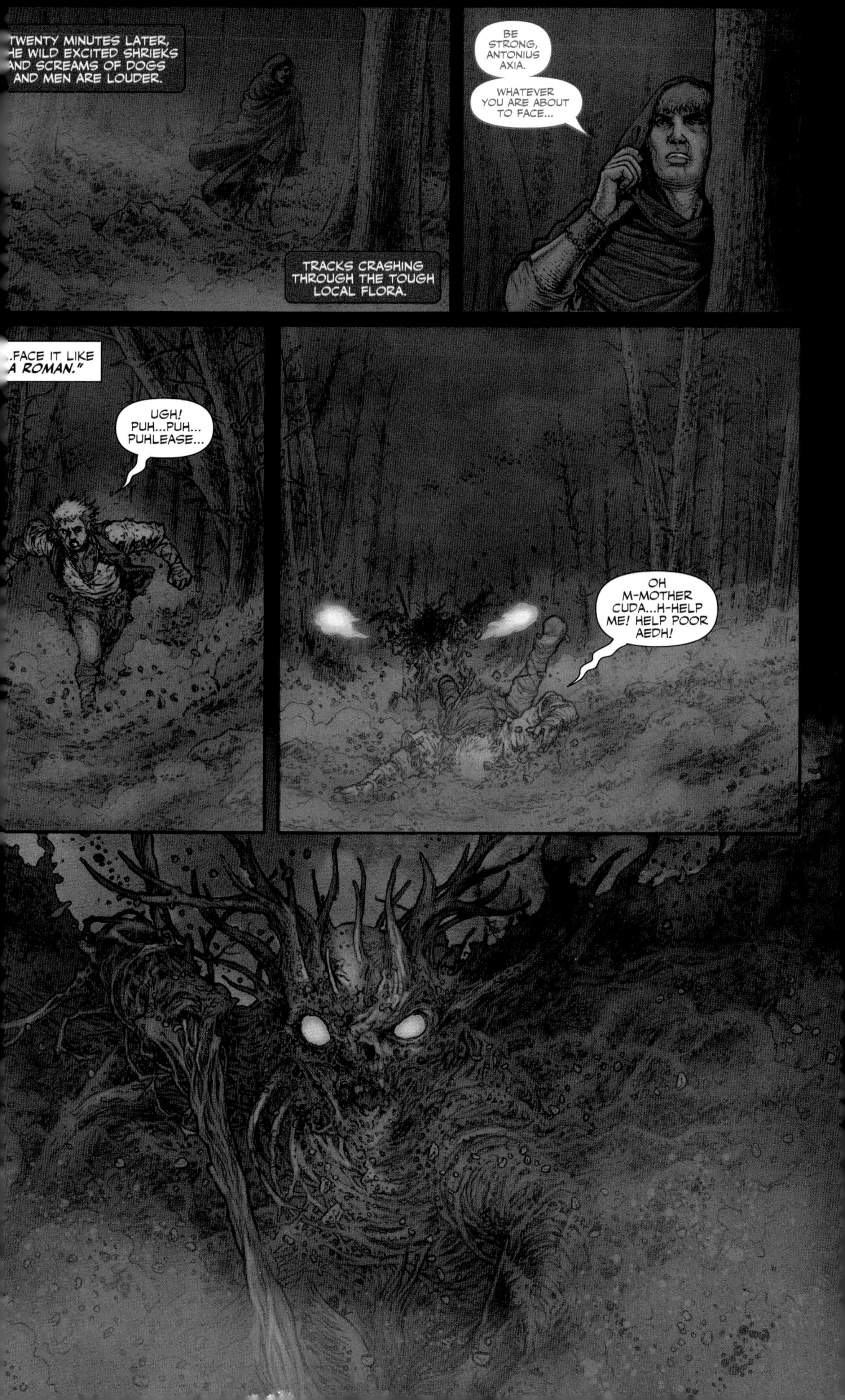
TWENTY MINUTES LATER, HE WILD EXCITED SHRIEKS AND SCREAMS OF DOGS AND MEN ARE LOUDER.
TRACKS CRASHING THROUGH THE TOUGH LOCAL FLORA.
BE STRONG, ANTONIUS AXIA.
WHATEVER YOU ARE ABOUT TO FACE...
..FACE IT LIKE A ROMAN."
UGH! PUH...PUH... PUHLEASE...
OH M-MOTHER CUDA...H-HELP ME! HELP POOR AEDH!

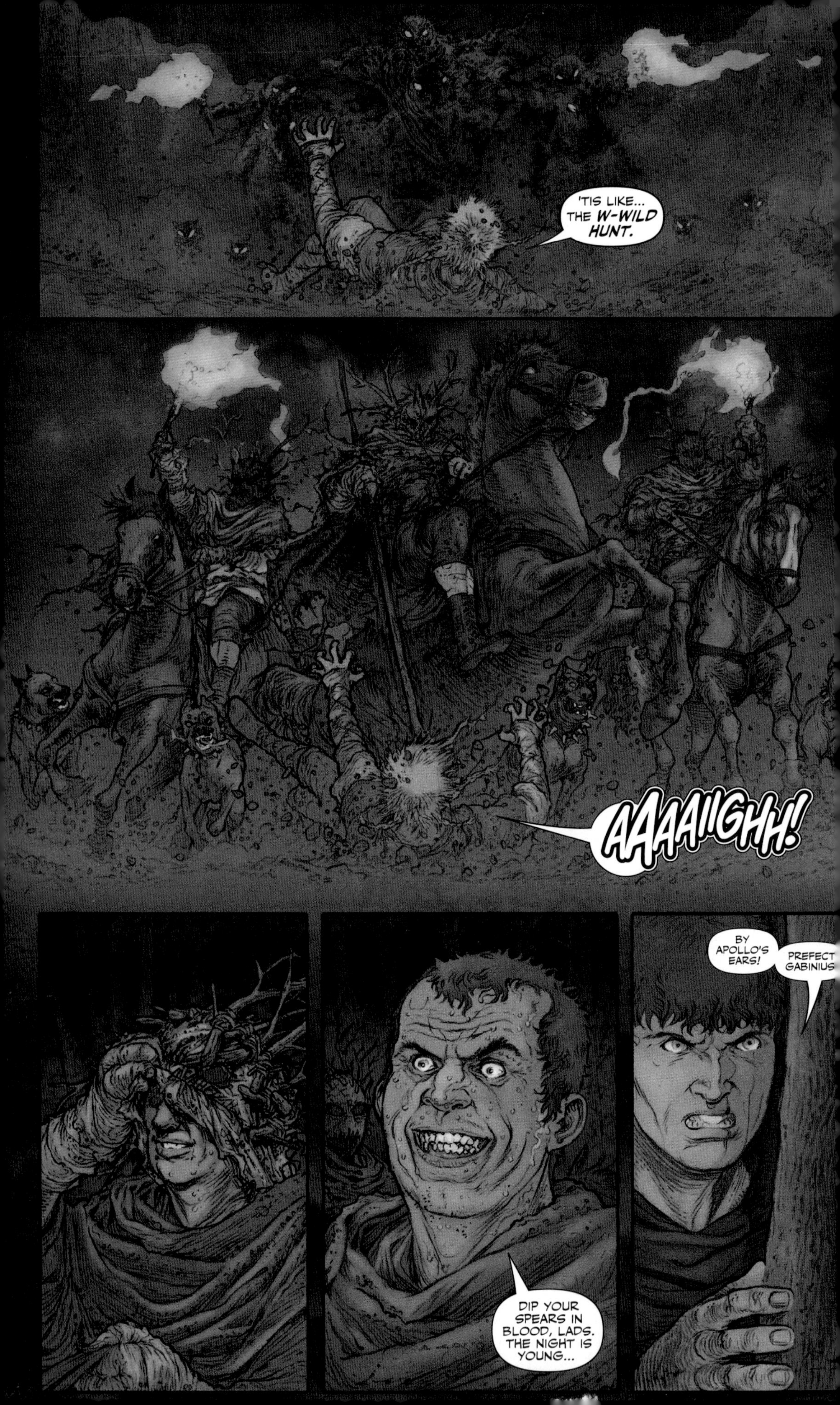
'TIS LIKE... THE W-WILD HUNT.
AAAAIIGHH!
DIP YOUR SPEARS IN BLOOD, LADS. THE NIGHT IS YOUNG...
BY APOLLO'S EARS!
PREFECT GABINIUS

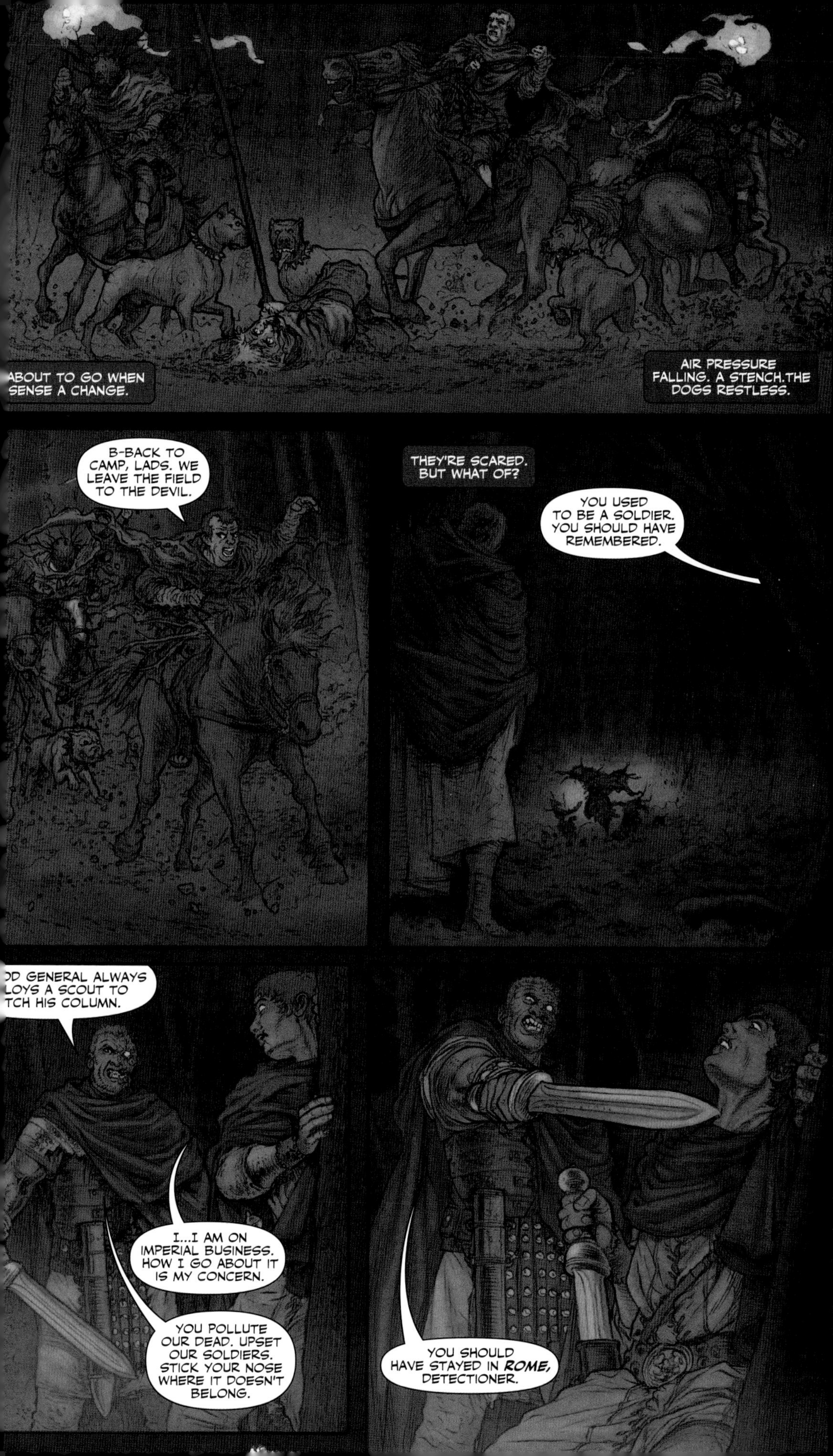

ABOUT TO GO WHEN
SENSE A CHANGE.
AIR PRESSURE FALLING. A STENCH.THE DOGS RESTLESS.
B-BACK TO CAMP, LADS. WE LEAVE THE FIELD TO THE DEVIL.
THEY'RE SCARED. BUT WHAT OF?
YOU USED TO BE A SOLDIER. YOU SHOULD HAVE REMEMBERED.
OD GENERAL ALWAYS
LOYS A SCOUT TO
TCH HIS COLUMN.
I...I AM ON IMPERIAL BUSINESS. HOW I GO ABOUT IT IS MY CONCERN.
YOU POLLUTE OUR DEAD. UPSET OUR SOLDIERS. STICK YOUR NOSE WHERE IT DOESN'T BELONG.
YOU SHOULD HAVE STAYED IN ROME, DETECTIONER.

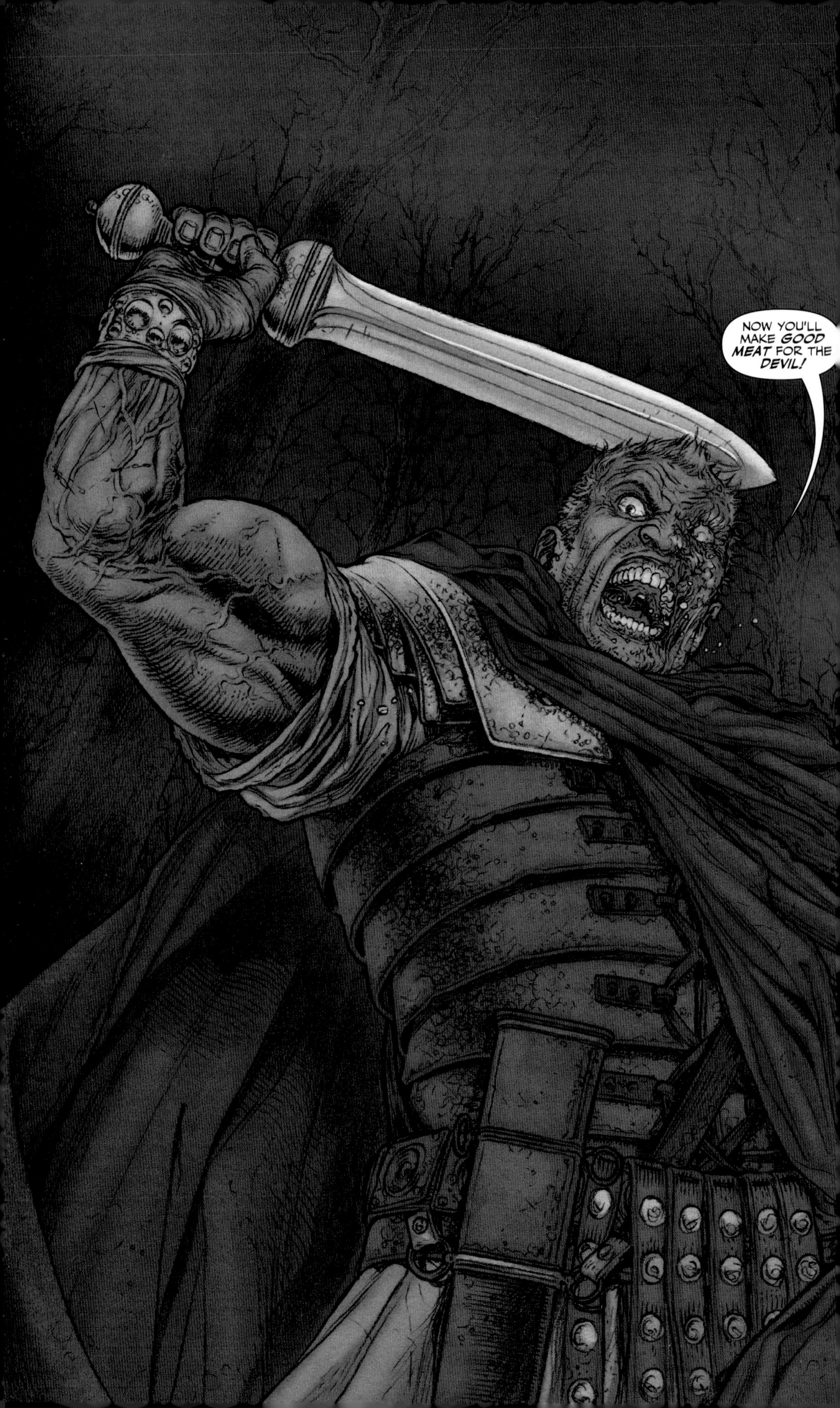
NOW YOU'LL MAKE *GOOD MEAT* FOR THE *DEVIL!*

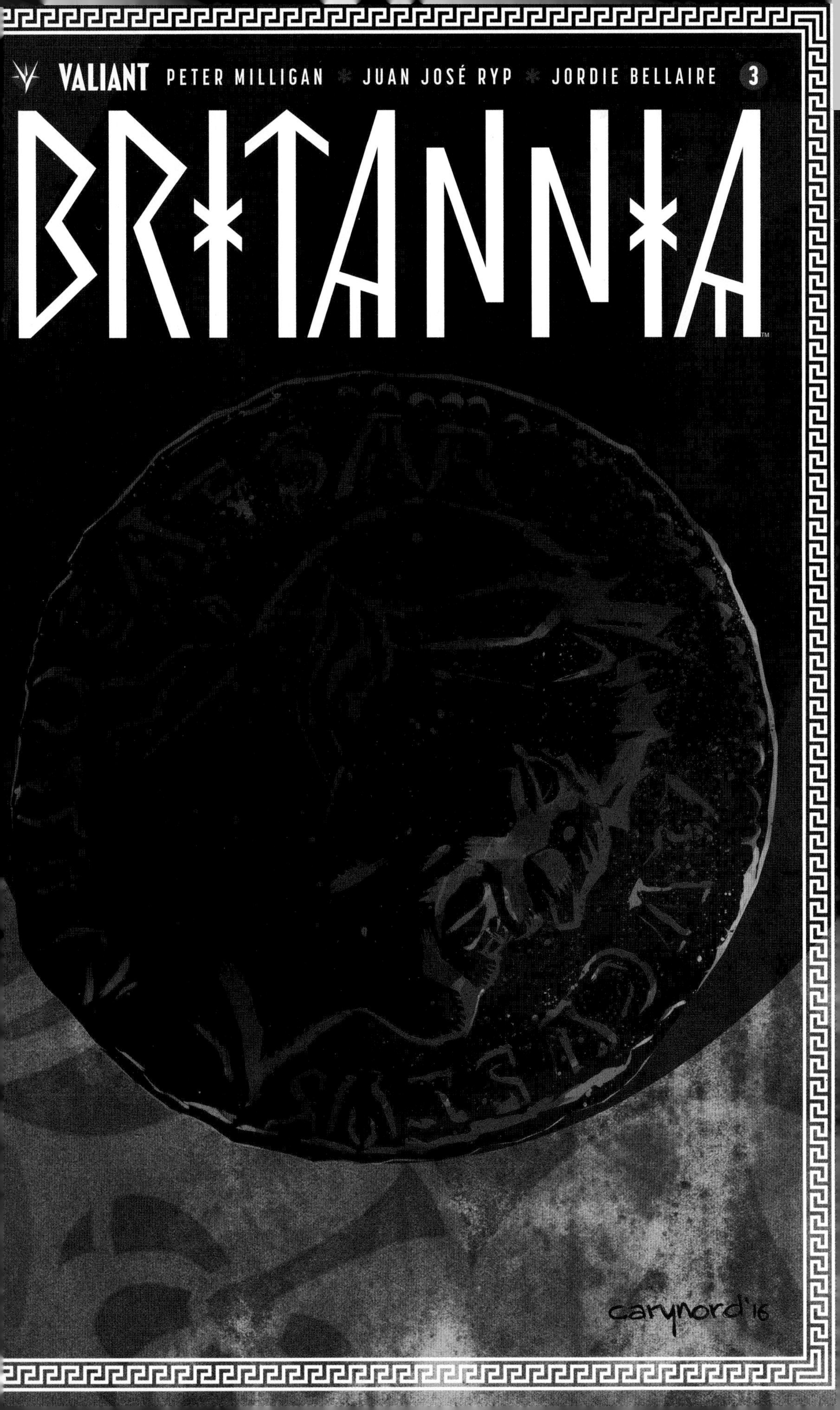
VALIANT
PETER MILLIGAN
JUAN JOSÉ RYP
JORDIE BELLAIRE
3
BRITANNIA
carynord'16

BOOK III

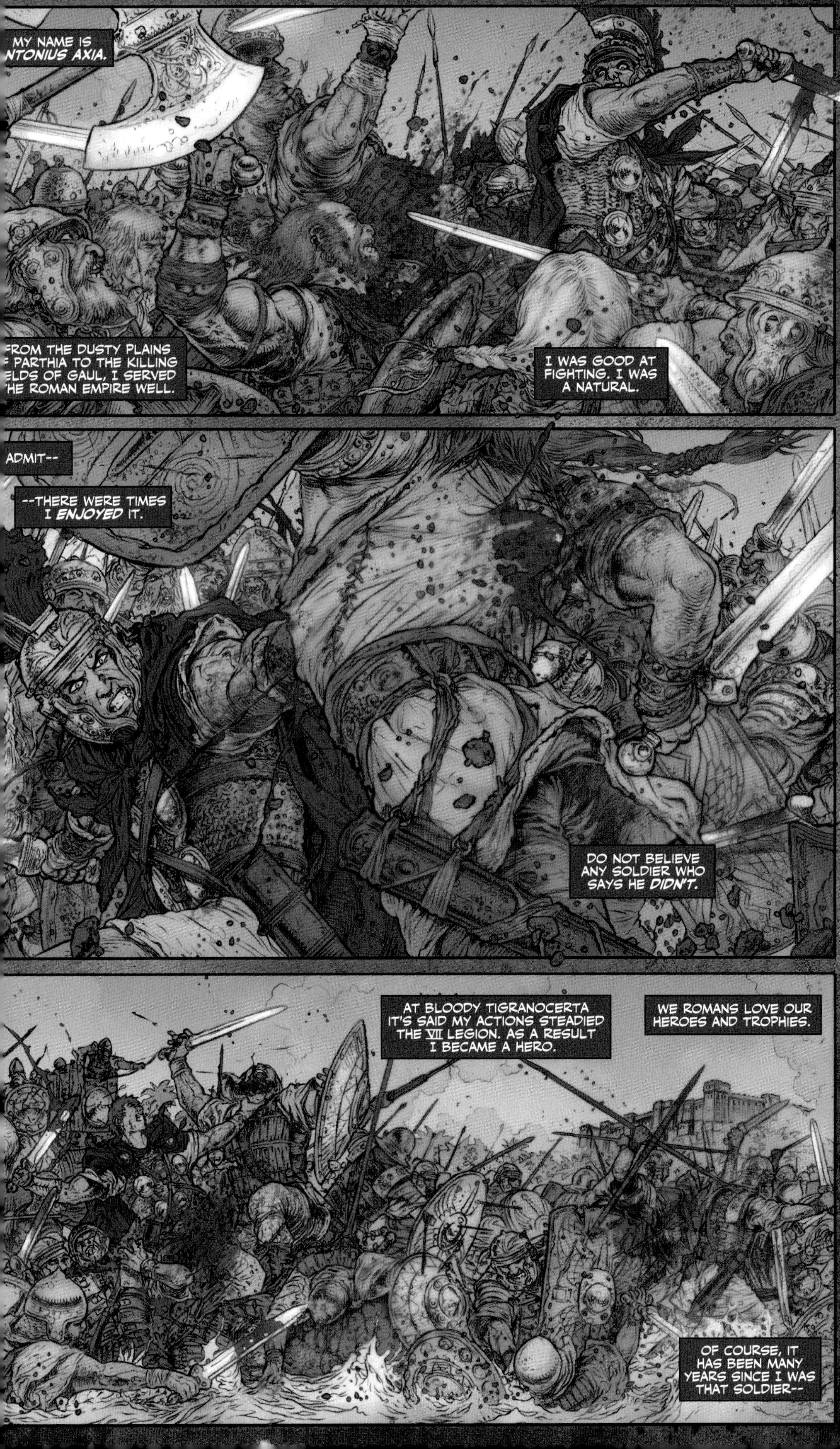
MY NAME IS NTONIUS AXIA.
FROM THE DUSTY PLAINS PARTHIA TO THE KILLING ELDS OF GAUL, I SERVED THE ROMAN EMPIRE WELL.
I WAS GOOD AT FIGHTING. I WAS A NATURAL.
ADMIT--
--THERE WERE TIMES I ENJOYED IT.
DO NOT BELIEVE ANY SOLDIER WHO SAYS HE DIDN'T.
AT BLOODY TIGRANOCERTA IT'S SAID MY ACTIONS STEADIED THE VII LEGION. AS A RESULT I BECAME A HERO.
WE ROMANS LOVE OUR HEROES AND TROPHIES.
OF COURSE, IT HAS BEEN MANY YEARS SINCE I WAS THAT SOLDIER--

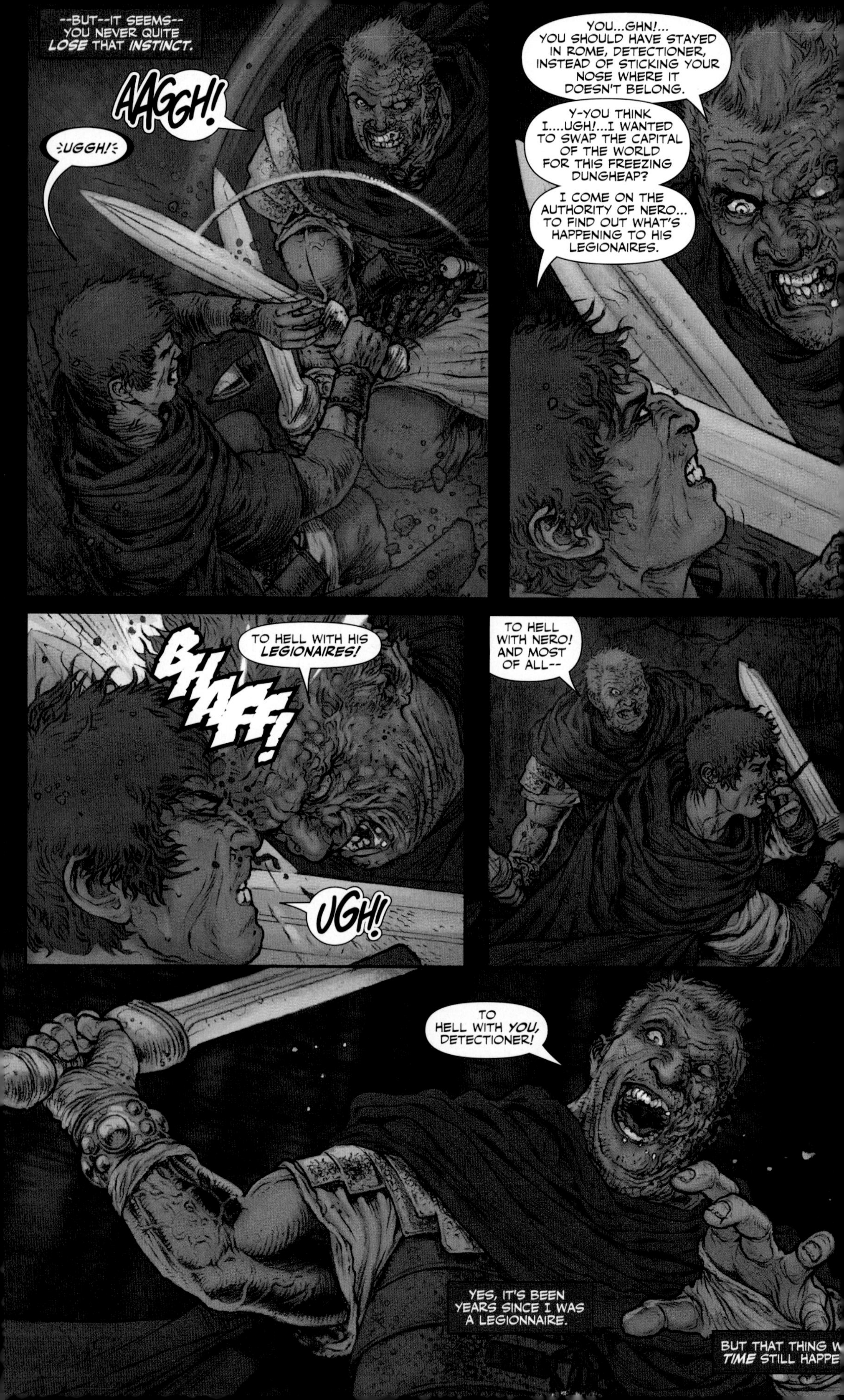
--BUT--IT SEEMS--
YOU NEVER QUITE
LOSE THAT INSTINCT.
AAGGH!
UGGH!
YOU...GHN!...
YOU SHOULD HAVE STAYED IN ROME, DETECTIONER, INSTEAD OF STICKING YOUR NOSE WHERE IT DOESN'T BELONG.
Y-YOU THINK I....UGH!...I WANTED TO SWAP THE CAPITAL OF THE WORLD FOR THIS FREEZING DUNGHEAP?
I COME ON THE AUTHORITY OF NERO... TO FIND OUT WHAT'S HAPPENING TO HIS LEGIONAIRES.
BHAFF!
TO HELL WITH HIS LEGIONAIRES!
UGH!
TO HELL WITH NERO! AND MOST OF ALL--
TO HELL WITH YOU, DETECTIONER!
YES, IT'S BEEN YEARS SINCE I WAS A LEGIONNAIRE.
BUT THAT THING W
TIME STILL HAPPE

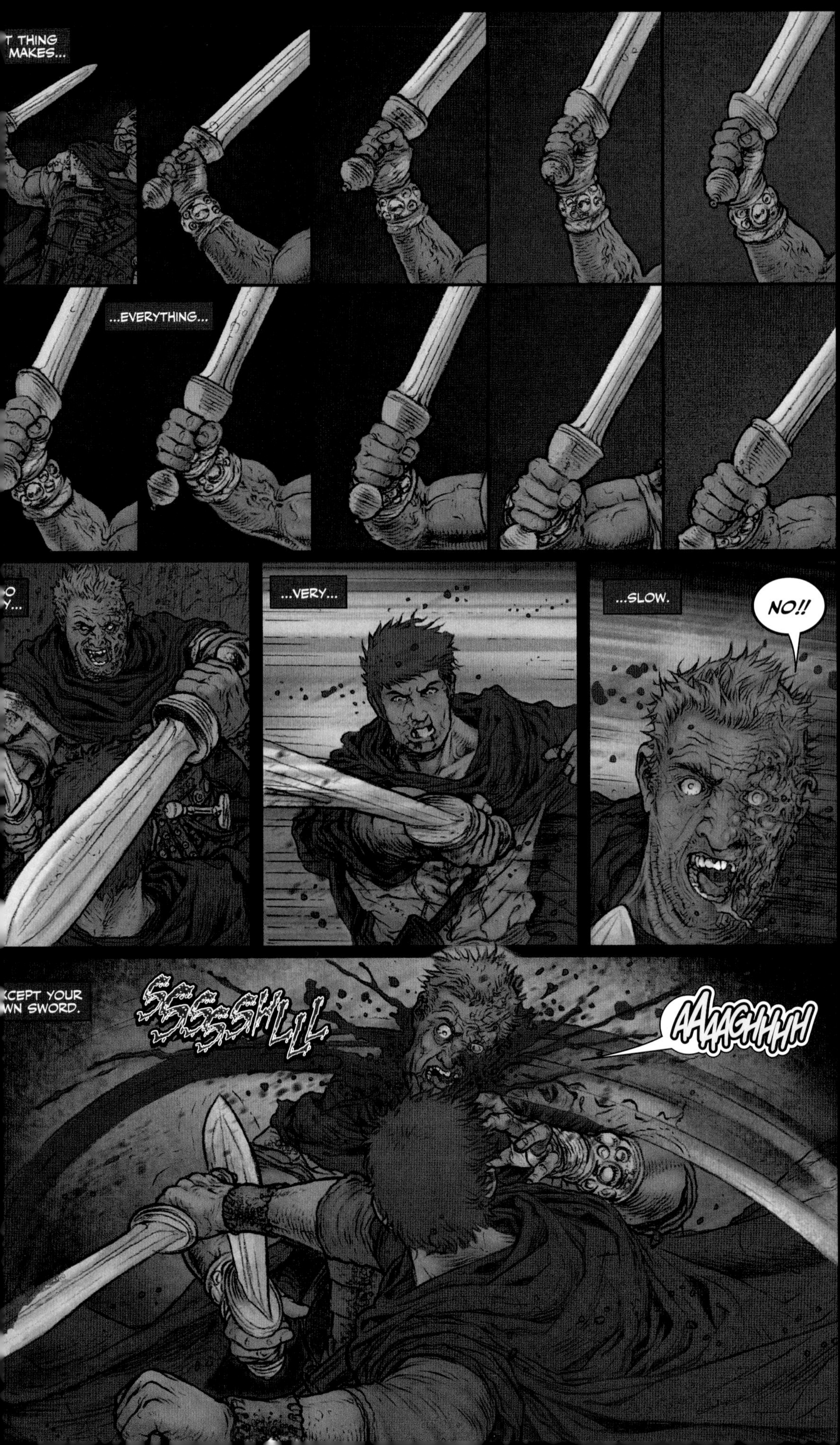
T THING
MAKES...
...EVERYTHING...
O
Y...
...VERY...
...SLOW.
NO!!
CCEPT YOUR
WN SWORD.
SSSSSHLL
AAAAGHHHHH

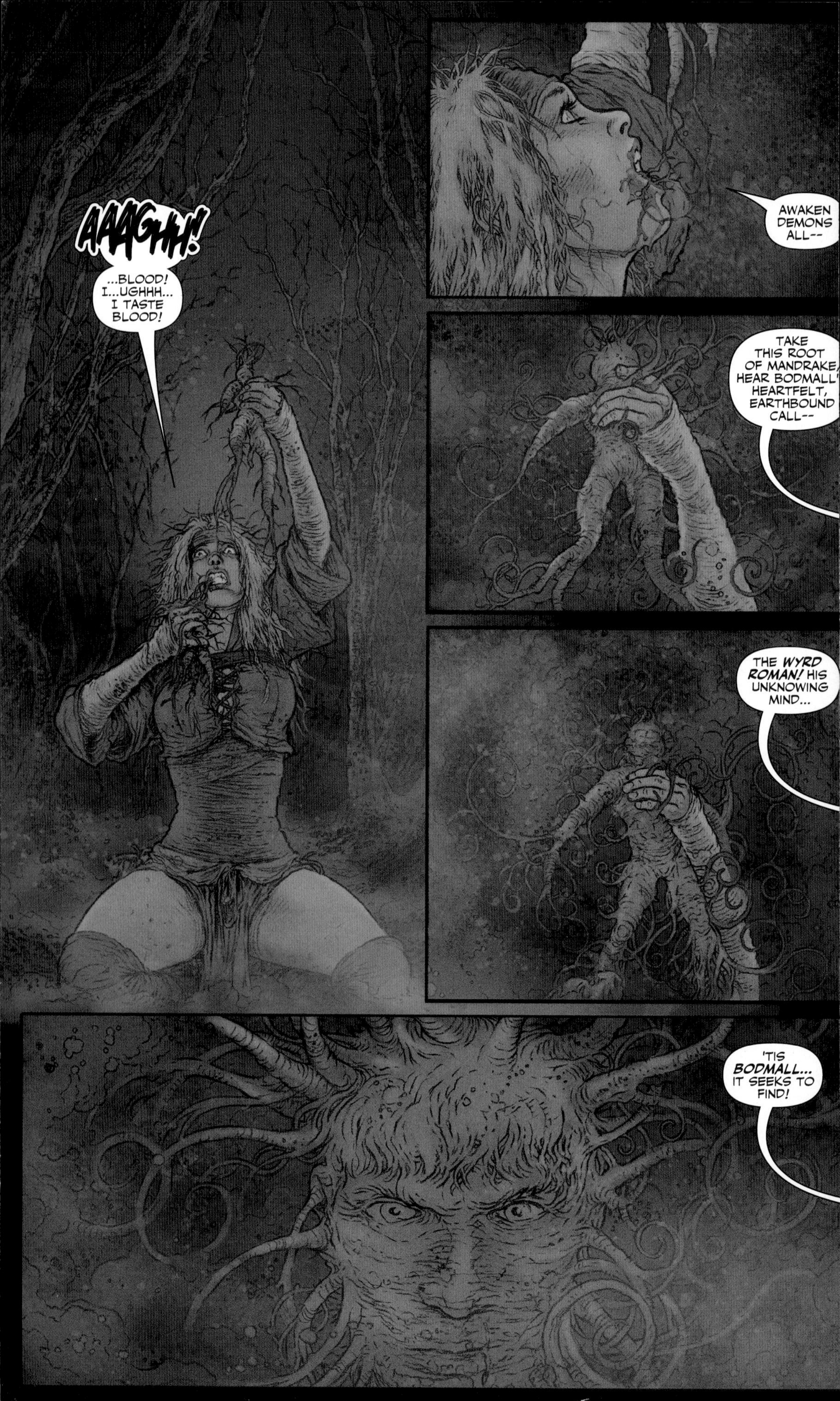
AAAGHH!
...BLOOD! I...UGHHH... I TASTE BLOOD!
AWAKEN DEMONS ALL--
TAKE THIS ROOT OF MANDRAKE, HEAR BODMALL'S HEARTFELT, EARTHBOUND CALL--
THE WYRD ROMAN! HIS UNKNOWING MIND...
'TIS BODMALL... IT SEEKS TO FIND!

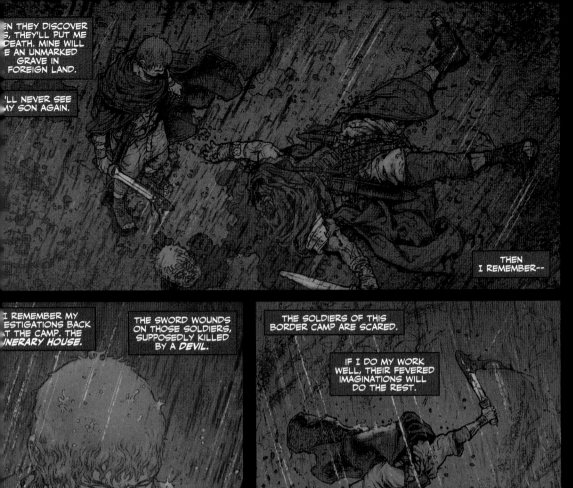

EN THEY DISCOVER [?], THEY'LL PUT ME [?]EATH. MINE WILL [?]E AN UNMARKED GRAVE IN [?] FOREIGN LAND.

['?]LL NEVER SEE [?]Y SON AGAIN.

THEN I REMEMBER--

I REMEMBER MY [?]ESTIGATIONS BACK [?]T THE CAMP. THE [?]NERARY HOUSE.

THE SWORD WOUNDS ON THOSE SOLDIERS, SUPPOSEDLY KILLED BY A *DEVIL*.

THE SOLDIERS OF THIS BORDER CAMP ARE SCARED.

IF I DO MY WORK WELL, THEIR FEVERED IMAGINATIONS WILL DO THE REST.

THEY'LL SEE THIS AS *DEVIL'S WORK*.

['?]M NO DEVIL, BUT [?]EITHER DO I FEEL [?]QUITE HUMAN. TO [?]UTILATE THE DEAD, IT'S *UN-ROMAN*.

BUT DEVILS ARE SO MUCH EASIER TO BELIEVE IN THAN GODS...

ANTONIUS... AXIA...

I WISH I STILL BELIEVED IN THE GODS, SO I COULD MAKE THE PRAYERS OF *PURIFICATION*.

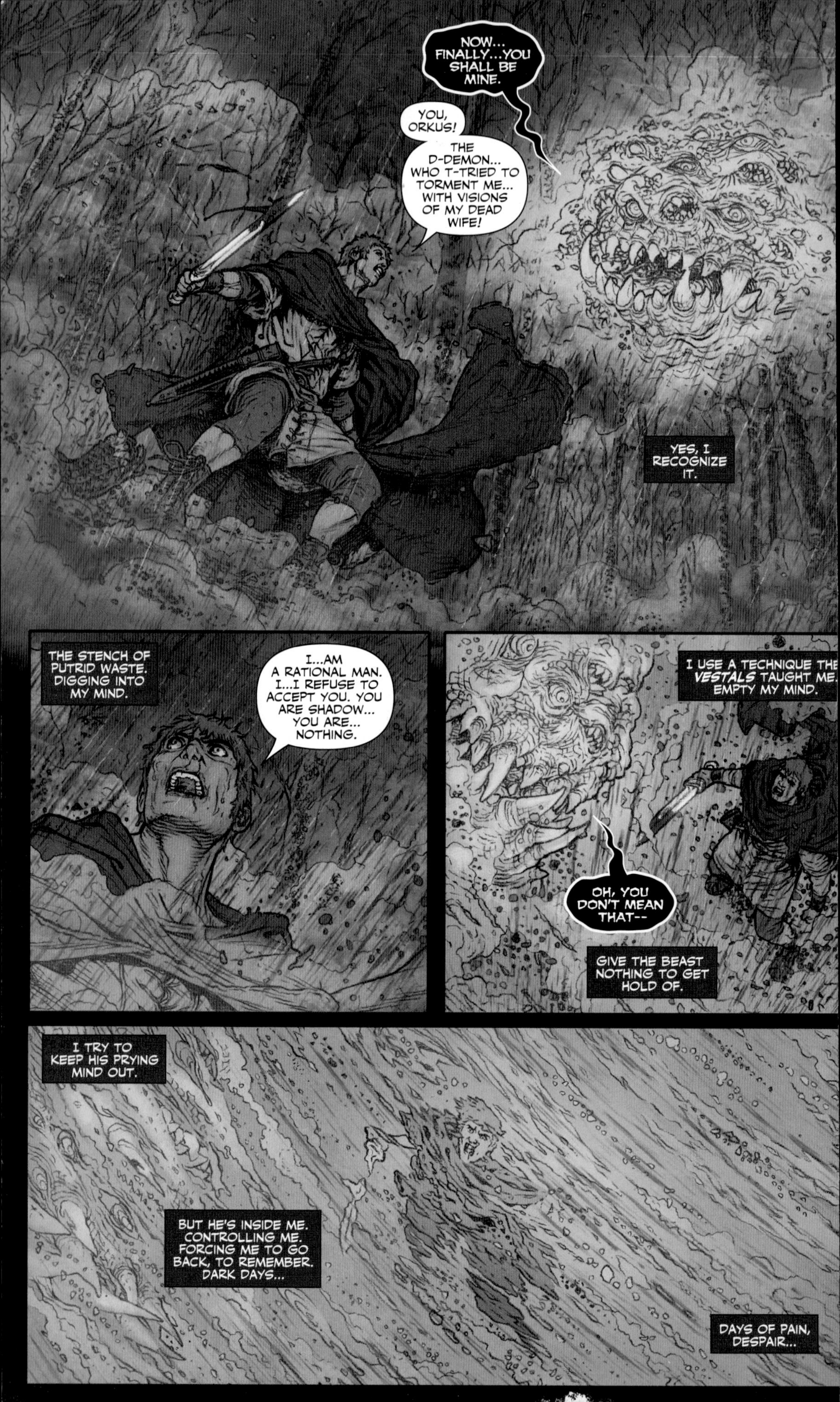
NOW... FINALLY...YOU SHALL BE MINE.
YOU, ORKUS!
THE D-DEMON... WHO T-TRIED TO TORMENT ME... WITH VISIONS OF MY DEAD WIFE!
YES, I RECOGNIZE IT.
THE STENCH OF PUTRID WASTE. DIGGING INTO MY MIND.
I...AM A RATIONAL MAN. I...I REFUSE TO ACCEPT YOU. YOU ARE SHADOW... YOU ARE... NOTHING.
I USE A TECHNIQUE THE VESTALS TAUGHT ME. EMPTY MY MIND.
OH, YOU DON'T MEAN THAT--
GIVE THE BEAST NOTHING TO GET HOLD OF.
I TRY TO KEEP HIS PRYING MIND OUT.
BUT HE'S INSIDE ME. CONTROLLING ME. FORCING ME TO GO BACK, TO REMEMBER. DARK DAYS...
DAYS OF PAIN, DESPAIR...

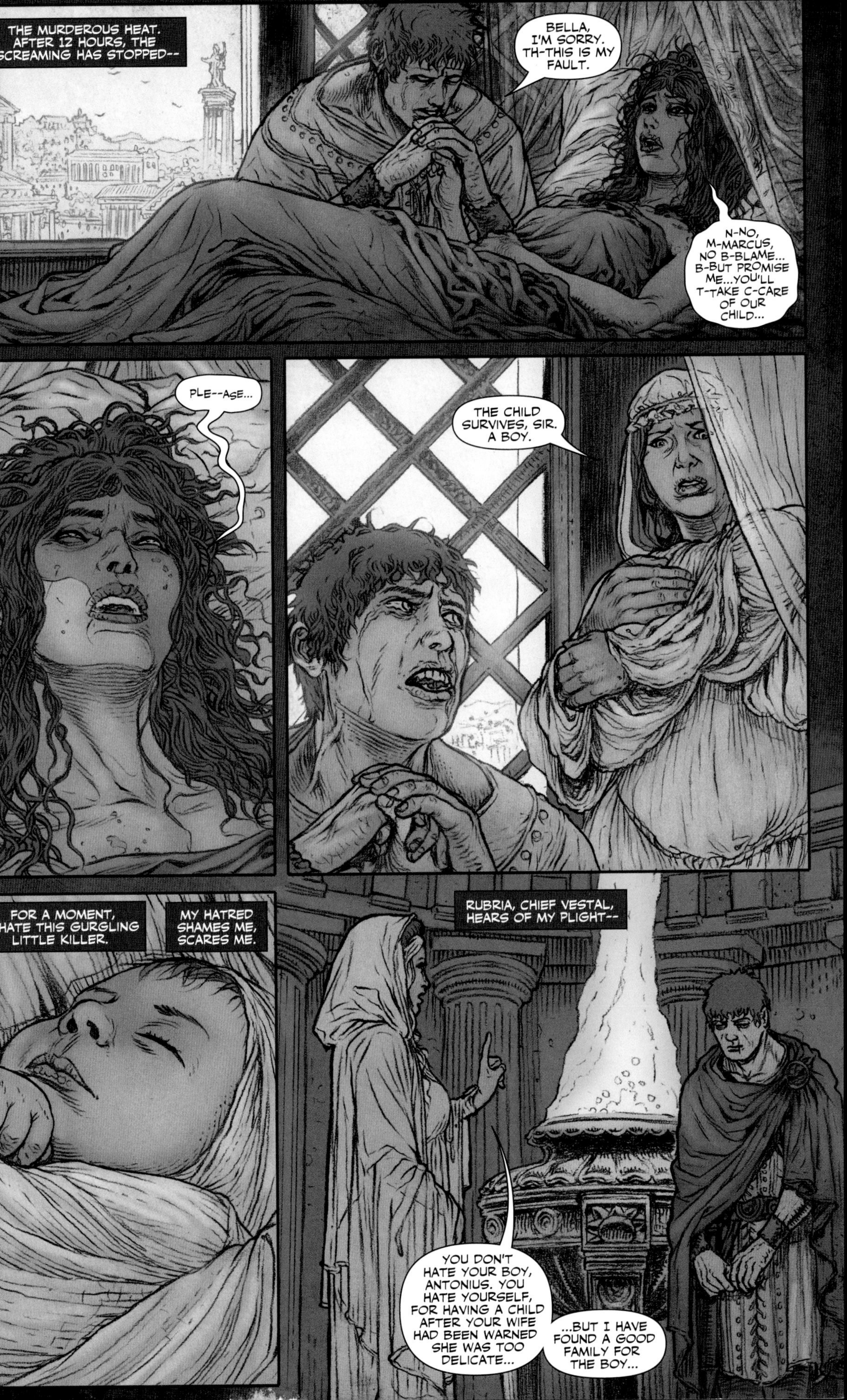
THE MURDEROUS HEAT. AFTER 12 HOURS, THE SCREAMING HAS STOPPED--
BELLA, I'M SORRY. TH-THIS IS MY FAULT.
N-NO, M-MARCUS, NO B-BLAME... B-BUT PROMISE ME...YOU'LL T-TAKE C-CARE OF OUR CHILD...
PLE--ASE...
THE CHILD SURVIVES, SIR. A BOY.
FOR A MOMENT, HATE THIS GURGLING LITTLE KILLER.
MY HATRED SHAMES ME, SCARES ME.
RUBRIA, CHIEF VESTAL, HEARS OF MY PLIGHT--
YOU DON'T HATE YOUR BOY, ANTONIUS. YOU HATE YOURSELF, FOR HAVING A CHILD AFTER YOUR WIFE HAD BEEN WARNED SHE WAS TOO DELICATE...
...BUT I HAVE FOUND A GOOD FAMILY FOR THE BOY...

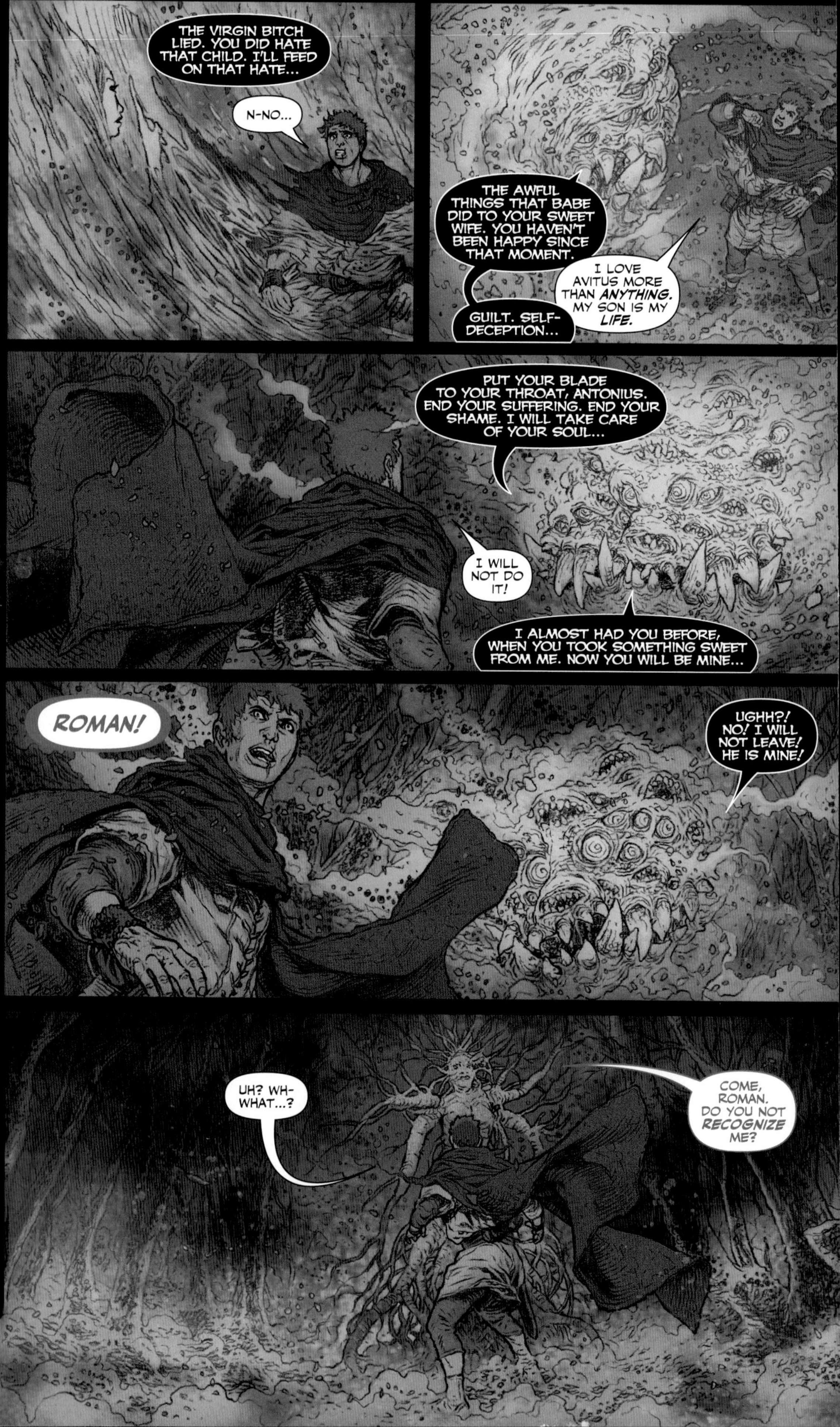
THE VIRGIN BITCH LIED. YOU DID HATE THAT CHILD. I'LL FEED ON THAT HATE...
N-NO...
THE AWFUL THINGS THAT BABE DID TO YOUR SWEET WIFE. YOU HAVEN'T BEEN HAPPY SINCE THAT MOMENT.
GUILT. SELF-DECEPTION...
I LOVE AVITUS MORE THAN ANYTHING. MY SON IS MY LIFE.
PUT YOUR BLADE TO YOUR THROAT, ANTONIUS. END YOUR SUFFERING. END YOUR SHAME. I WILL TAKE CARE OF YOUR SOUL...
I WILL NOT DO IT!
I ALMOST HAD YOU BEFORE, WHEN YOU TOOK SOMETHING SWEET FROM ME. NOW YOU WILL BE MINE...
ROMAN!
UGHH?! NO! I WILL NOT LEAVE! HE IS MINE!
UH? WH-WHAT...?
COME, ROMAN. DO YOU NOT RECOGNIZE ME?

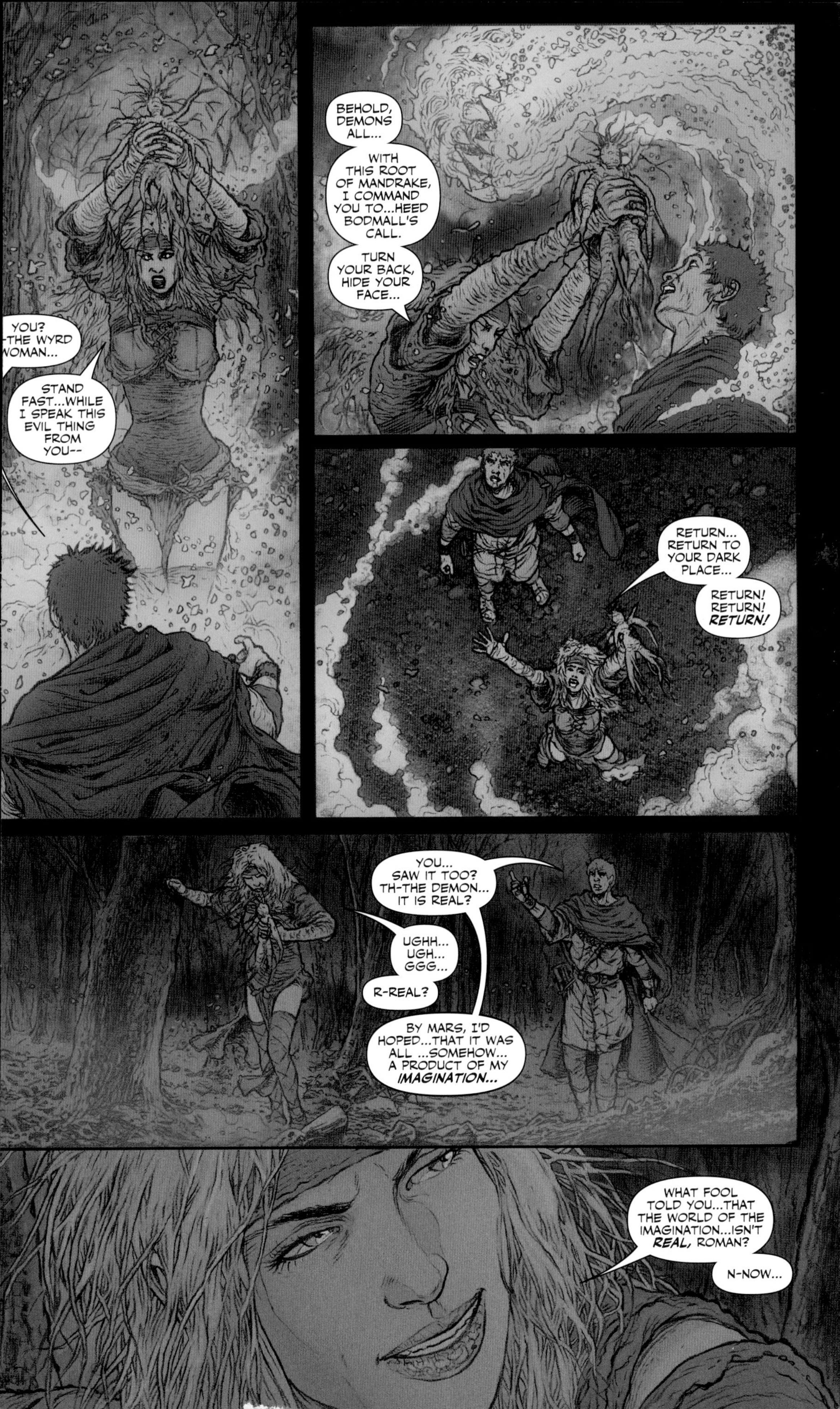
YOU? -THE WYRD WOMAN...
STAND FAST...WHILE I SPEAK THIS EVIL THING FROM YOU--
BEHOLD, DEMONS ALL...
WITH THIS ROOT OF MANDRAKE, I COMMAND YOU TO...HEED BODMALL'S CALL.
TURN YOUR BACK, HIDE YOUR FACE...
RETURN... RETURN TO YOUR DARK PLACE...
RETURN! RETURN! RETURN!
YOU... SAW IT TOO? TH-THE DEMON... IT IS REAL?
UGHH... UGH... GGG...
R-REAL?
BY MARS, I'D HOPED...THAT IT WAS ALL ...SOMEHOW... A PRODUCT OF MY IMAGINATION...
WHAT FOOL TOLD YOU...THAT THE WORLD OF THE IMAGINATION...ISN'T REAL, ROMAN?
N-NOW...

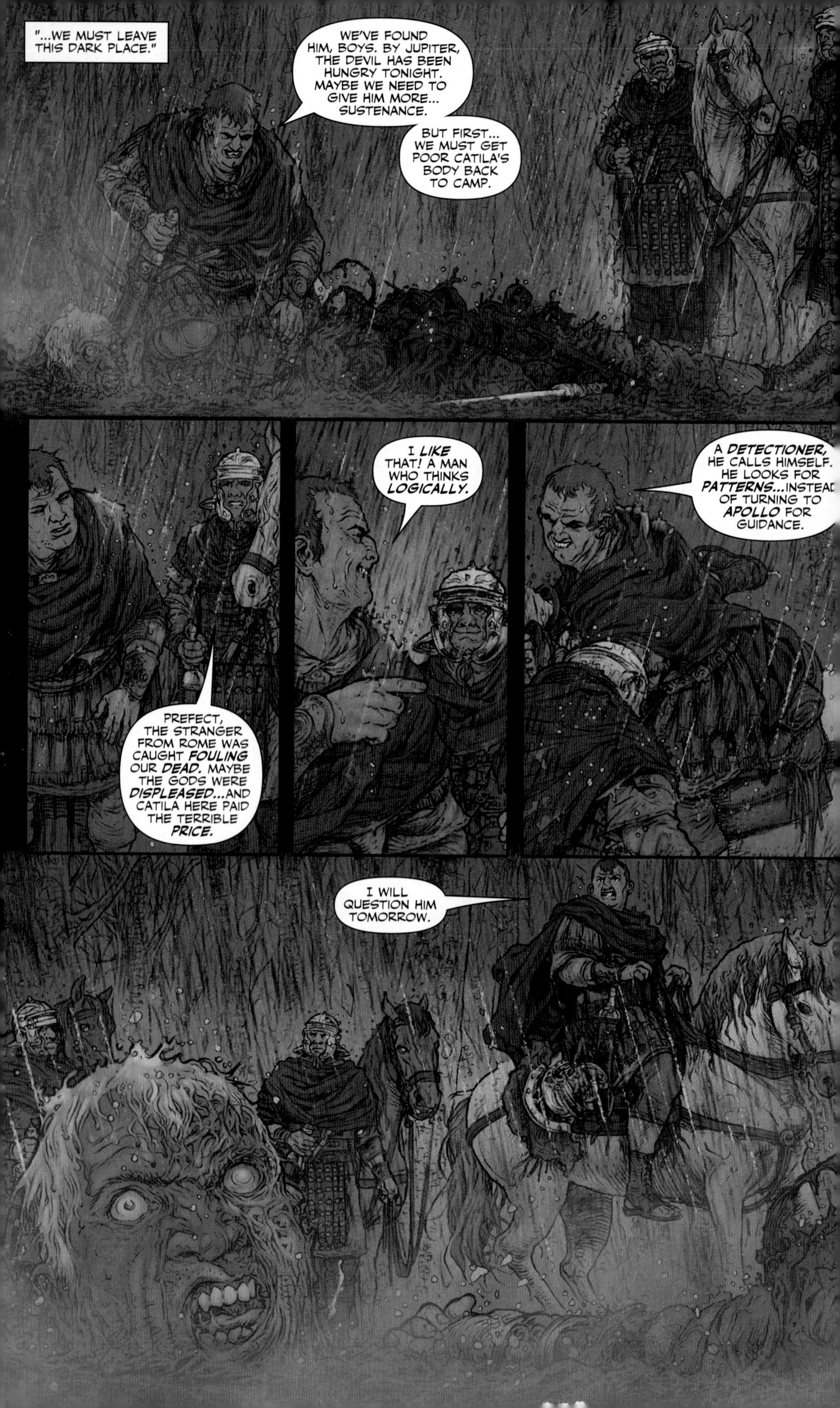

"...WE MUST LEAVE THIS DARK PLACE."
WE'VE FOUND HIM, BOYS. BY JUPITER, THE DEVIL HAS BEEN HUNGRY TONIGHT. MAYBE WE NEED TO GIVE HIM MORE... SUSTENANCE.
BUT FIRST... WE MUST GET POOR CATILA'S BODY BACK TO CAMP.
PREFECT, THE STRANGER FROM ROME WAS CAUGHT FOULING OUR DEAD. MAYBE THE GODS WERE DISPLEASED...AND CATILA HERE PAID THE TERRIBLE PRICE.
I LIKE THAT! A MAN WHO THINKS LOGICALLY.
A DETECTIONER, HE CALLS HIMSELF. HE LOOKS FOR PATTERNS...INSTEAD OF TURNING TO APOLLO FOR GUIDANCE.
I WILL QUESTION HIM TOMORROW.

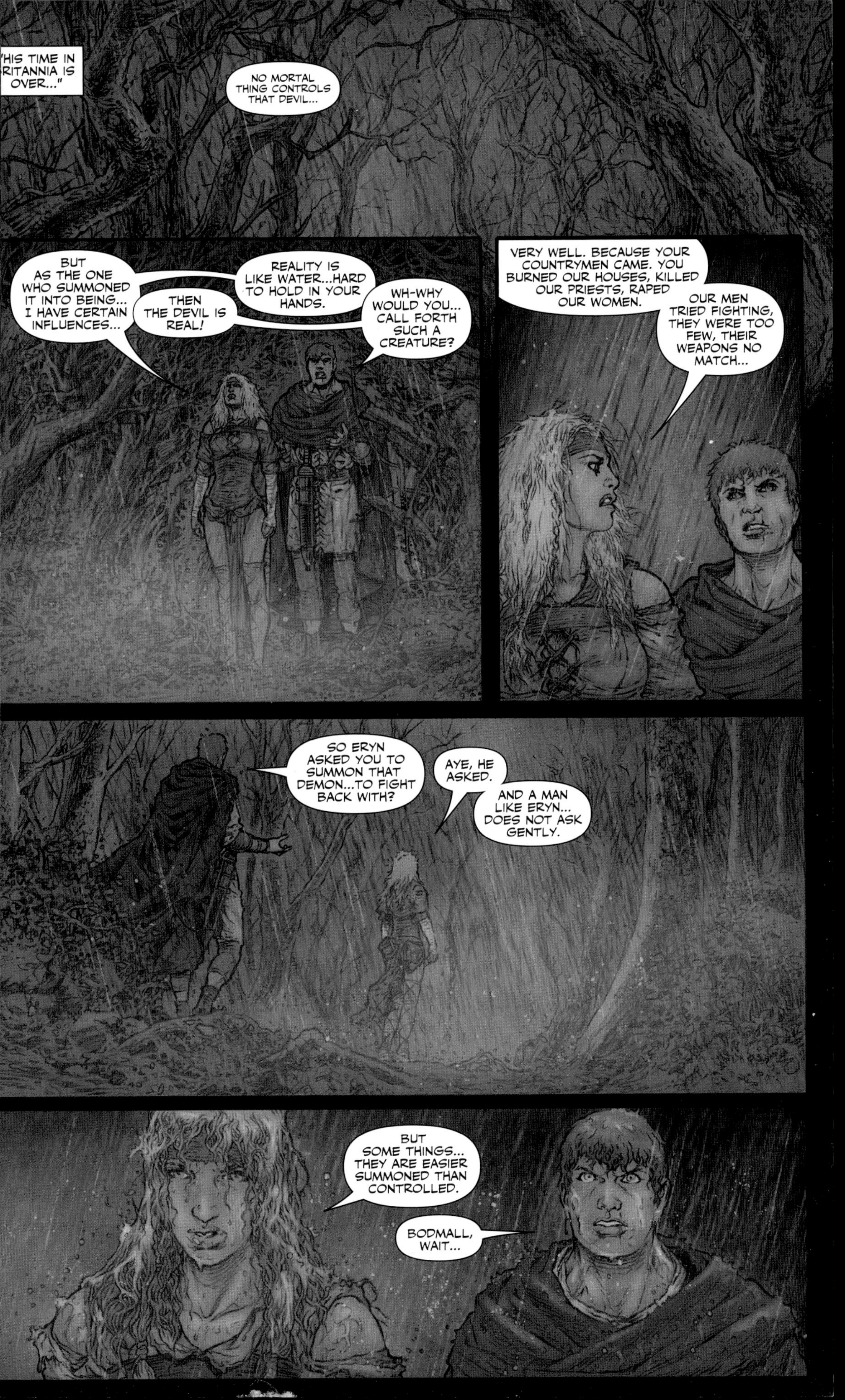
"HIS TIME IN
RITANNIA IS
OVER..."
NO MORTAL THING CONTROLS THAT DEVIL...
BUT AS THE ONE WHO SUMMONED IT INTO BEING... I HAVE CERTAIN INFLUENCES...
REALITY IS LIKE WATER...HARD TO HOLD IN YOUR HANDS.
THEN THE DEVIL IS REAL!
WH-WHY WOULD YOU... CALL FORTH SUCH A CREATURE?
VERY WELL. BECAUSE YOUR COUNTRYMEN CAME. YOU BURNED OUR HOUSES, KILLED OUR PRIESTS, RAPED OUR WOMEN.
OUR MEN TRIED FIGHTING, THEY WERE TOO FEW, THEIR WEAPONS NO MATCH...
SO ERYN ASKED YOU TO SUMMON THAT DEMON...TO FIGHT BACK WITH?
AYE, HE ASKED.
AND A MAN LIKE ERYN... DOES NOT ASK GENTLY.
BUT SOME THINGS... THEY ARE EASIER SUMMONED THAN CONTROLLED.
BODMALL, WAIT...

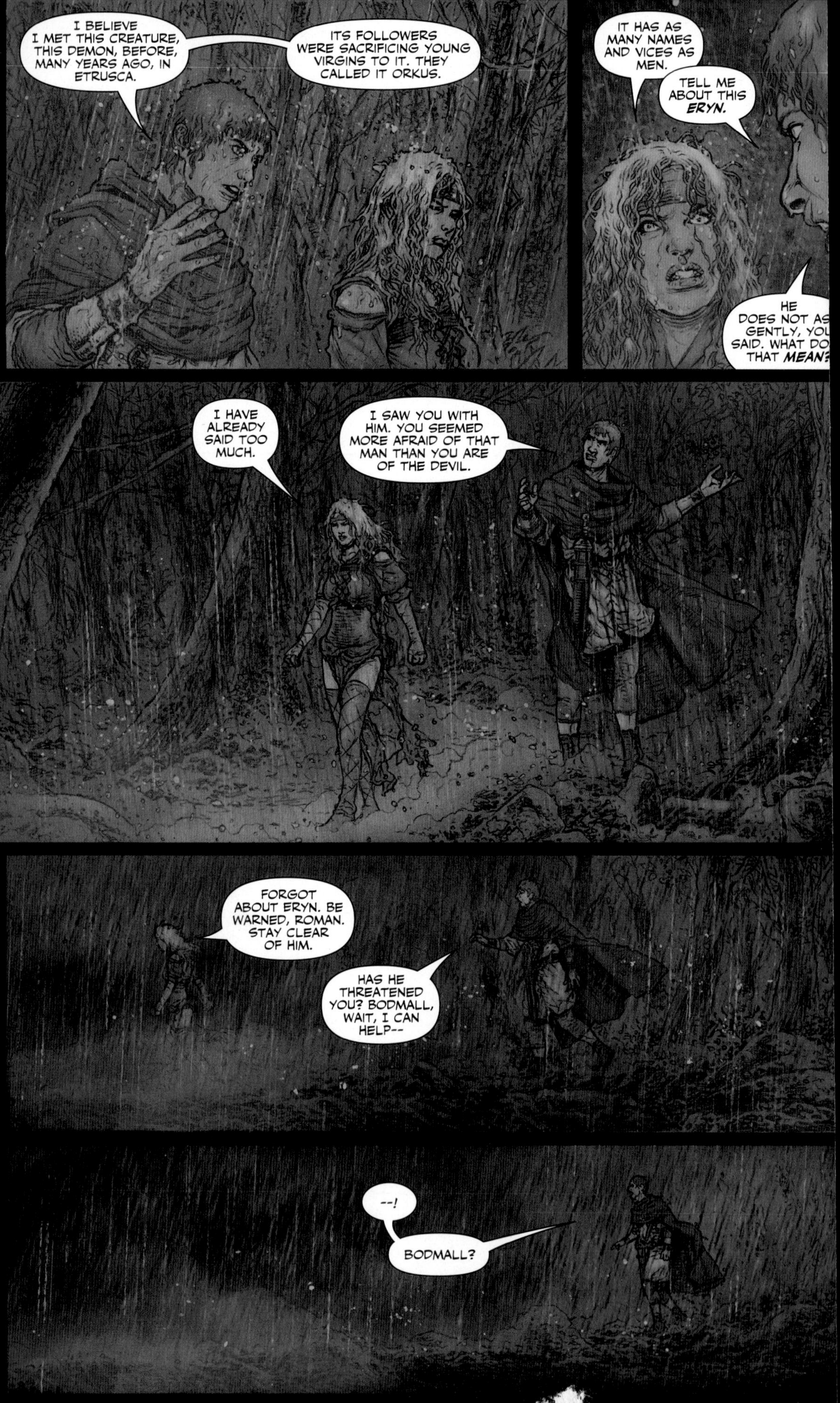
I BELIEVE I MET THIS CREATURE, THIS DEMON, BEFORE, MANY YEARS AGO, IN ETRUSCA.
ITS FOLLOWERS WERE SACRIFICING YOUNG VIRGINS TO IT. THEY CALLED IT ORKUS.
IT HAS AS MANY NAMES AND VICES AS MEN.
TELL ME ABOUT THIS *ERYN.*
HE DOES NOT AS GENTLY, YOU SAID. WHAT DO THAT *MEAN?*
I HAVE ALREADY SAID TOO MUCH.
I SAW YOU WITH HIM. YOU SEEMED MORE AFRAID OF THAT MAN THAN YOU ARE OF THE DEVIL.
FORGOT ABOUT ERYN. BE WARNED, ROMAN. STAY CLEAR OF HIM.
HAS HE THREATENED YOU? BODMALL, WAIT, I CAN HELP--
--!
BODMALL?

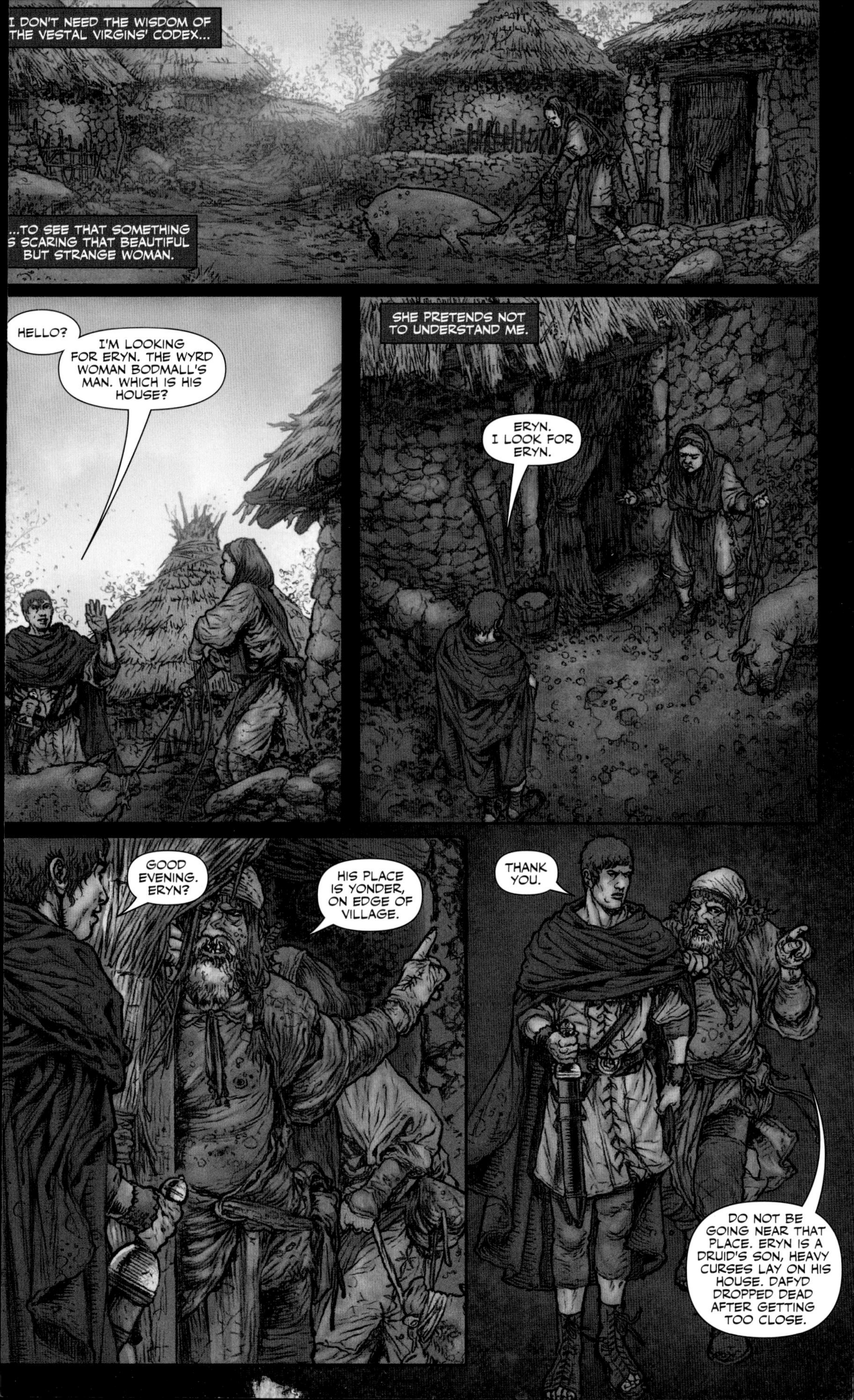
I DON'T NEED THE WISDOM OF THE VESTAL VIRGINS' CODEX...
...TO SEE THAT SOMETHING IS SCARING THAT BEAUTIFUL BUT STRANGE WOMAN.
HELLO?
I'M LOOKING FOR ERYN. THE WYRD WOMAN BODMALL'S MAN. WHICH IS HIS HOUSE?
SHE PRETENDS NOT TO UNDERSTAND ME.
ERYN. I LOOK FOR ERYN.
GOOD EVENING. ERYN?
HIS PLACE IS YONDER, ON EDGE OF VILLAGE.
THANK YOU.
DO NOT BE GOING NEAR THAT PLACE. ERYN IS A DRUID'S SON, HEAVY CURSES LAY ON HIS HOUSE. DAFYD DROPPED DEAD AFTER GETTING TOO CLOSE.

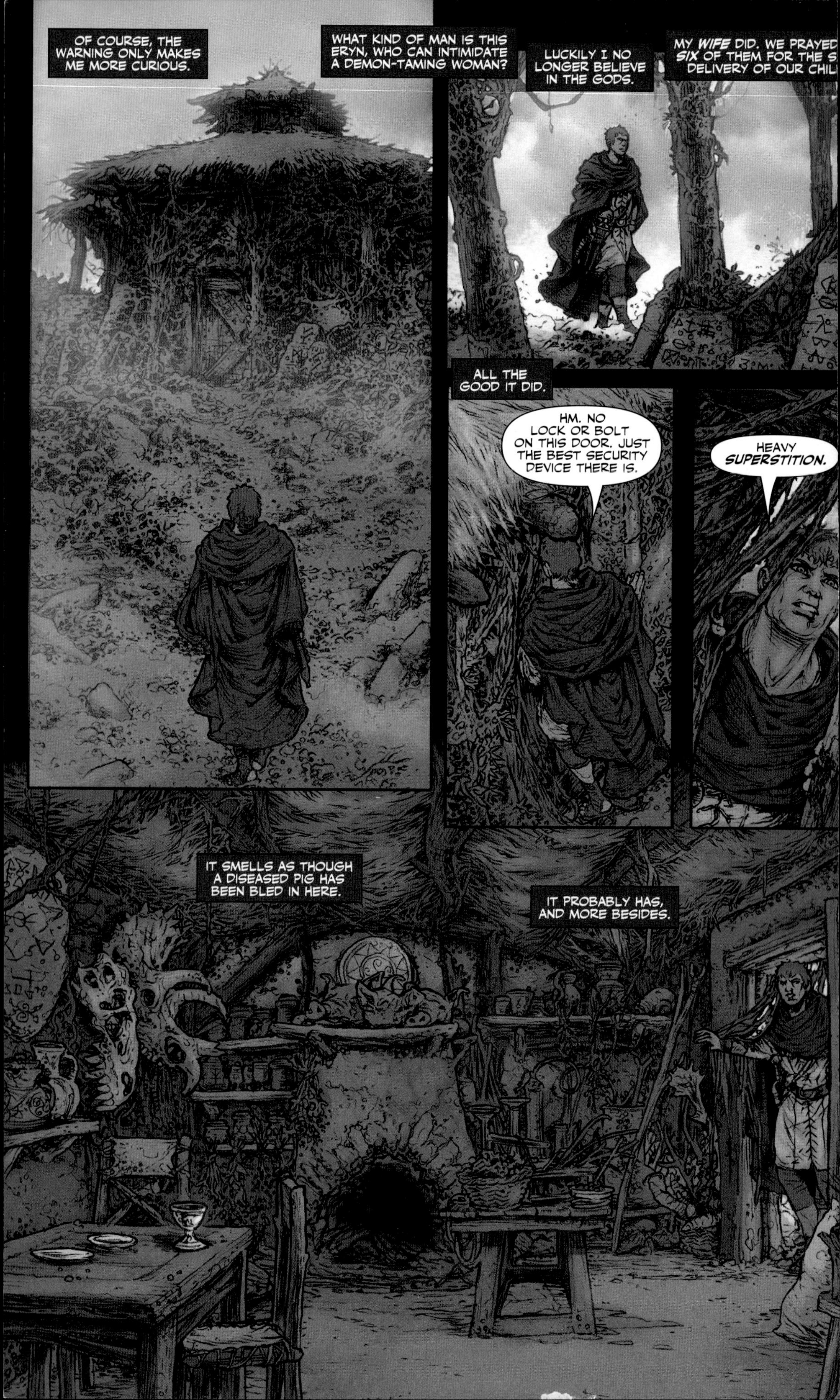

OF COURSE, THE WARNING ONLY MAKES ME MORE CURIOUS.
WHAT KIND OF MAN IS THIS ERYN, WHO CAN INTIMIDATE A DEMON-TAMING WOMAN?
LUCKILY I NO LONGER BELIEVE IN THE GODS.
MY *WIFE* DID. WE PRAYED *SIX* OF THEM FOR THE S DELIVERY OF OUR CHIL
ALL THE GOOD IT DID.
HM. NO LOCK OR BOLT ON THIS DOOR. JUST THE BEST SECURITY DEVICE THERE IS.
HEAVY *SUPERSTITION.*
IT SMELLS AS THOUGH A DISEASED PIG HAS BEEN BLED IN HERE.
IT PROBABLY HAS, AND MORE BESIDES.

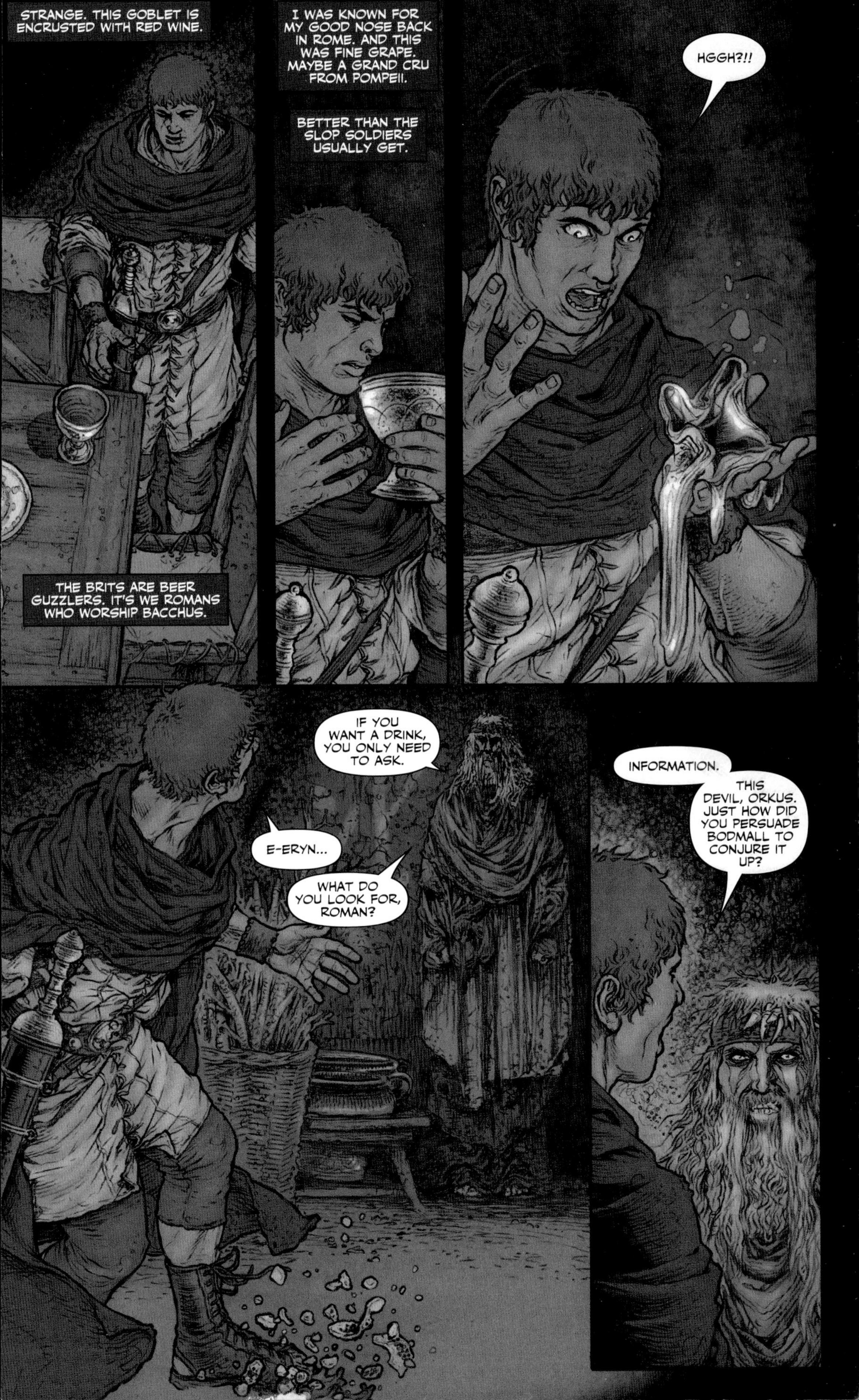
STRANGE. THIS GOBLET IS ENCRUSTED WITH RED WINE.
THE BRITS ARE BEER GUZZLERS. IT'S WE ROMANS WHO WORSHIP BACCHUS.
I WAS KNOWN FOR MY GOOD NOSE BACK IN ROME. AND THIS WAS FINE GRAPE. MAYBE A GRAND CRU FROM POMPEII.
BETTER THAN THE SLOP SOLDIERS USUALLY GET.
HGGH?!!
IF YOU WANT A DRINK, YOU ONLY NEED TO ASK.
E-ERYN...
WHAT DO YOU LOOK FOR, ROMAN?
INFORMATION.
THIS DEVIL, ORKUS. JUST HOW DID YOU PERSUADE BODMALL TO CONJURE IT UP?

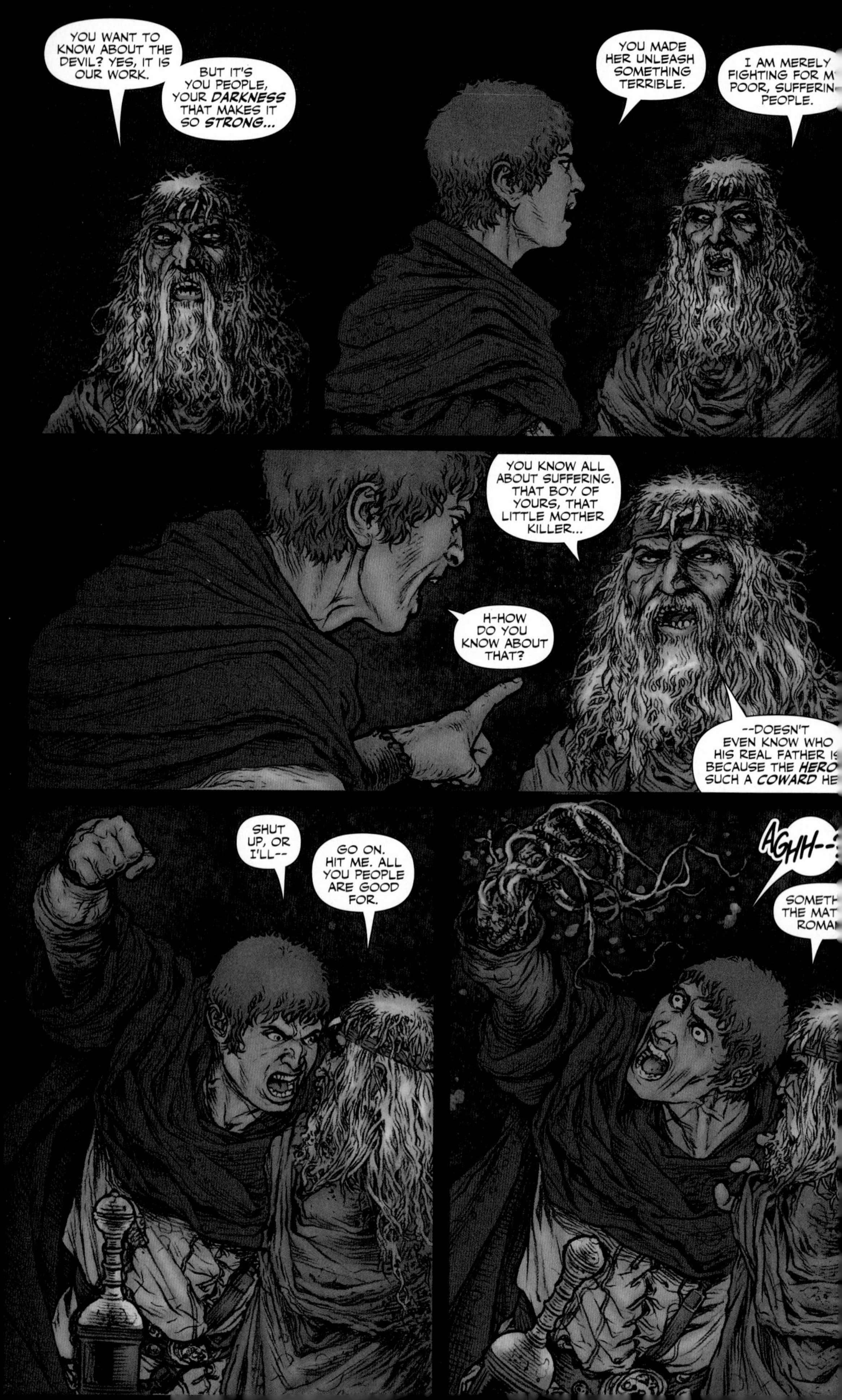
YOU WANT TO KNOW ABOUT THE DEVIL? YES, IT IS OUR WORK.
BUT IT'S YOU PEOPLE, YOUR DARKNESS THAT MAKES IT SO STRONG...
YOU MADE HER UNLEASH SOMETHING TERRIBLE.
I AM MERELY FIGHTING FOR M POOR, SUFFERIN PEOPLE.
YOU KNOW ALL ABOUT SUFFERING. THAT BOY OF YOURS, THAT LITTLE MOTHER KILLER...
H-HOW DO YOU KNOW ABOUT THAT?
--DOESN'T EVEN KNOW WHO HIS REAL FATHER IS BECAUSE THE HERO SUCH A COWARD HE
SHUT UP, OR I'LL--
GO ON. HIT ME. ALL YOU PEOPLE ARE GOOD FOR.
AGHH--
SOMETH THE MAT ROMA

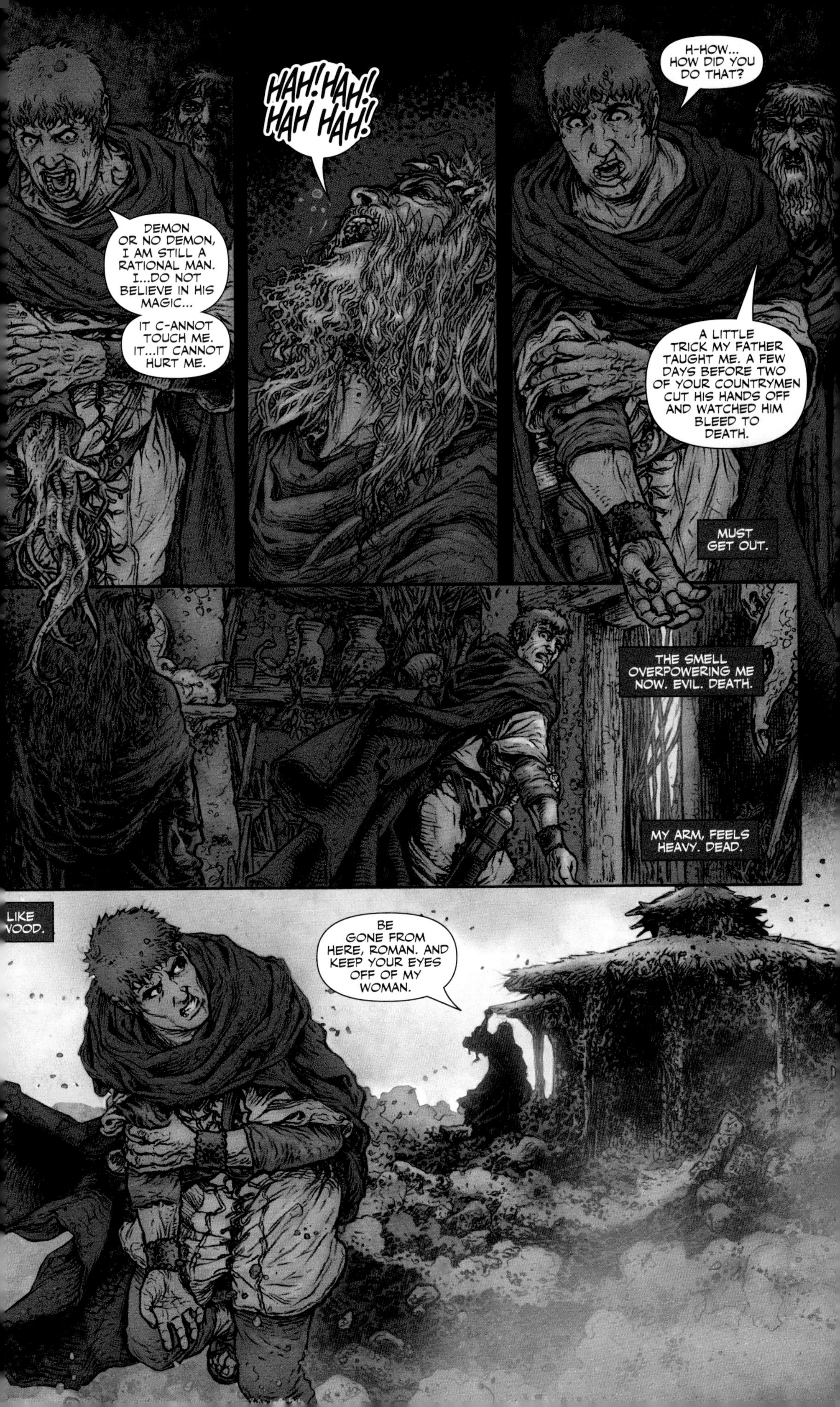

DEMON OR NO DEMON, I AM STILL A RATIONAL MAN. I...DO NOT BELIEVE IN HIS MAGIC...
IT C-ANNOT TOUCH ME. IT...IT CANNOT HURT ME.
HAH! HAH! HAH HAH!
H-HOW... HOW DID YOU DO THAT?
A LITTLE TRICK MY FATHER TAUGHT ME. A FEW DAYS BEFORE TWO OF YOUR COUNTRYMEN CUT HIS HANDS OFF AND WATCHED HIM BLEED TO DEATH.
MUST GET OUT.
THE SMELL OVERPOWERING ME NOW. EVIL. DEATH.
MY ARM, FEELS HEAVY. DEAD.
LIKE WOOD.
BE GONE FROM HERE, ROMAN. AND KEEP YOUR EYES OFF OF MY WOMAN.

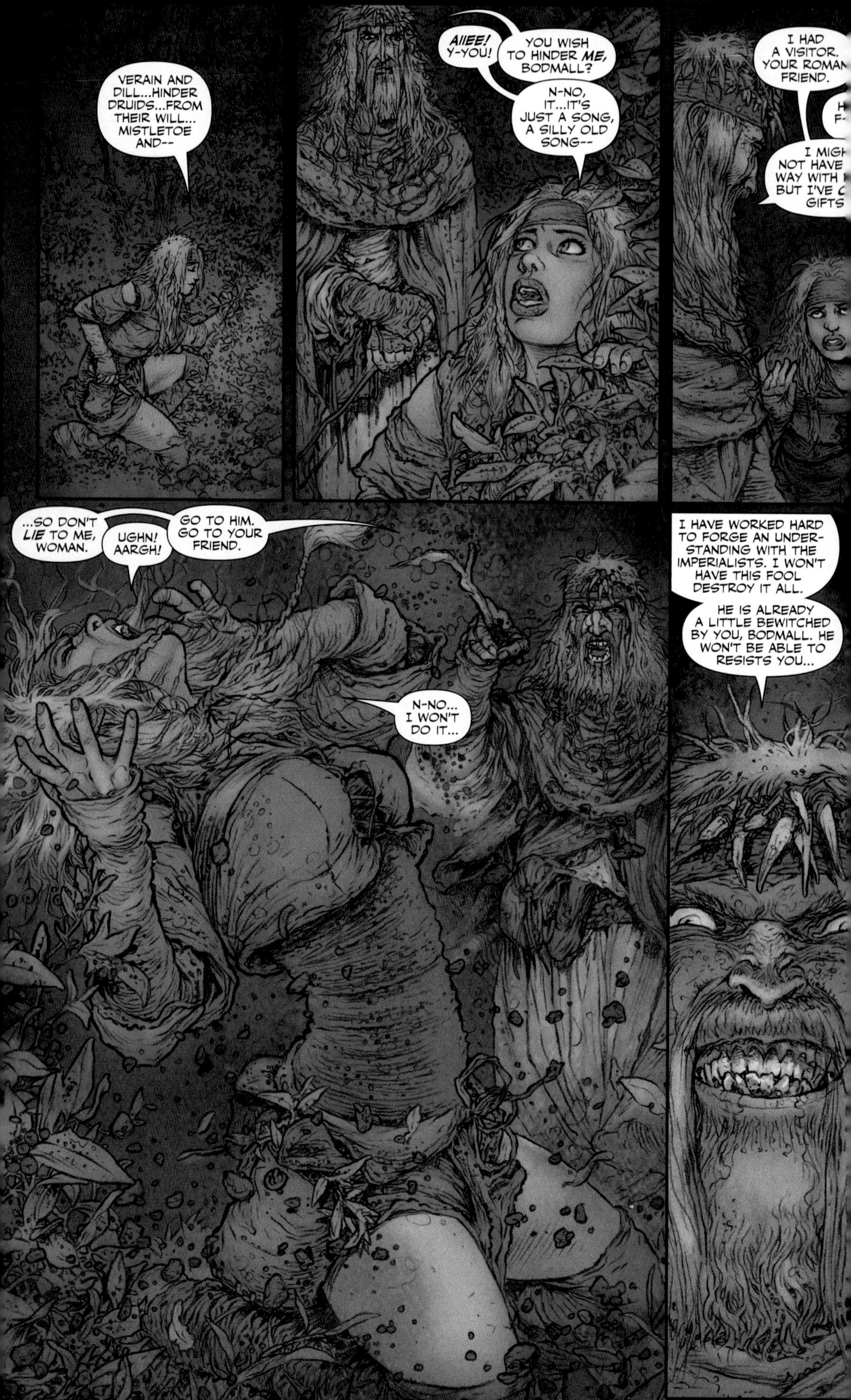

VERAIN AND DILL...HINDER DRUIDS...FROM THEIR WILL... MISTLETOE AND--
AIIEE! Y-YOU!
YOU WISH TO HINDER ME, BODMALL?
N-NO, IT...IT'S JUST A SONG, A SILLY OLD SONG--
I HAD A VISITOR. YOUR ROMAN FRIEND.
I MIGH NOT HAVE WAY WITH BUT I'VE GIFTS
...SO DON'T LIE TO ME, WOMAN.
UGHN! AARGH!
GO TO HIM. GO TO YOUR FRIEND.
N-NO... I WON'T DO IT...
I HAVE WORKED HARD TO FORGE AN UNDERSTANDING WITH THE IMPERIALISTS. I WON'T HAVE THIS FOOL DESTROY IT ALL.
HE IS ALREADY A LITTLE BEWITCHED BY YOU, BODMALL. HE WON'T BE ABLE TO RESISTS YOU...

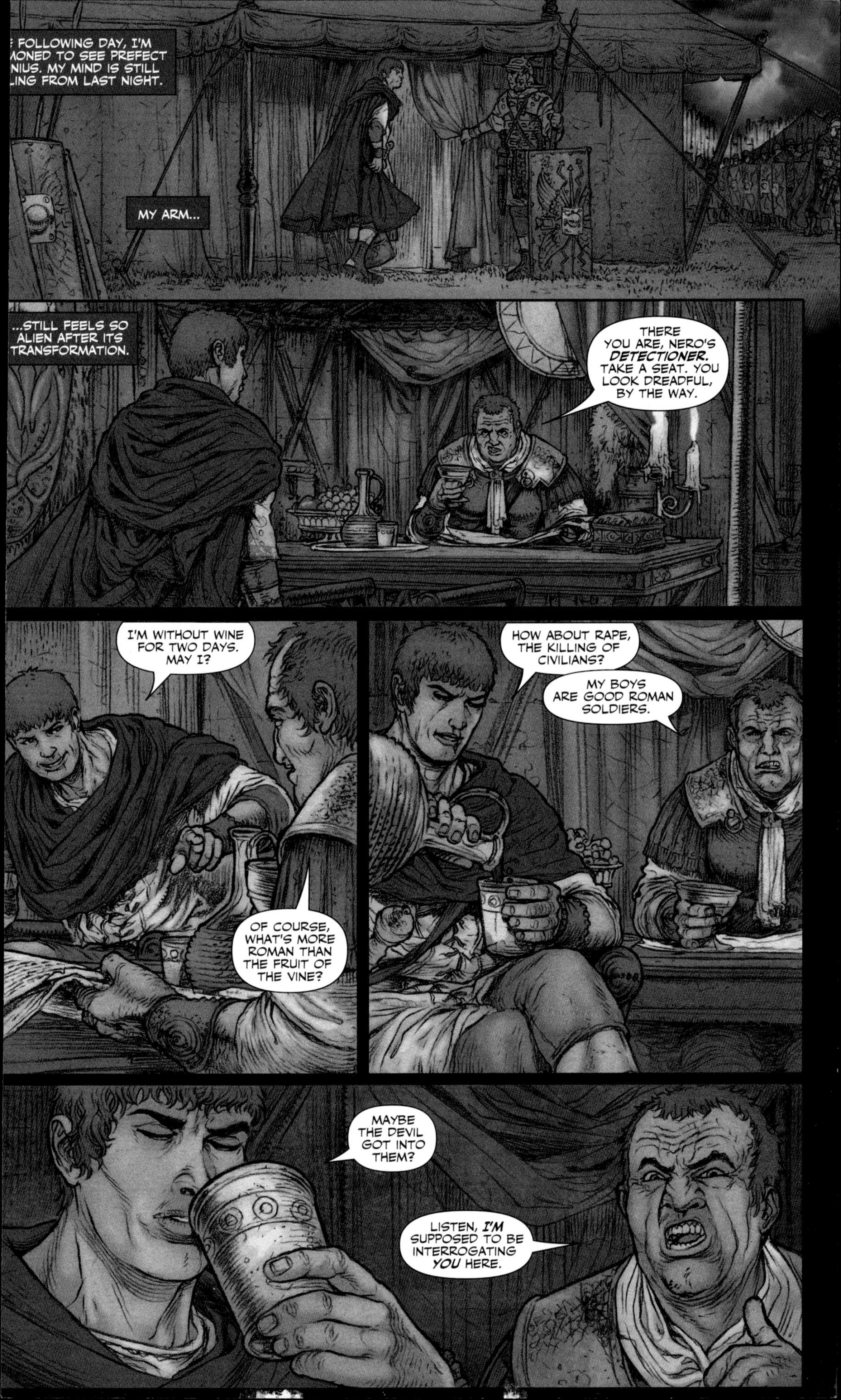

E FOLLOWING DAY, I'M MONED TO SEE PREFECT NIUS. MY MIND IS STILL LING FROM LAST NIGHT.
MY ARM...
...STILL FEELS SO ALIEN AFTER ITS TRANSFORMATION.
THERE YOU ARE, NERO'S DETECTIONER. TAKE A SEAT. YOU LOOK DREADFUL, BY THE WAY.
I'M WITHOUT WINE FOR TWO DAYS. MAY I?
OF COURSE, WHAT'S MORE ROMAN THAN THE FRUIT OF THE VINE?
HOW ABOUT RAPE, THE KILLING OF CIVILIANS?
MY BOYS ARE GOOD ROMAN SOLDIERS.
MAYBE THE DEVIL GOT INTO THEM?
LISTEN, I'M SUPPOSED TO BE INTERROGATING YOU HERE.

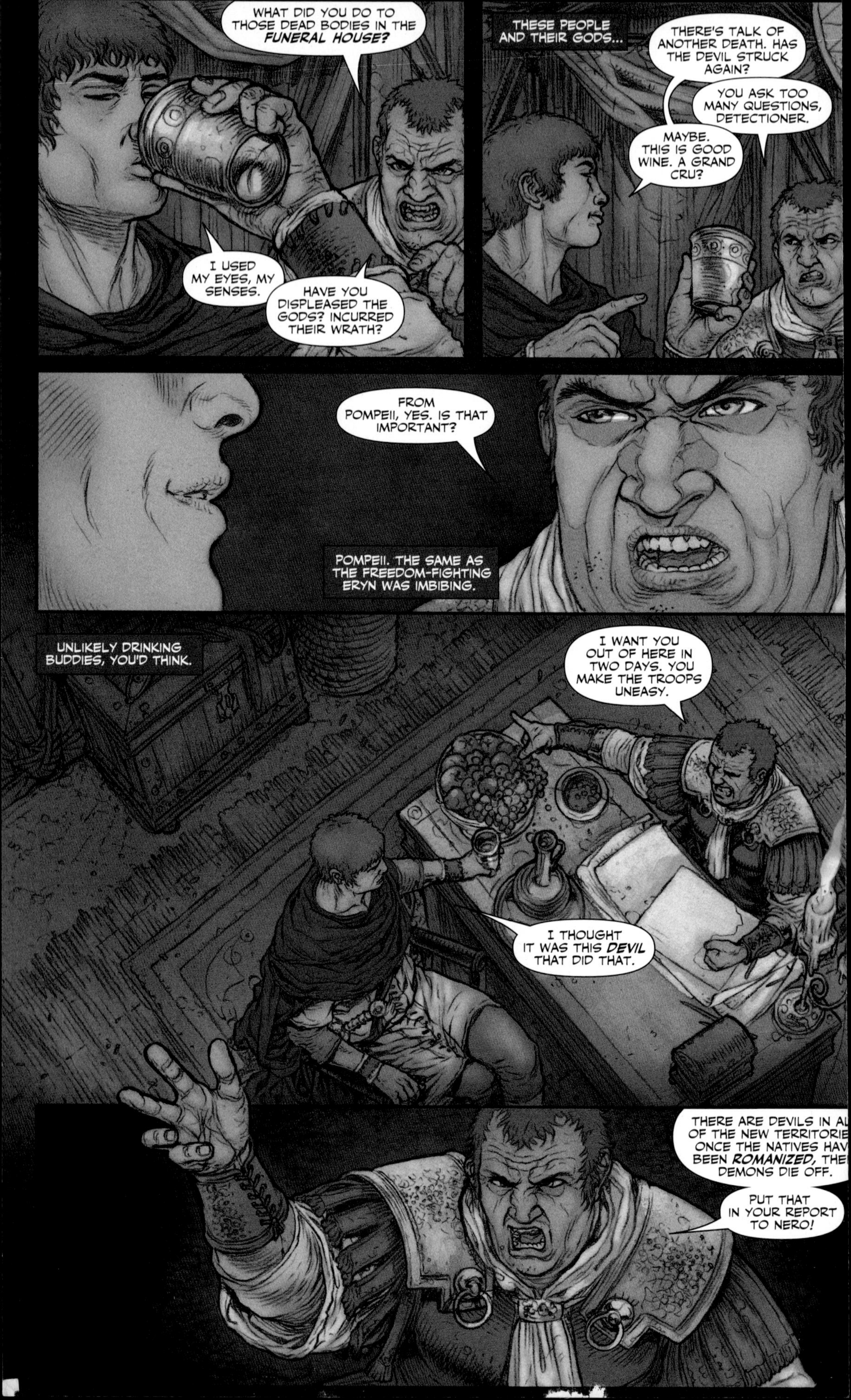
WHAT DID YOU DO TO THOSE DEAD BODIES IN THE FUNERAL HOUSE?
I USED MY EYES, MY SENSES.
HAVE YOU DISPLEASED THE GODS? INCURRED THEIR WRATH?
THESE PEOPLE AND THEIR GODS...
THERE'S TALK OF ANOTHER DEATH. HAS THE DEVIL STRUCK AGAIN?
MAYBE. THIS IS GOOD WINE. A GRAND CRU?
YOU ASK TOO MANY QUESTIONS, DETECTIONER.
FROM POMPEII, YES. IS THAT IMPORTANT?
POMPEII. THE SAME AS THE FREEDOM-FIGHTING ERYN WAS IMBIBING.
UNLIKELY DRINKING BUDDIES, YOU'D THINK.
I WANT YOU OUT OF HERE IN TWO DAYS. YOU MAKE THE TROOPS UNEASY.
I THOUGHT IT WAS THIS DEVIL THAT DID THAT.
THERE ARE DEVILS IN AL OF THE NEW TERRITORIE ONCE THE NATIVES HAV BEEN ROMANIZED, THE DEMONS DIE OFF.
PUT THAT IN YOUR REPORT TO NERO!

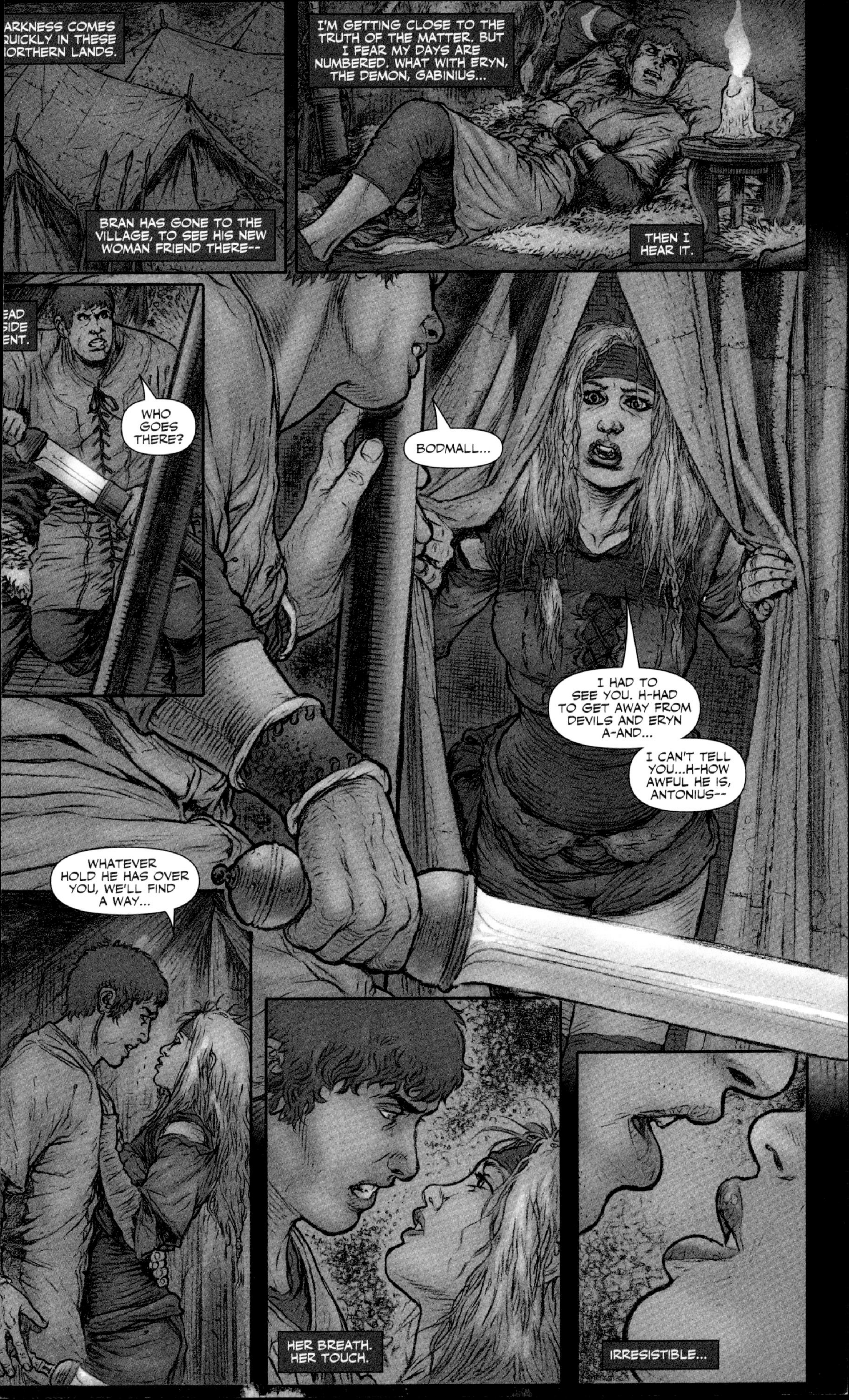
ARKNESS COMES
QUICKLY IN THESE
NORTHERN LANDS.
BRAN HAS GONE TO THE
VILLAGE, TO SEE HIS NEW
WOMAN FRIEND THERE--
I'M GETTING CLOSE TO THE
TRUTH OF THE MATTER. BUT
I FEAR MY DAYS ARE
NUMBERED. WHAT WITH ERYN,
THE DEMON, GABINIUS...
THEN I
HEAR IT.
EAD
SIDE
ENT.
WHO
GOES
THERE?
BODMALL...
I HAD TO
SEE YOU. H-HAD
TO GET AWAY FROM
DEVILS AND ERYN
A-AND...
I CAN'T TELL
YOU...H-HOW
AWFUL HE IS,
ANTONIUS--
WHATEVER
HOLD HE HAS OVER
YOU, WE'LL FIND
A WAY...
HER BREATH.
HER TOUCH.
IRRESISTIBLE...

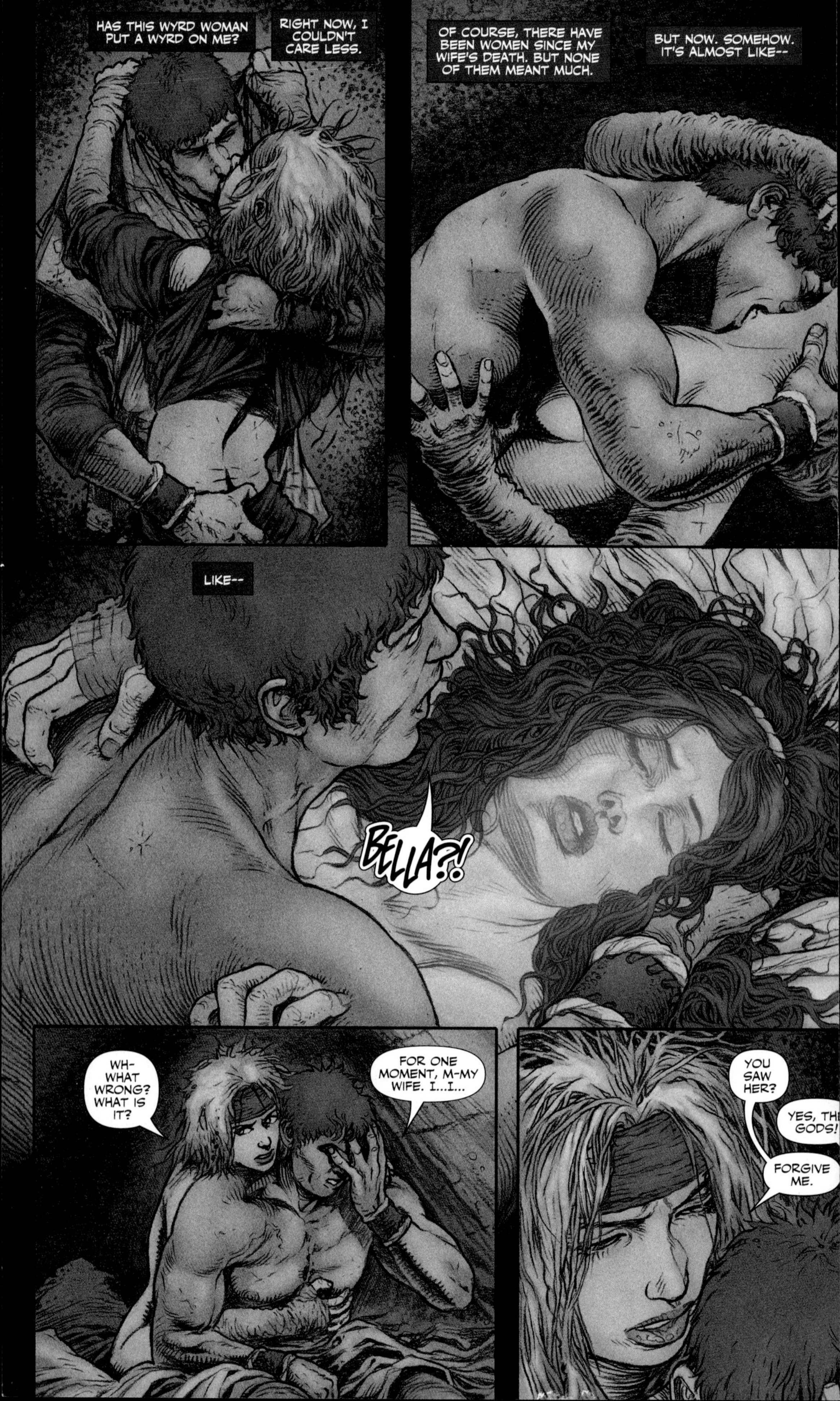
HAS THIS WYRD WOMAN PUT A WYRD ON ME?
RIGHT NOW, I COULDN'T CARE LESS.
OF COURSE, THERE HAVE BEEN WOMEN SINCE MY WIFE'S DEATH. BUT NONE OF THEM MEANT MUCH.
BUT NOW. SOMEHOW. IT'S ALMOST LIKE--
LIKE--
BELLA?!
WH-WHAT WRONG? WHAT IS IT?
FOR ONE MOMENT, M-MY WIFE. I...I...
YOU SAW HER?
YES, TH GODS!
FORGIVE ME.

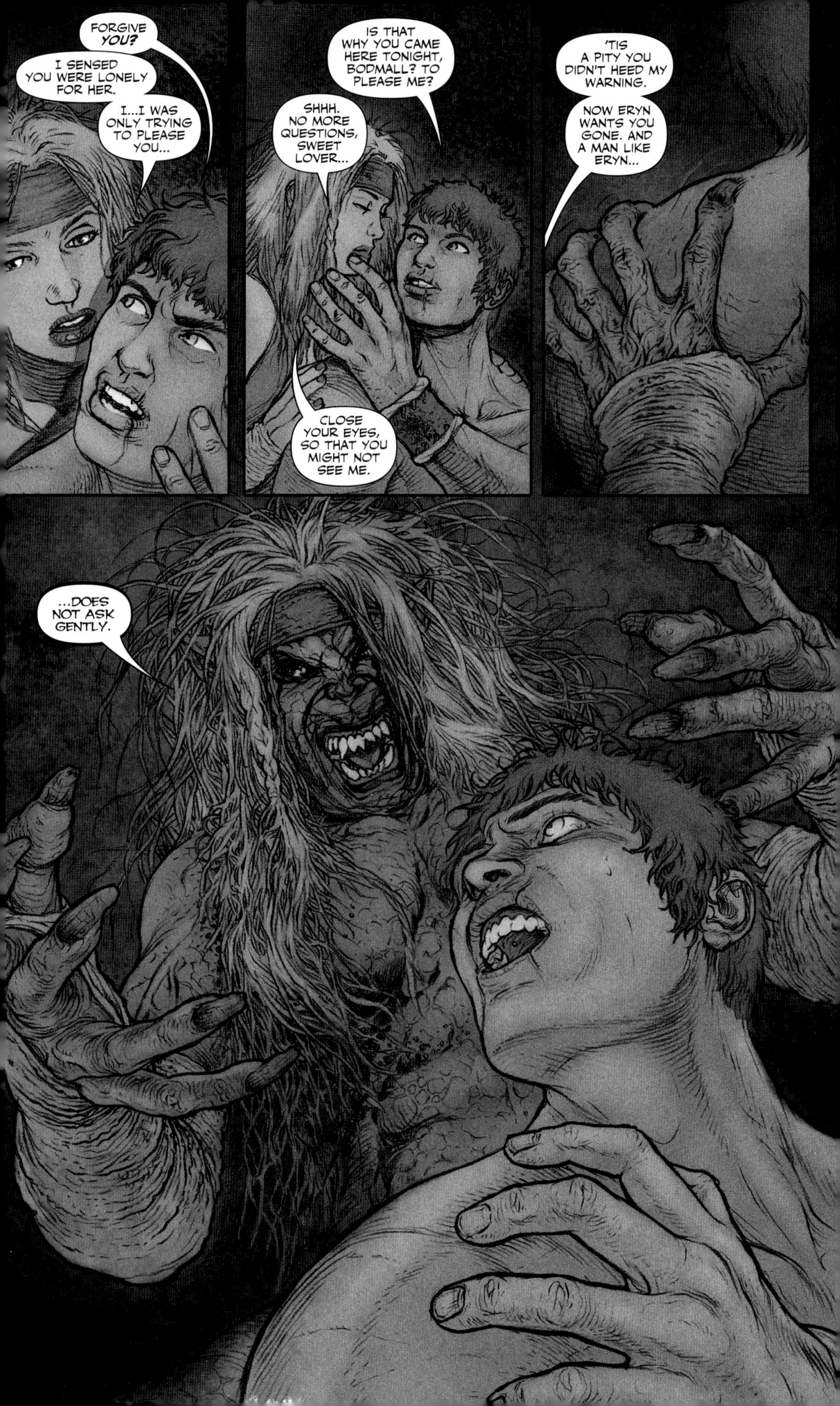
FORGIVE *YOU?*
I SENSED YOU WERE LONELY FOR HER.
I...I WAS ONLY TRYING TO PLEASE YOU...
IS THAT WHY YOU CAME HERE TONIGHT, BODMALL? TO PLEASE ME?
SHHH. NO MORE QUESTIONS, SWEET LOVER...
CLOSE YOUR EYES, SO THAT YOU MIGHT NOT SEE ME.
'TIS A PITY YOU DIDN'T HEED MY WARNING.
NOW ERYN WANTS YOU GONE. AND A MAN LIKE ERYN...
...DOES NOT ASK GENTLY.

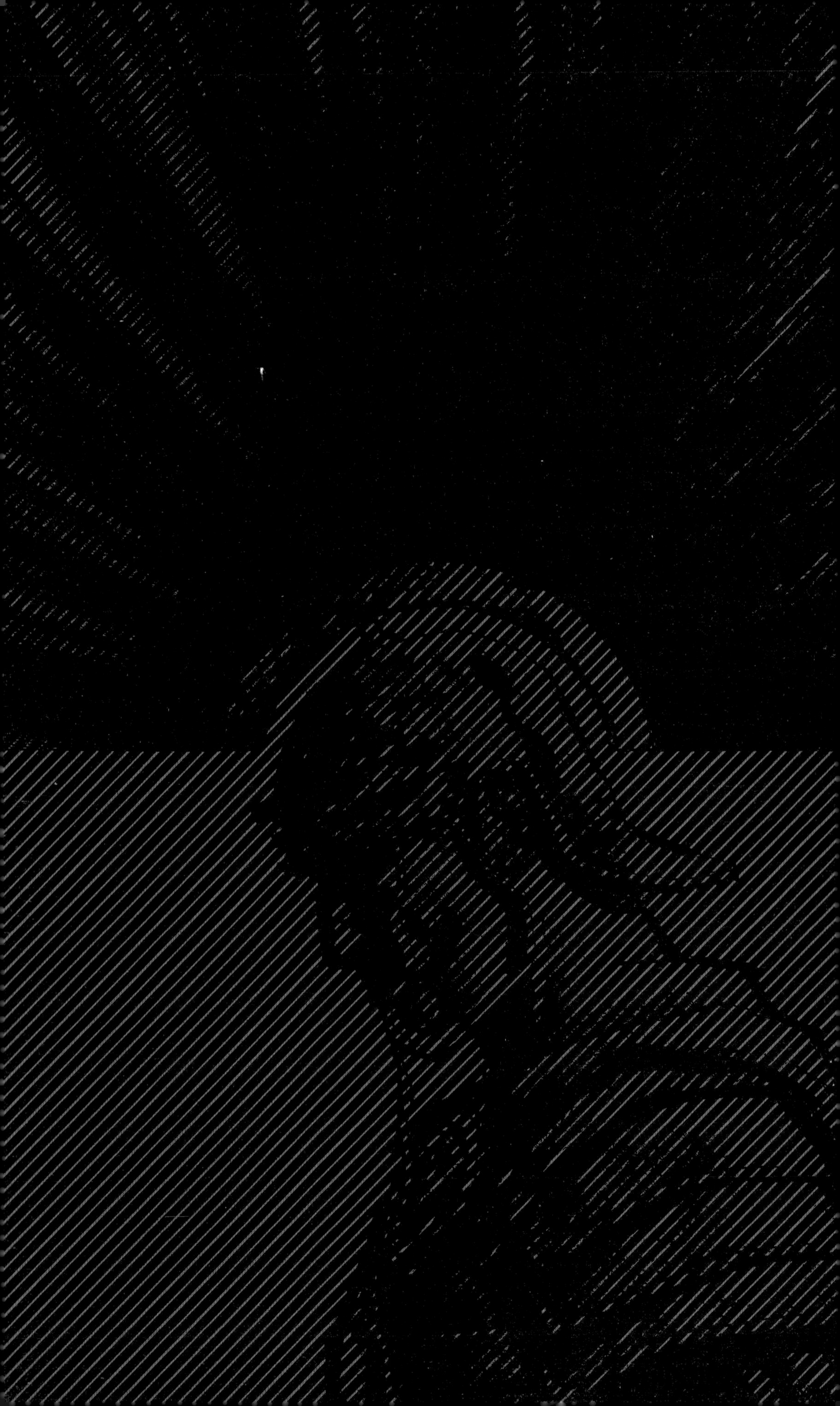

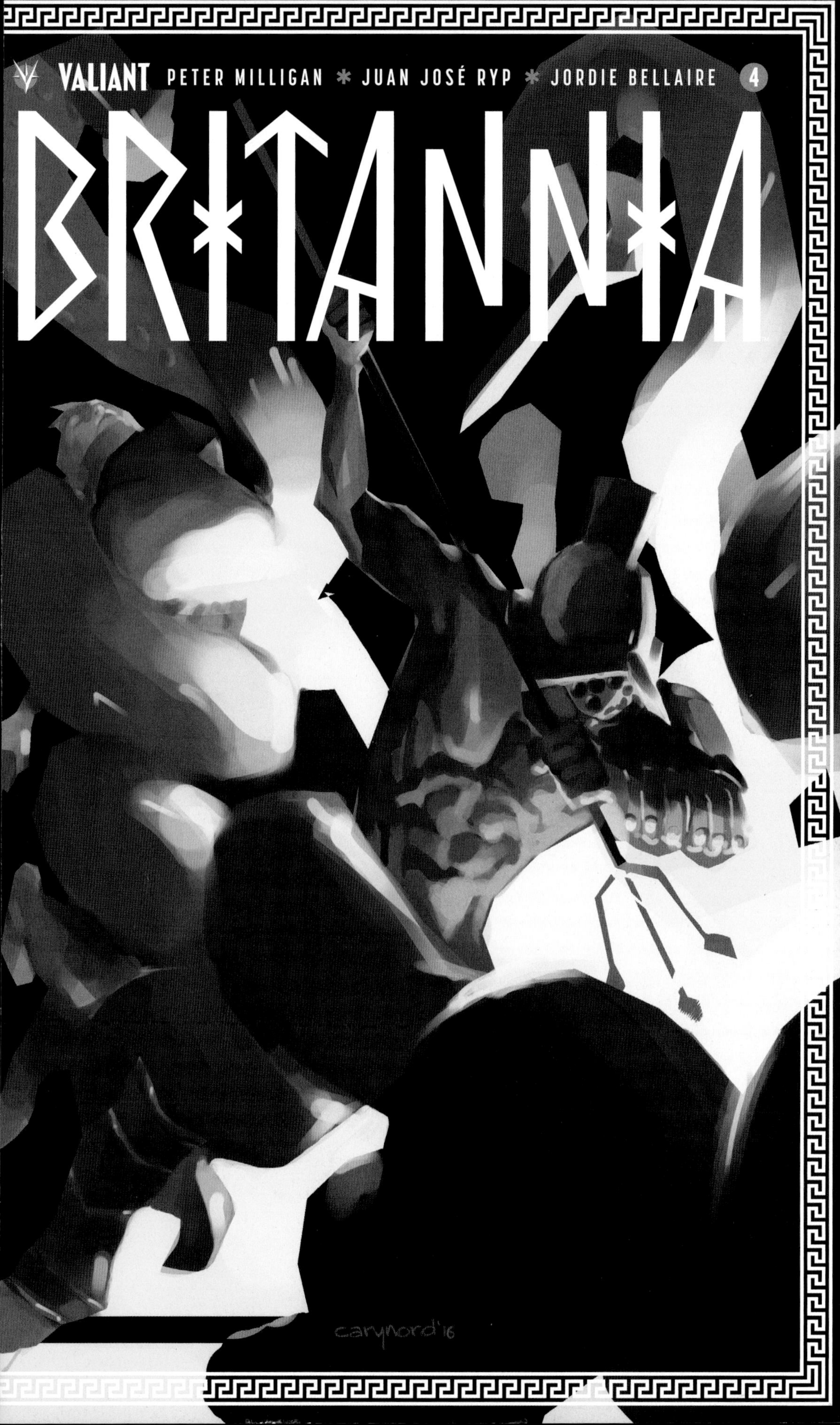
VALIANT
PETER MILLIGAN * JUAN JOSÉ RYP * JORDIE BELLAIRE
4
BRITANNIA
carynord'16

BOOK IV

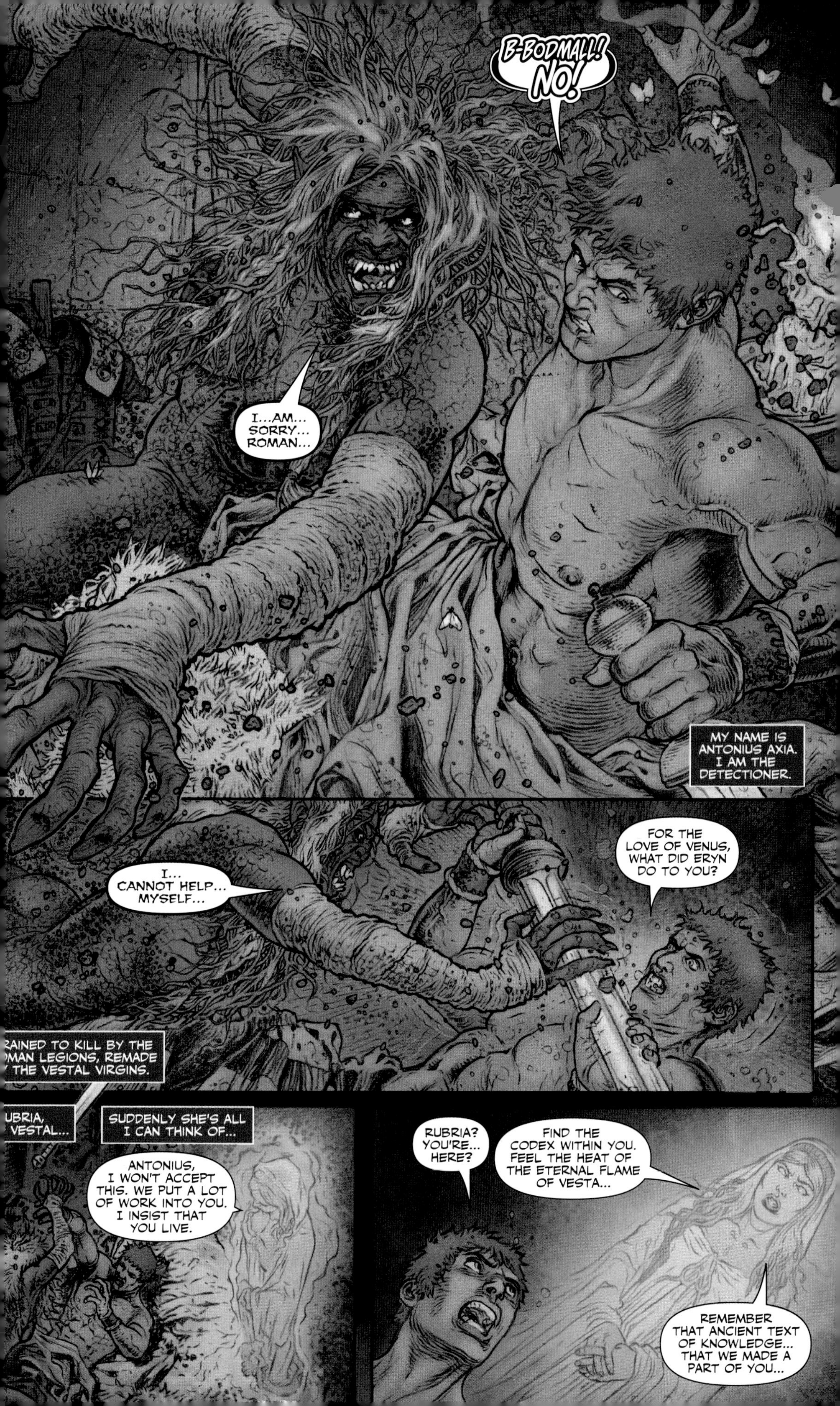

B-BODMALL! NO!
I...AM... SORRY... ROMAN...
MY NAME IS ANTONIUS AXIA. I AM THE DETECTIONER.
I... CANNOT HELP... MYSELF...
FOR THE LOVE OF VENUS, WHAT DID ERYN DO TO YOU?
RAINED TO KILL BY THE
OMAN LEGIONS, REMADE
THE VESTAL VIRGINS.
UBRIA,
VESTAL...
SUDDENLY SHE'S ALL I CAN THINK OF...
ANTONIUS, I WON'T ACCEPT THIS. WE PUT A LOT OF WORK INTO YOU. I INSIST THAT YOU LIVE.
RUBRIA? YOU'RE... HERE?
FIND THE CODEX WITHIN YOU. FEEL THE HEAT OF THE ETERNAL FLAME OF VESTA...
REMEMBER THAT ANCIENT TEXT OF KNOWLEDGE... THAT WE MADE A PART OF YOU...

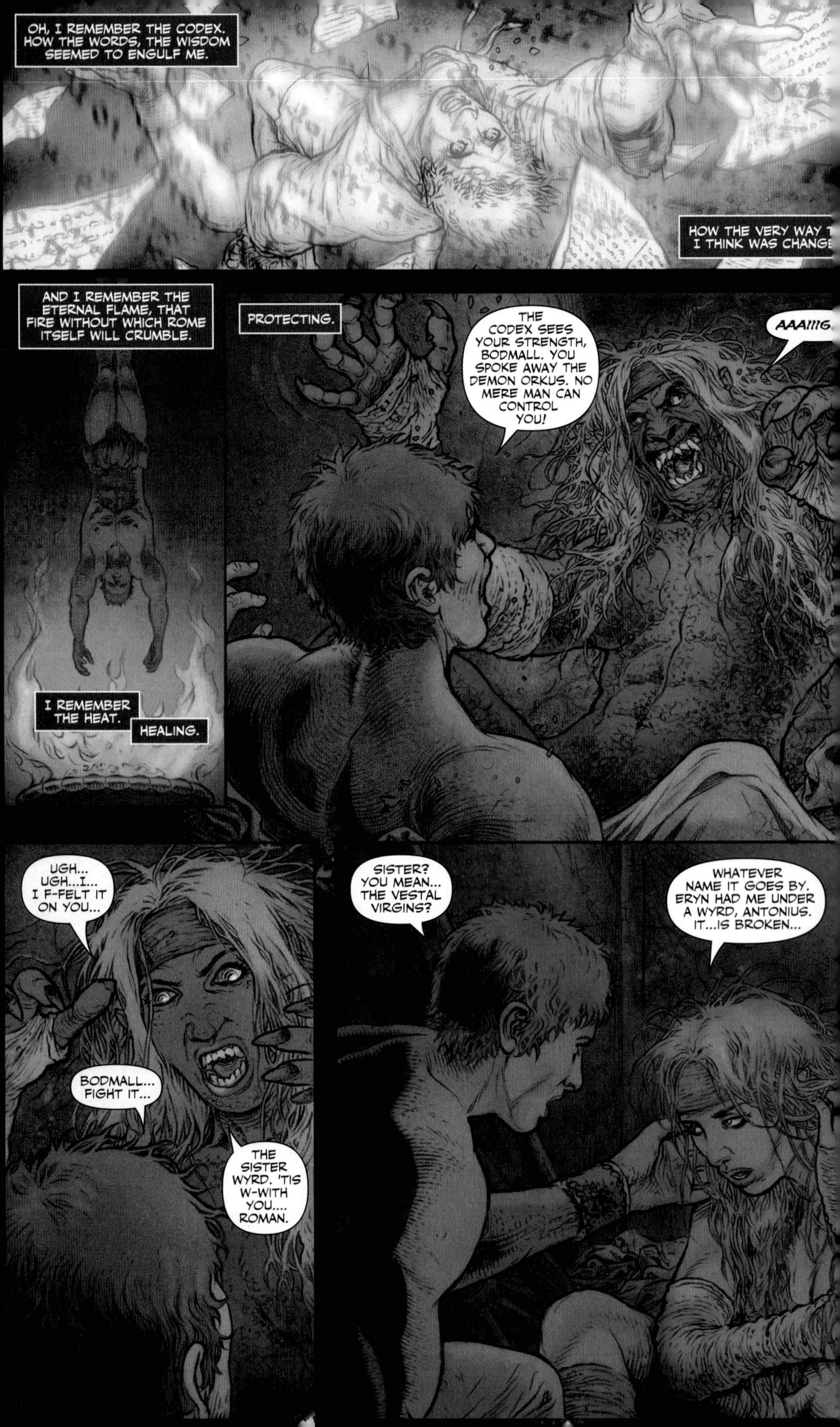
OH, I REMEMBER THE CODEX. HOW THE WORDS, THE WISDOM SEEMED TO ENGULF ME.
HOW THE VERY WAY I THINK WAS CHANGE
AND I REMEMBER THE ETERNAL FLAME, THAT FIRE WITHOUT WHICH ROME ITSELF WILL CRUMBLE.
I REMEMBER THE HEAT.
HEALING.
PROTECTING.
THE CODEX SEES YOUR STRENGTH, BODMALL. YOU SPOKE AWAY THE DEMON ORKUS. NO MERE MAN CAN CONTROL YOU!
AAAIIIG
UGH... UGH...I... I F-FELT IT ON YOU...
BODMALL... FIGHT IT...
THE SISTER WYRD. 'TIS W-WITH YOU.... ROMAN.
SISTER? YOU MEAN... THE VESTAL VIRGINS?
WHATEVER NAME IT GOES BY. ERYN HAD ME UNDER A WYRD, ANTONIUS. IT...IS BROKEN...

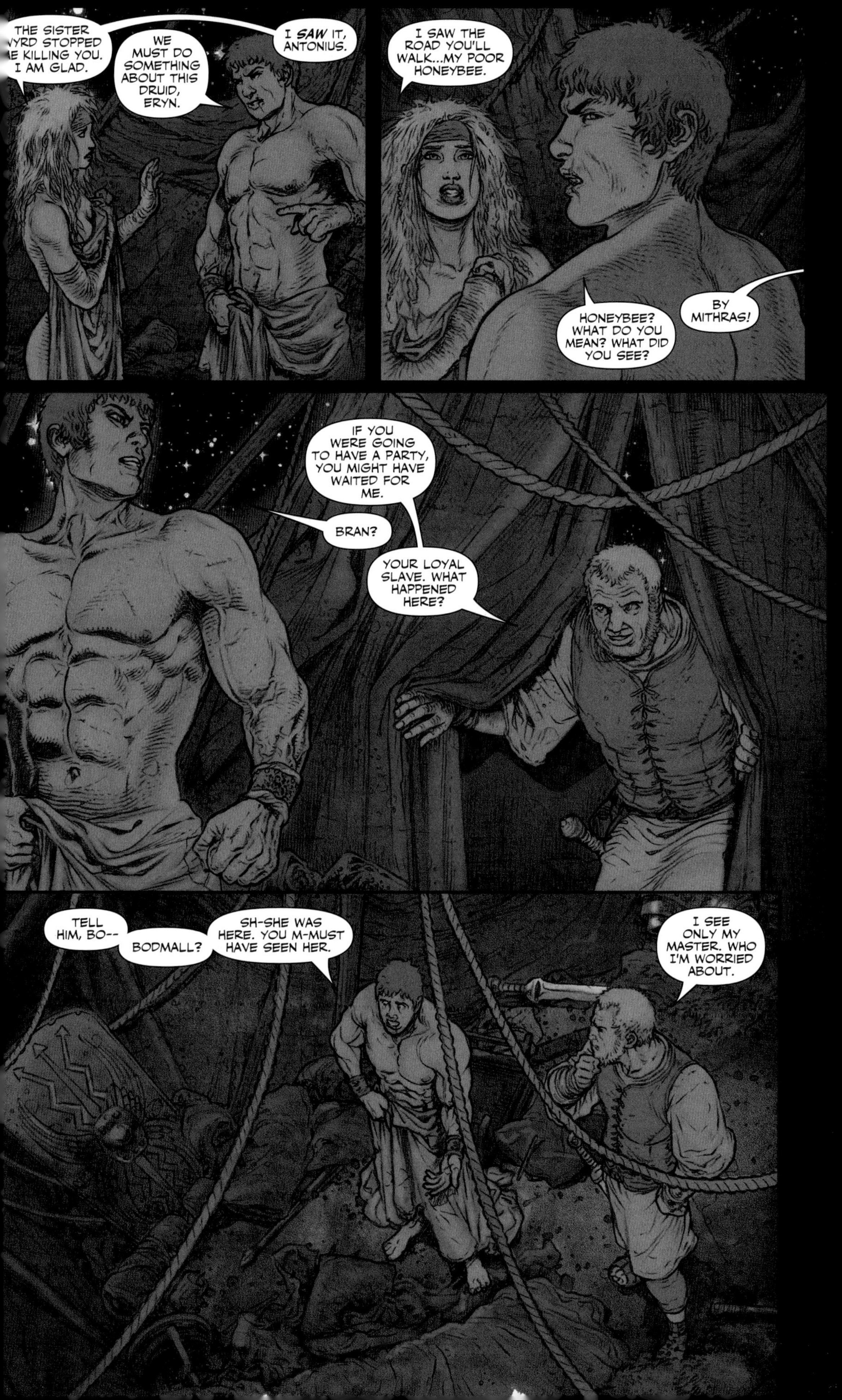

THE SISTER WYRD STOPPED ME KILLING YOU. I AM GLAD.
WE MUST DO SOMETHING ABOUT THIS DRUID, ERYN.
I SAW IT, ANTONIUS.
I SAW THE ROAD YOU'LL WALK...MY POOR HONEYBEE.
HONEYBEE? WHAT DO YOU MEAN? WHAT DID YOU SEE?
BY MITHRAS!
IF YOU WERE GOING TO HAVE A PARTY, YOU MIGHT HAVE WAITED FOR ME.
BRAN?
YOUR LOYAL SLAVE. WHAT HAPPENED HERE?
TELL HIM, BO--
BODMALL?
SH-SHE WAS HERE. YOU M-MUST HAVE SEEN HER.
I SEE ONLY MY MASTER. WHO I'M WORRIED ABOUT.

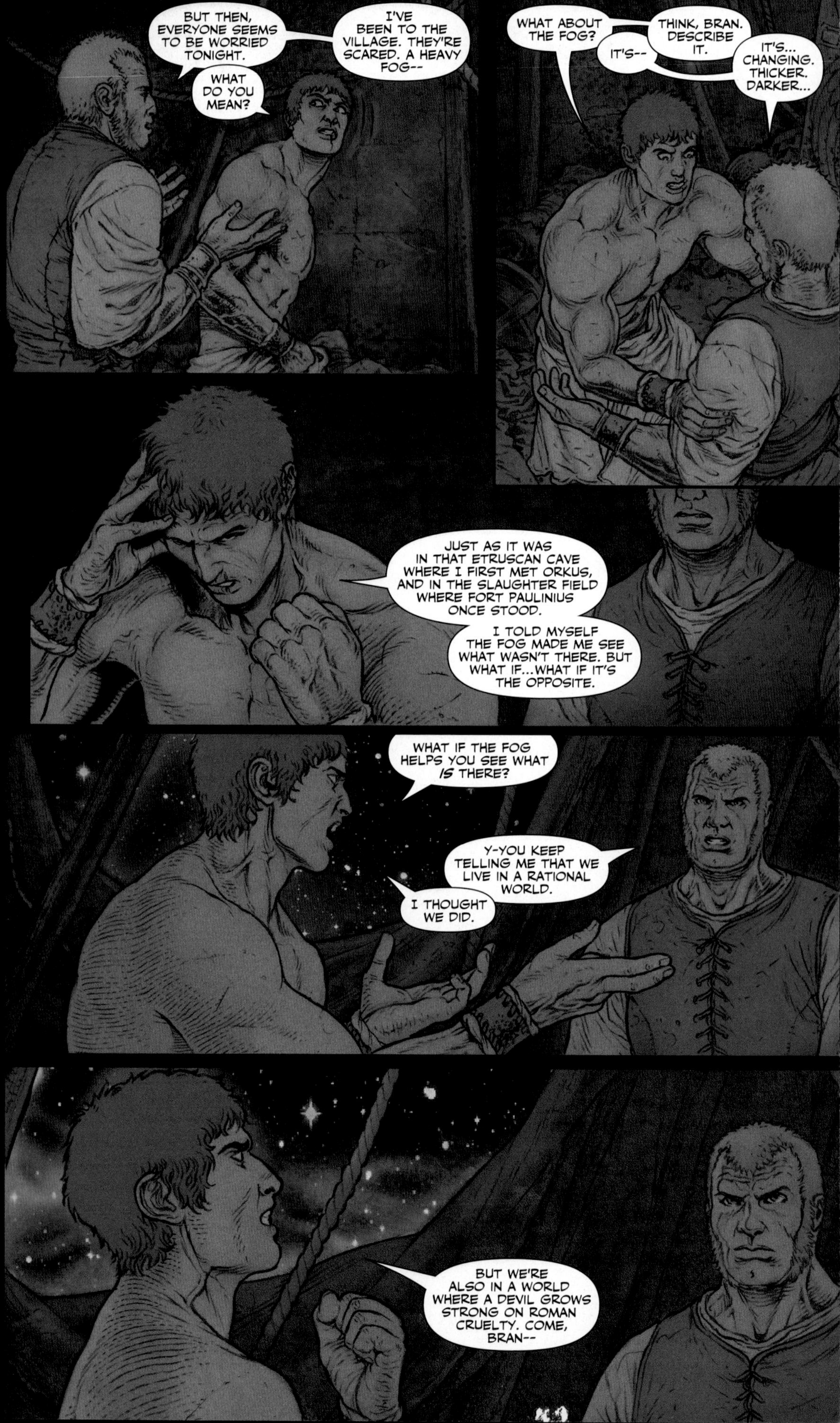
BUT THEN, EVERYONE SEEMS TO BE WORRIED TONIGHT.
WHAT DO YOU MEAN?
I'VE BEEN TO THE VILLAGE. THEY'RE SCARED. A HEAVY FOG--
WHAT ABOUT THE FOG?
IT'S--
THINK, BRAN. DESCRIBE IT.
IT'S... CHANGING. THICKER. DARKER...
JUST AS IT WAS IN THAT ETRUSCAN CAVE WHERE I FIRST MET ORKUS, AND IN THE SLAUGHTER FIELD WHERE FORT PAULINIUS ONCE STOOD.
I TOLD MYSELF THE FOG MADE ME SEE WHAT WASN'T THERE. BUT WHAT IF...WHAT IF IT'S THE OPPOSITE.
WHAT IF THE FOG HELPS YOU SEE WHAT *IS* THERE?
Y-YOU KEEP TELLING ME THAT WE LIVE IN A RATIONAL WORLD.
I THOUGHT WE DID.
BUT WE'RE ALSO IN A WORLD WHERE A DEVIL GROWS STRONG ON ROMAN CRUELTY. COME, BRAN--

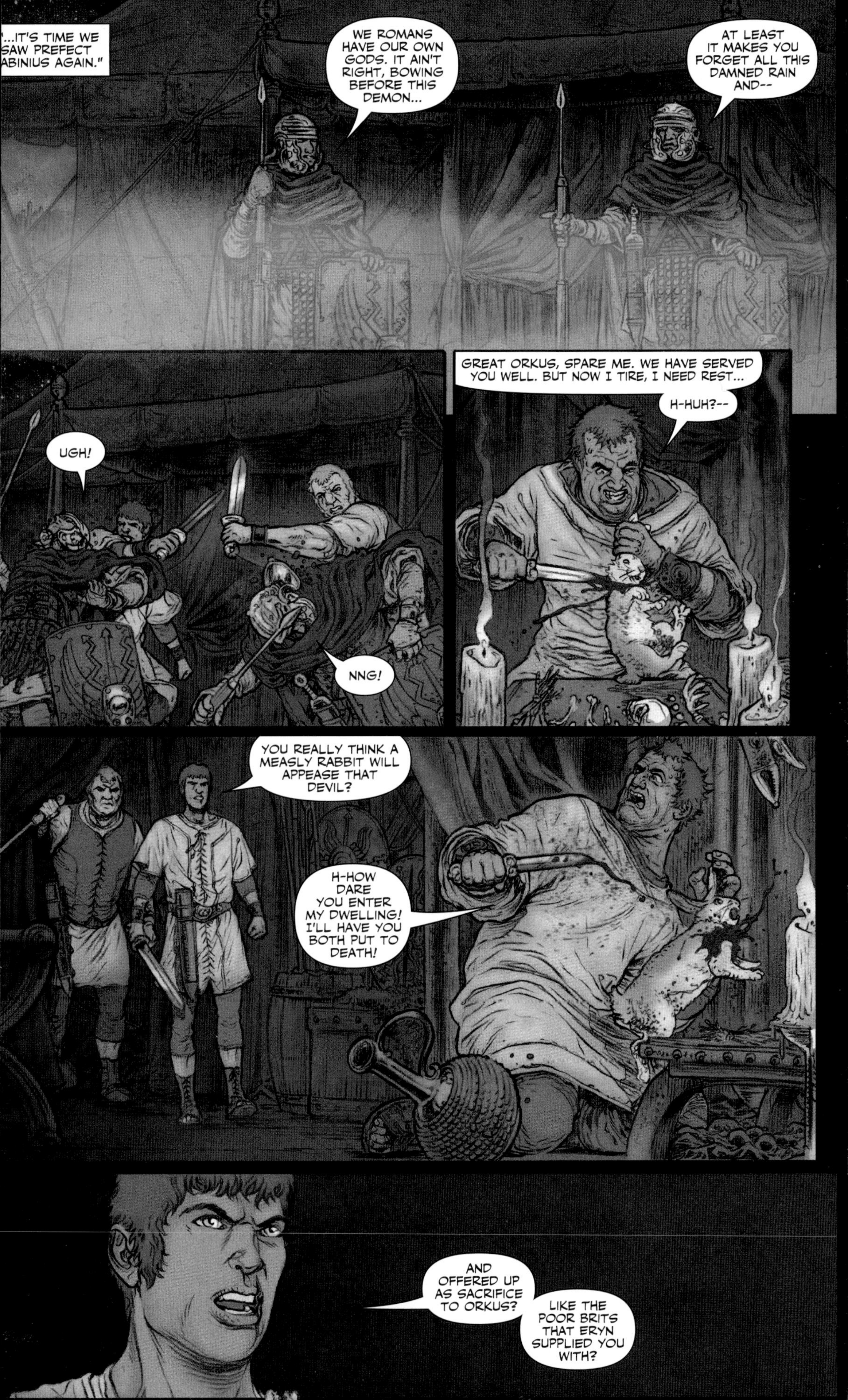
"...IT'S TIME WE SAW PREFECT ABINIUS AGAIN."
WE ROMANS HAVE OUR OWN GODS. IT AIN'T RIGHT, BOWING BEFORE THIS DEMON...
AT LEAST IT MAKES YOU FORGET ALL THIS DAMNED RAIN AND--
UGH!
NNG!
GREAT ORKUS, SPARE ME. WE HAVE SERVED YOU WELL. BUT NOW I TIRE, I NEED REST...
H-HUH?--
YOU REALLY THINK A MEASLY RABBIT WILL APPEASE THAT DEVIL?
H-HOW DARE YOU ENTER MY DWELLING! I'LL HAVE YOU BOTH PUT TO DEATH!
AND OFFERED UP AS SACRIFICE TO ORKUS?
LIKE THE POOR BRITS THAT ERYN SUPPLIED YOU WITH?

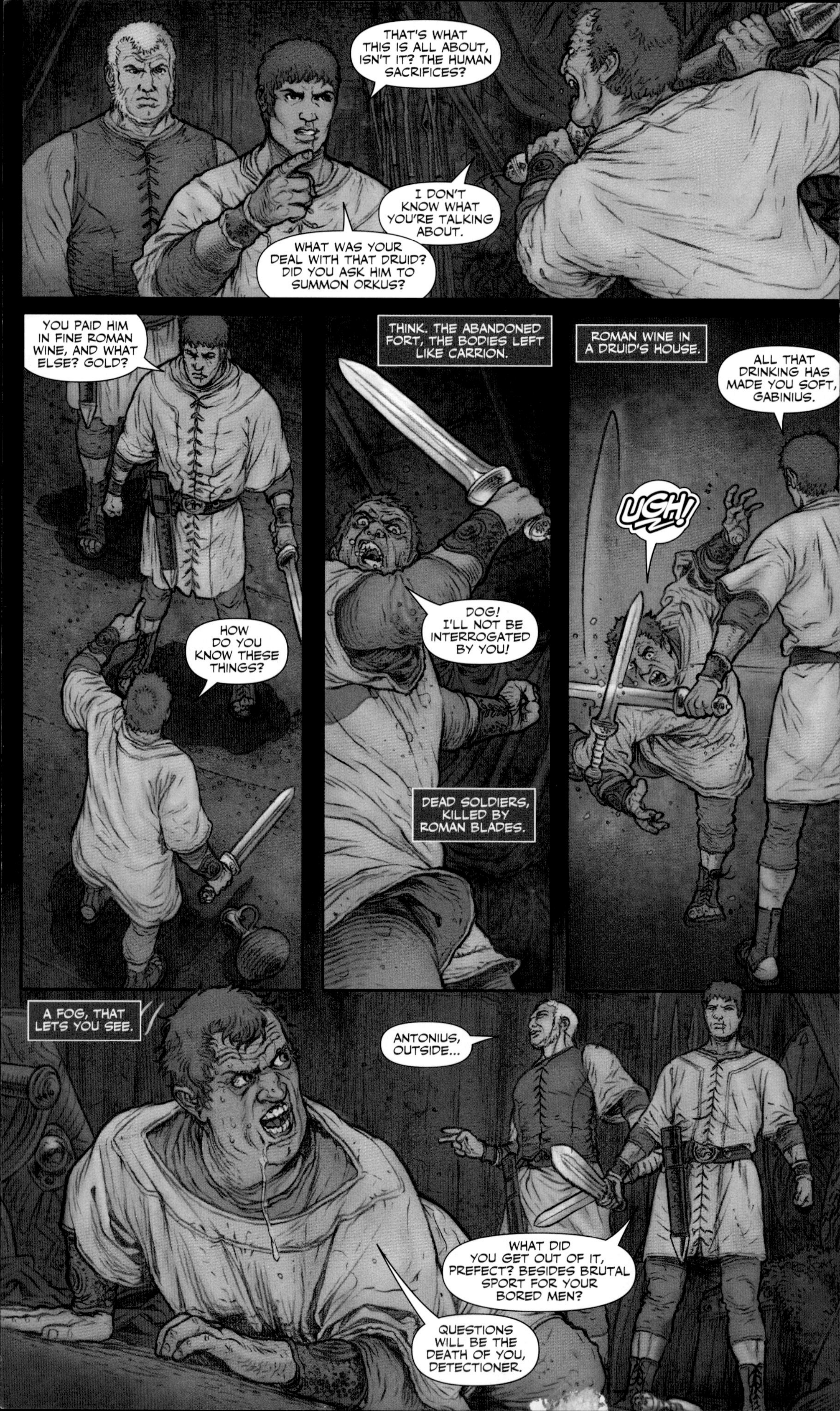

THAT'S WHAT THIS IS ALL ABOUT, ISN'T IT? THE HUMAN SACRIFICES?
I DON'T KNOW WHAT YOU'RE TALKING ABOUT.
WHAT WAS YOUR DEAL WITH THAT DRUID? DID YOU ASK HIM TO SUMMON ORKUS?
YOU PAID HIM IN FINE ROMAN WINE, AND WHAT ELSE? GOLD?
HOW DO YOU KNOW THESE THINGS?
THINK. THE ABANDONED FORT, THE BODIES LEFT LIKE CARRION.
DOG! I'LL NOT BE INTERROGATED BY YOU!
DEAD SOLDIERS, KILLED BY ROMAN BLADES.
ROMAN WINE IN A DRUID'S HOUSE.
ALL THAT DRINKING HAS MADE YOU SOFT, GABINIUS.
UGH!
A FOG, THAT LETS YOU SEE.
ANTONIUS, OUTSIDE...
WHAT DID YOU GET OUT OF IT, PREFECT? BESIDES BRUTAL SPORT FOR YOUR BORED MEN?
QUESTIONS WILL BE THE DEATH OF YOU, DETECTIONER.

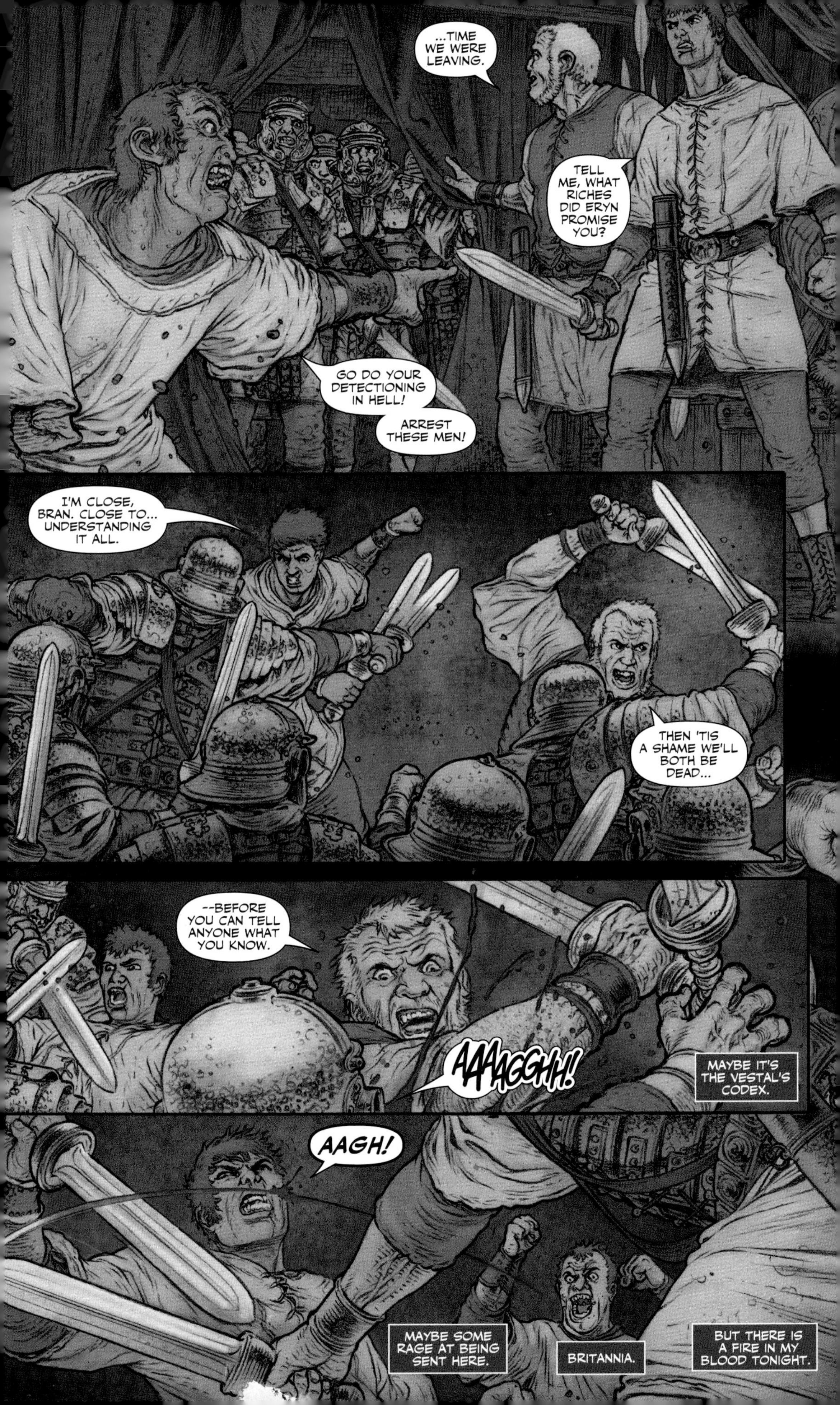

...TIME WE WERE LEAVING.
TELL ME, WHAT RICHES DID ERYN PROMISE YOU?
GO DO YOUR DETECTIONING IN HELL!
ARREST THESE MEN!
I'M CLOSE, BRAN. CLOSE TO... UNDERSTANDING IT ALL.
THEN 'TIS A SHAME WE'LL BOTH BE DEAD...
--BEFORE YOU CAN TELL ANYONE WHAT YOU KNOW.
AAAAGGHH!
MAYBE IT'S THE VESTAL'S CODEX.
AAGH!
MAYBE SOME RAGE AT BEING SENT HERE.
BRITANNIA.
BUT THERE IS A FIRE IN MY BLOOD TONIGHT.

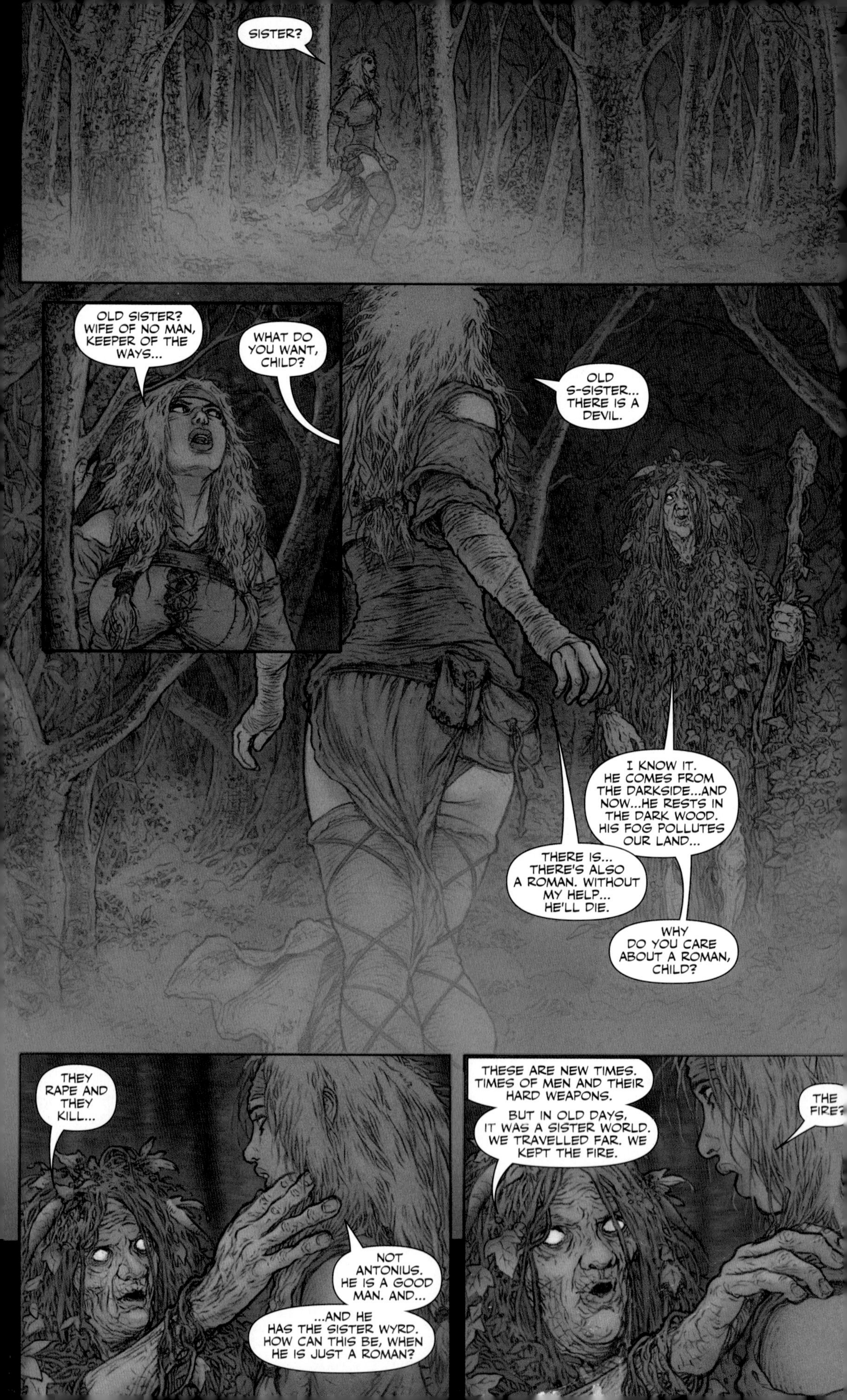
SISTER?
OLD SISTER? WIFE OF NO MAN, KEEPER OF THE WAYS...
WHAT DO YOU WANT, CHILD?
OLD S-SISTER... THERE IS A DEVIL.
I KNOW IT. HE COMES FROM THE DARKSIDE...AND NOW...HE RESTS IN THE DARK WOOD. HIS FOG POLLUTES OUR LAND...
THERE IS... THERE'S ALSO A ROMAN. WITHOUT MY HELP... HE'LL DIE.
WHY DO YOU CARE ABOUT A ROMAN, CHILD?
THEY RAPE AND THEY KILL...
NOT ANTONIUS. HE IS A GOOD MAN. AND...
...AND HE HAS THE SISTER WYRD. HOW CAN THIS BE, WHEN HE IS JUST A ROMAN?
THESE ARE NEW TIMES. TIMES OF MEN AND THEIR HARD WEAPONS.
BUT IN OLD DAYS, IT WAS A SISTER WORLD. WE TRAVELLED FAR. WE KEPT THE FIRE.
THE FIRE?

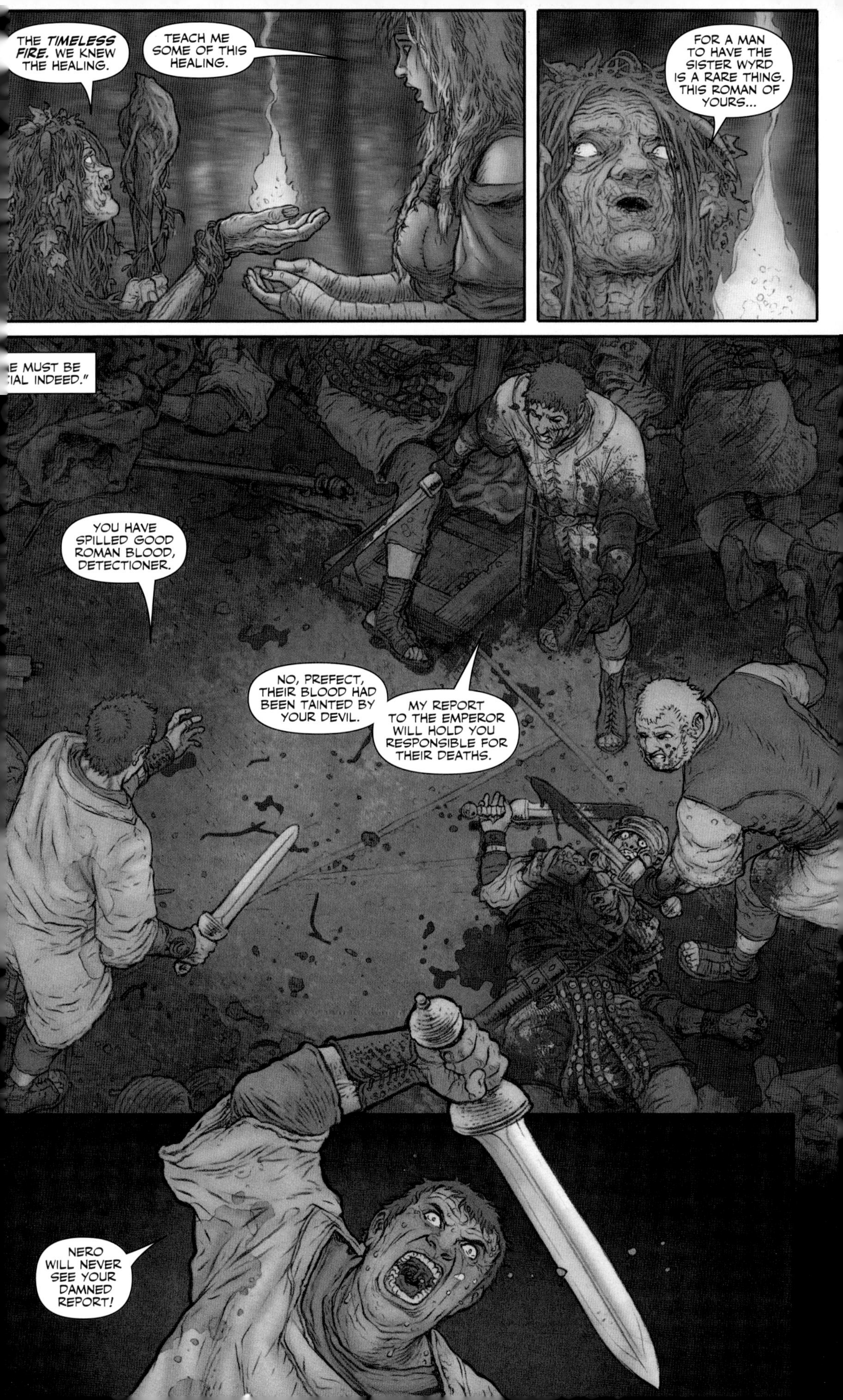
THE *TIMELESS FIRE*. WE KNEW THE HEALING.
TEACH ME SOME OF THIS HEALING.
FOR A MAN TO HAVE THE SISTER WYRD IS A RARE THING. THIS ROMAN OF YOURS...
E MUST BE CIAL INDEED."
YOU HAVE SPILLED GOOD ROMAN BLOOD, DETECTIONER.
NO, PREFECT, THEIR BLOOD HAD BEEN TAINTED BY YOUR DEVIL.
MY REPORT TO THE EMPEROR WILL HOLD YOU RESPONSIBLE FOR THEIR DEATHS.
NERO WILL NEVER SEE YOUR DAMNED REPORT!

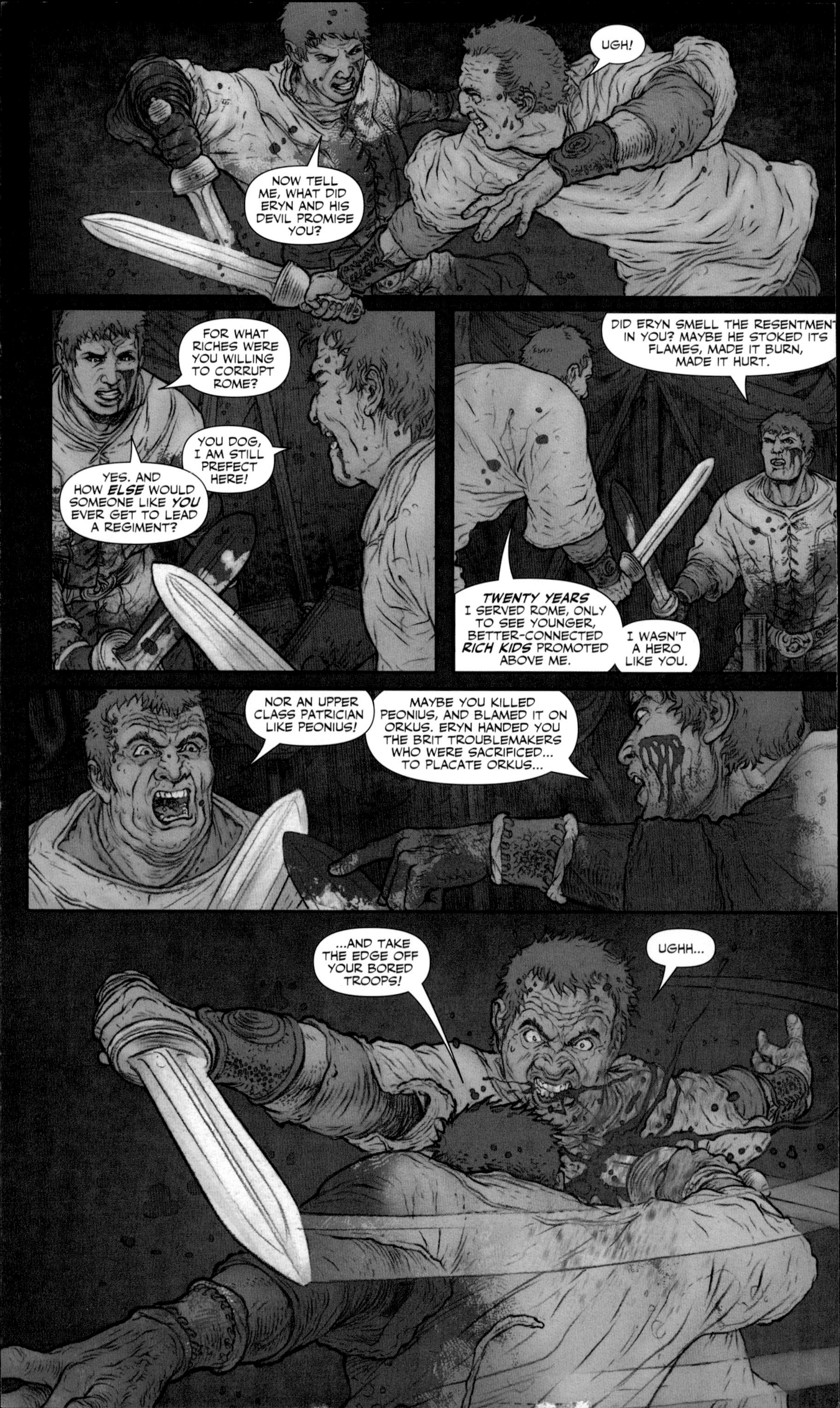
UGH!
NOW TELL ME, WHAT DID ERYN AND HIS DEVIL PROMISE YOU?
FOR WHAT RICHES WERE YOU WILLING TO CORRUPT ROME?
YOU DOG, I AM STILL PREFECT HERE!
YES. AND HOW *ELSE* WOULD SOMEONE LIKE *YOU* EVER GET TO LEAD A REGIMENT?
DID ERYN SMELL THE RESENTMENT IN YOU? MAYBE HE STOKED ITS FLAMES, MADE IT BURN, MADE IT HURT.
TWENTY YEARS I SERVED ROME, ONLY TO SEE YOUNGER, BETTER-CONNECTED ***RICH KIDS*** PROMOTED ABOVE ME.
I WASN'T A HERO LIKE YOU.
NOR AN UPPER CLASS PATRICIAN LIKE PEONIUS!
MAYBE YOU KILLED PEONIUS, AND BLAMED IT ON ORKUS. ERYN HANDED YOU THE BRIT TROUBLEMAKERS WHO WERE SACRIFICED... TO PLACATE ORKUS...
...AND TAKE THE EDGE OFF YOUR BORED TROOPS!
UGHH...

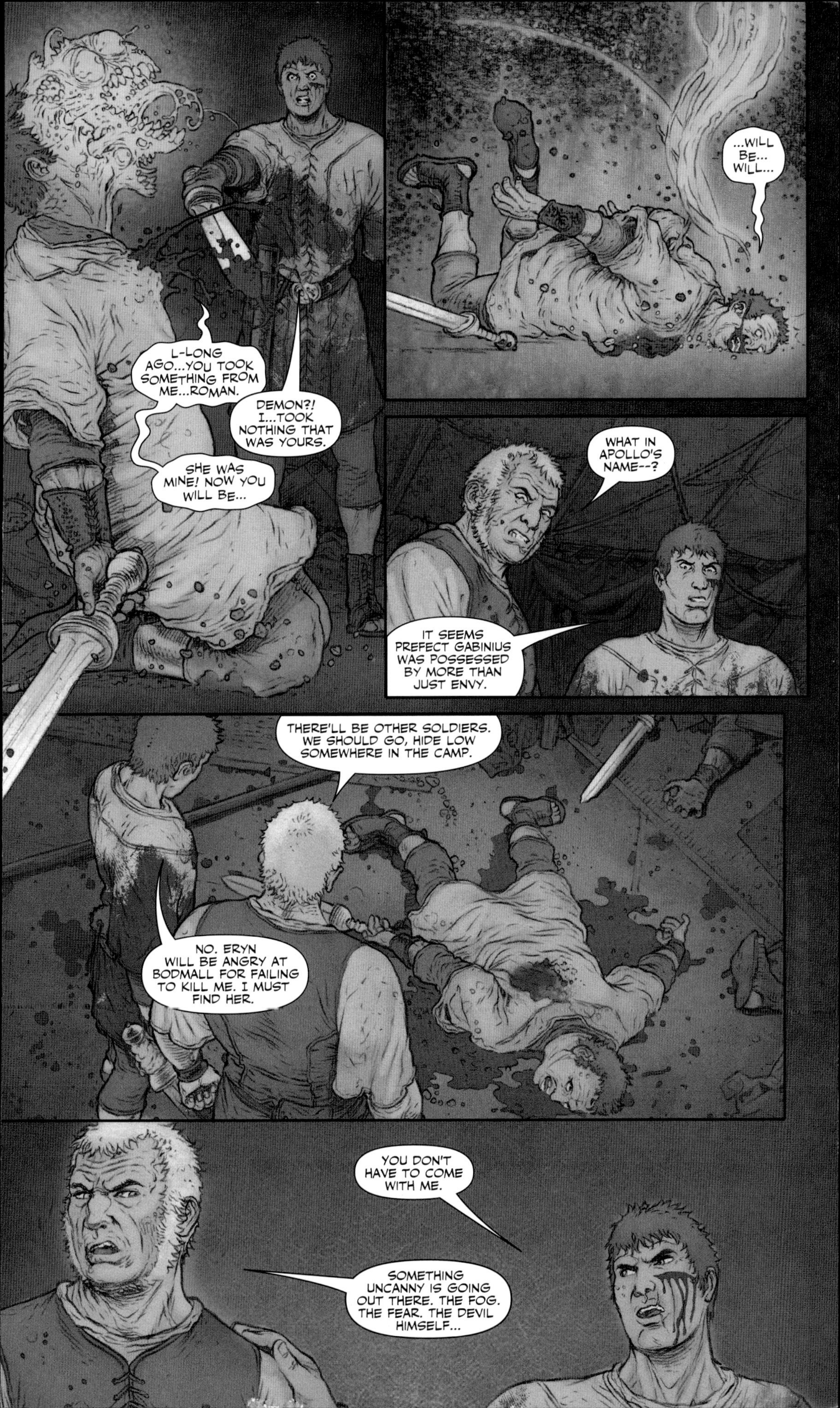
L-LONG AGO...YOU TOOK SOMETHING FROM ME...ROMAN.
DEMON?! I...TOOK NOTHING THAT WAS YOURS.
SHE WAS MINE! NOW YOU WILL BE...
...WILL BE... WILL...
WHAT IN APOLLO'S NAME--?
IT SEEMS PREFECT GABINIUS WAS POSSESSED BY MORE THAN JUST ENVY.
THERE'LL BE OTHER SOLDIERS. WE SHOULD GO, HIDE LOW SOMEWHERE IN THE CAMP.
NO. ERYN WILL BE ANGRY AT BODMALL FOR FAILING TO KILL ME. I MUST FIND HER.
YOU DON'T HAVE TO COME WITH ME.
SOMETHING UNCANNY IS GOING OUT THERE. THE FOG. THE FEAR. THE DEVIL HIMSELF...

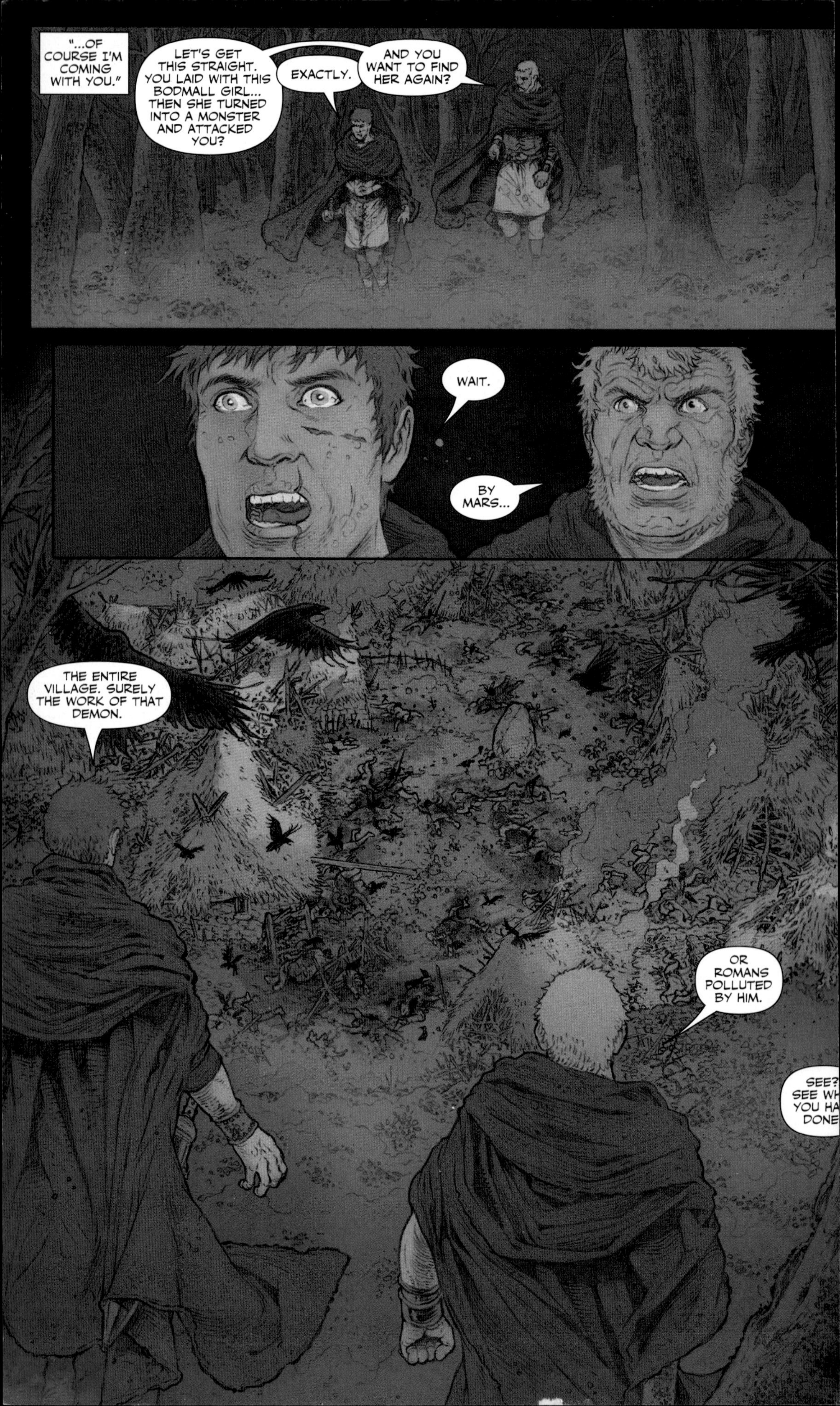
"...OF COURSE I'M COMING WITH YOU."
LET'S GET THIS STRAIGHT. YOU LAID WITH THIS BODMALL GIRL... THEN SHE TURNED INTO A MONSTER AND ATTACKED YOU?
EXACTLY.
AND YOU WANT TO FIND HER AGAIN?
WAIT.
BY MARS...
THE ENTIRE VILLAGE. SURELY THE WORK OF THAT DEMON.
OR ROMANS POLLUTED BY HIM.
SEE? SEE WH YOU HA DONE

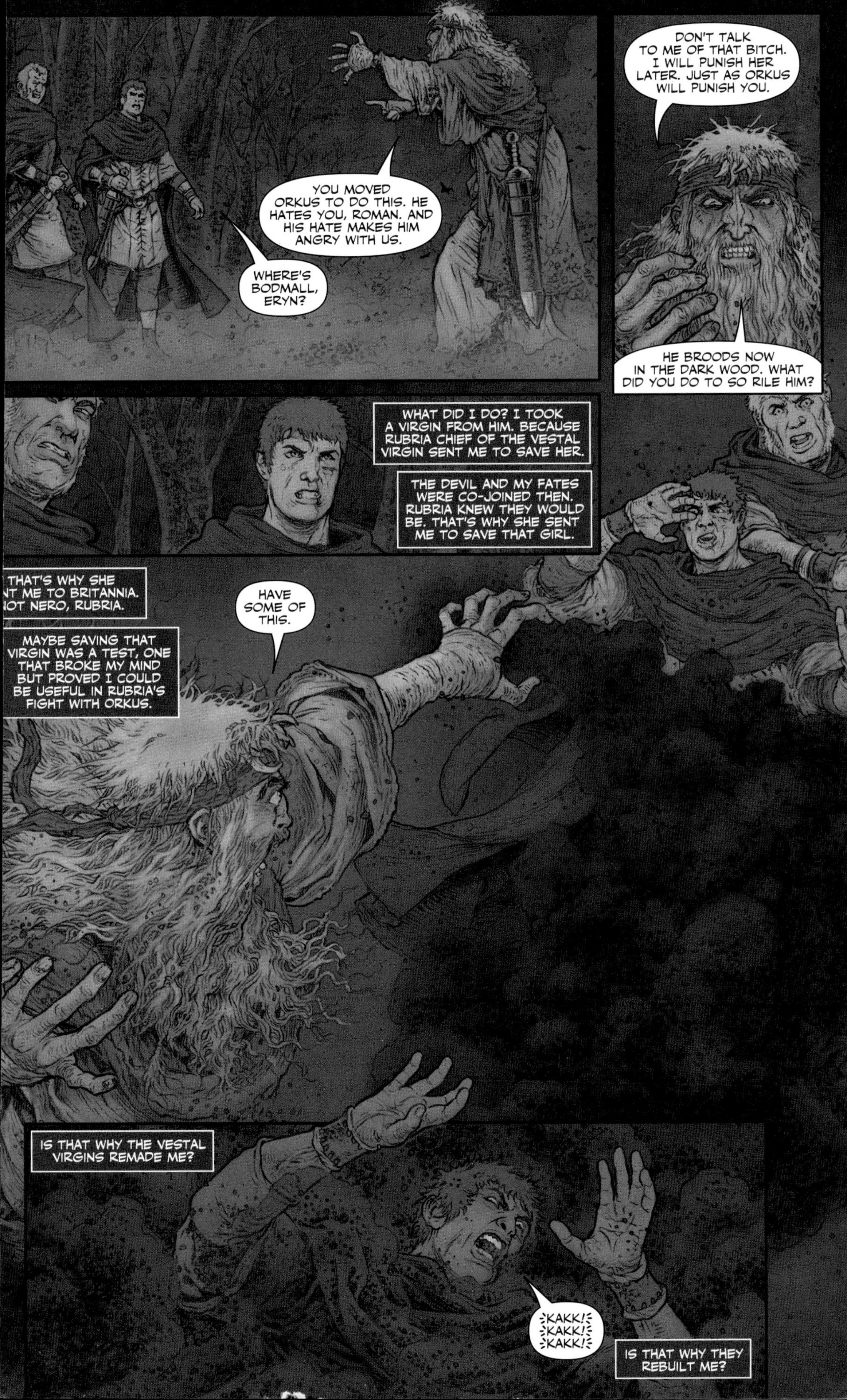
YOU MOVED ORKUS TO DO THIS. HE HATES YOU, ROMAN. AND HIS HATE MAKES HIM ANGRY WITH US.
WHERE'S BODMALL, ERYN?
DON'T TALK TO ME OF THAT BITCH. I WILL PUNISH HER LATER. JUST AS ORKUS WILL PUNISH YOU.
HE BROODS NOW IN THE DARK WOOD. WHAT DID YOU DO TO SO RILE HIM?
WHAT DID I DO? I TOOK A VIRGIN FROM HIM. BECAUSE RUBRIA CHIEF OF THE VESTAL VIRGIN SENT ME TO SAVE HER.
THE DEVIL AND MY FATES WERE CO-JOINED THEN. RUBRIA KNEW THEY WOULD BE. THAT'S WHY SHE SENT ME TO SAVE THAT GIRL.
THAT'S WHY SHE NT ME TO BRITANNIA. NOT NERO, RUBRIA.
HAVE SOME OF THIS.
MAYBE SAVING THAT VIRGIN WAS A TEST, ONE THAT BROKE MY MIND BUT PROVED I COULD BE USEFUL IN RUBRIA'S FIGHT WITH ORKUS.
IS THAT WHY THE VESTAL VIRGINS REMADE ME?
KAKK! KAKK! KAKK!
IS THAT WHY THEY REBUILT ME?

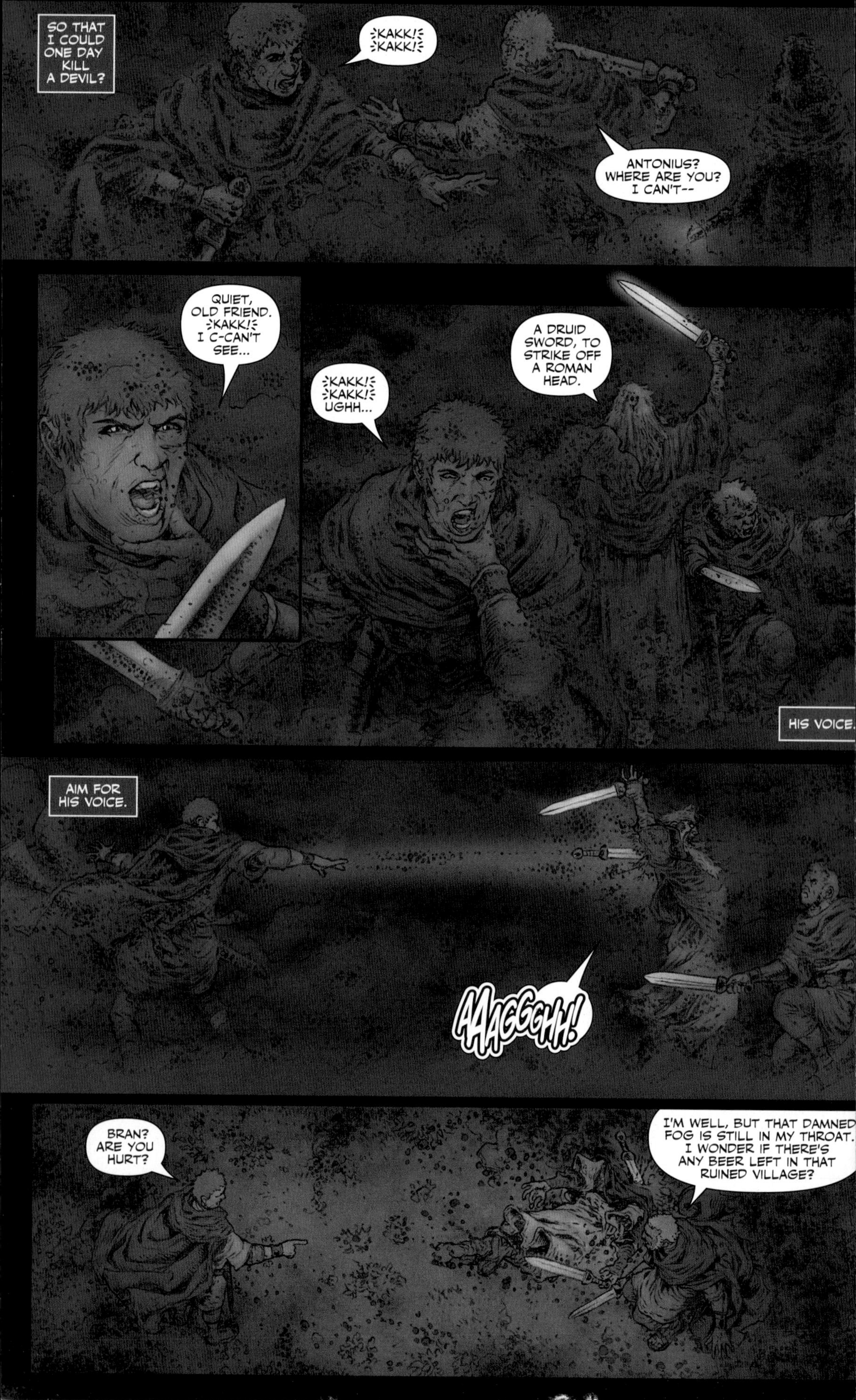
SO THAT I COULD ONE DAY KILL A DEVIL?
KAKK! KAKK!
ANTONIUS? WHERE ARE YOU? I CAN'T--
QUIET, OLD FRIEND. KAKK! I C-CAN'T SEE...
KAKK! KAKK! UGHH...
A DRUID SWORD, TO STRIKE OFF A ROMAN HEAD.
HIS VOICE.
AIM FOR HIS VOICE.
AAAGGGHH!
BRAN? ARE YOU HURT?
I'M WELL, BUT THAT DAMNED FOG IS STILL IN MY THROAT. I WONDER IF THERE'S ANY BEER LEFT IN THAT RUINED VILLAGE?

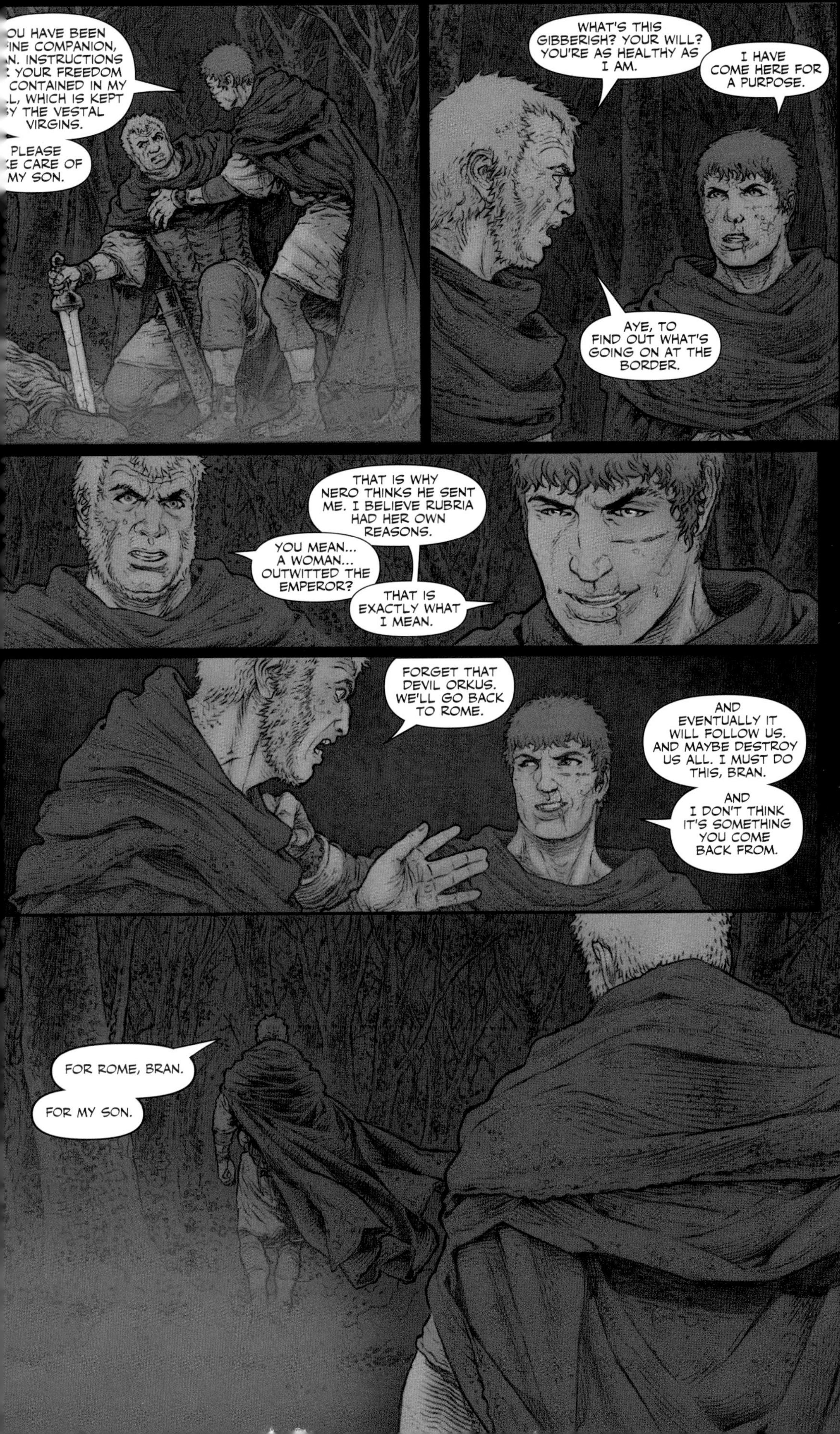
OU HAVE BEEN FINE COMPANION, N. INSTRUCTIONS YOUR FREEDOM CONTAINED IN MY L, WHICH IS KEPT Y THE VESTAL VIRGINS.
PLEASE E CARE OF MY SON.
WHAT'S THIS GIBBERISH? YOUR WILL? YOU'RE AS HEALTHY AS I AM.
I HAVE COME HERE FOR A PURPOSE.
AYE, TO FIND OUT WHAT'S GOING ON AT THE BORDER.
THAT IS WHY NERO THINKS HE SENT ME. I BELIEVE RUBRIA HAD HER OWN REASONS.
YOU MEAN... A WOMAN... OUTWITTED THE EMPEROR?
THAT IS EXACTLY WHAT I MEAN.
FORGET THAT DEVIL ORKUS. WE'LL GO BACK TO ROME.
AND EVENTUALLY IT WILL FOLLOW US. AND MAYBE DESTROY US ALL. I MUST DO THIS, BRAN.
AND I DON'T THINK IT'S SOMETHING YOU COME BACK FROM.
FOR ROME, BRAN.
FOR MY SON.

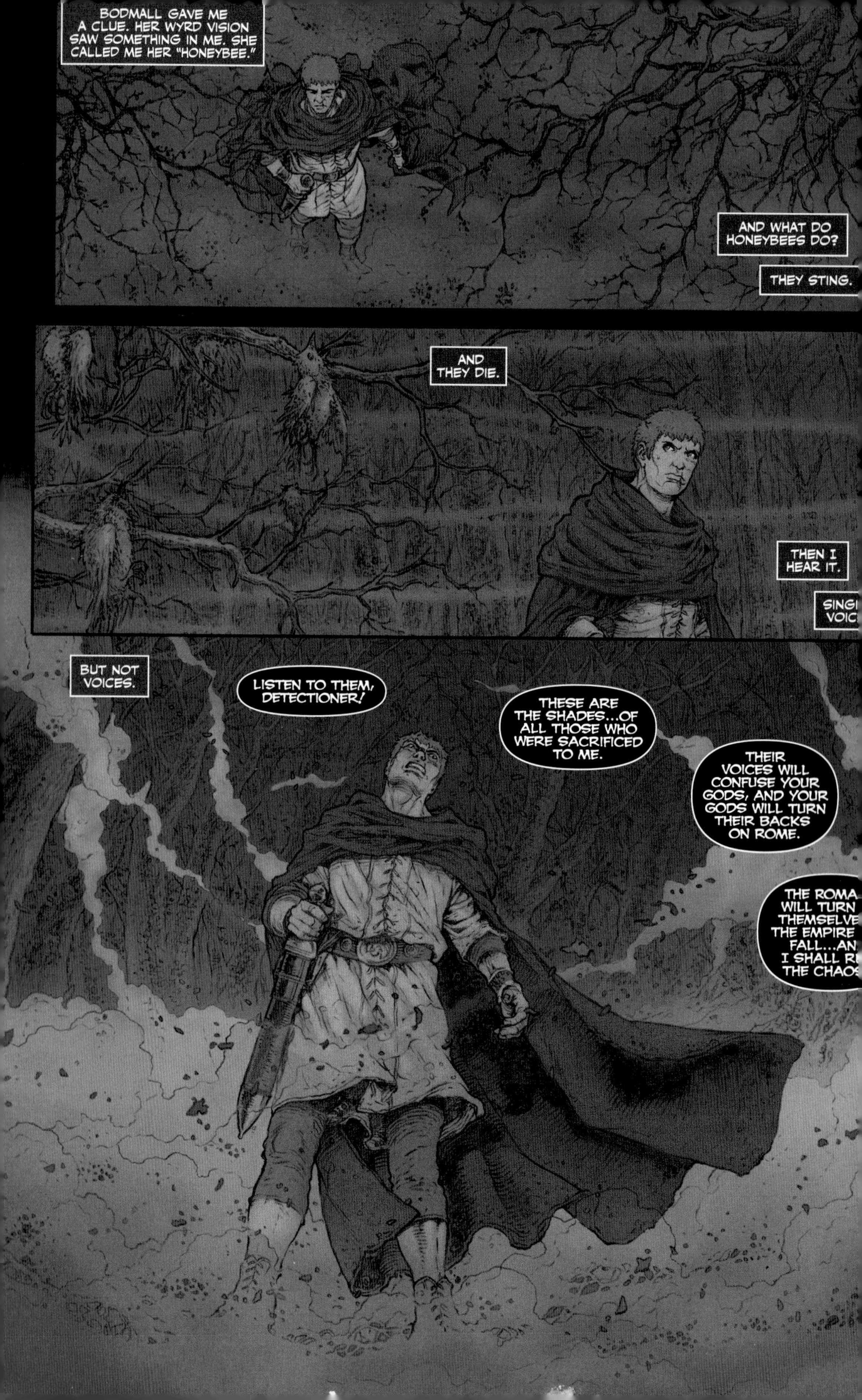
BODMALL GAVE ME A CLUE. HER WYRD VISION SAW SOMETHING IN ME. SHE CALLED ME HER "HONEYBEE."
AND WHAT DO HONEYBEES DO?
THEY STING.
AND THEY DIE.
THEN I HEAR IT.
BUT NOT VOICES.
LISTEN TO THEM, DETECTIONER!
THESE ARE THE SHADES...OF ALL THOSE WHO WERE SACRIFICED TO ME.
THEIR VOICES WILL CONFUSE YOUR GODS, AND YOUR GODS WILL TURN THEIR BACKS ON ROME.

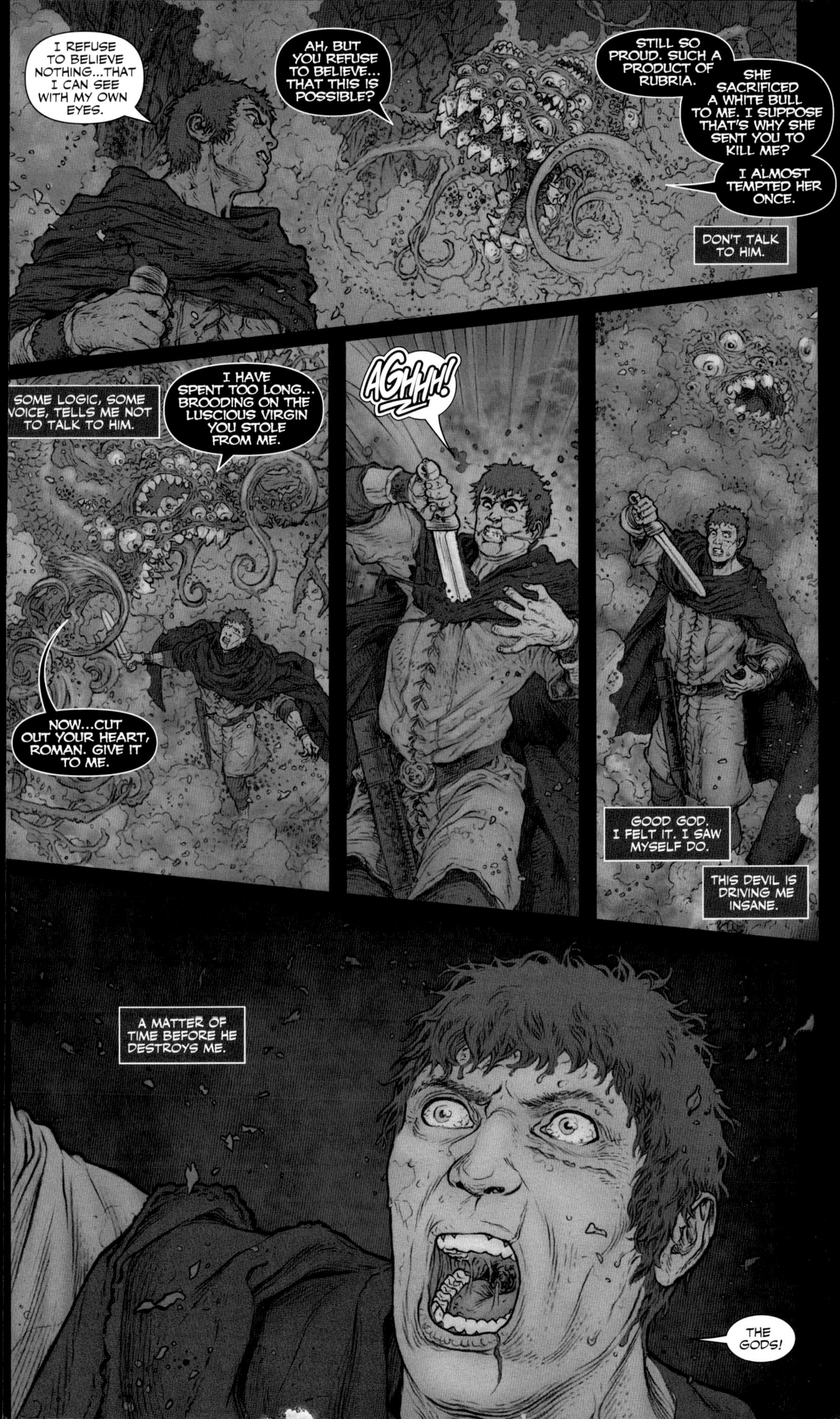
I REFUSE TO BELIEVE NOTHING...THAT I CAN SEE WITH MY OWN EYES.
AH, BUT YOU REFUSE TO BELIEVE... THAT THIS IS POSSIBLE?
STILL SO PROUD. SUCH A PRODUCT OF RUBRIA.
SHE SACRIFICED A WHITE BULL TO ME. I SUPPOSE THAT'S WHY SHE SENT YOU TO KILL ME?
I ALMOST TEMPTED HER ONCE.
DON'T TALK TO HIM.
SOME LOGIC, SOME VOICE, TELLS ME NOT TO TALK TO HIM.
I HAVE SPENT TOO LONG... BROODING ON THE LUSCIOUS VIRGIN YOU STOLE FROM ME.
NOW...CUT OUT YOUR HEART, ROMAN. GIVE IT TO ME.
AGHHH!
GOOD GOD. I FELT IT. I SAW MYSELF DO.
THIS DEVIL IS DRIVING ME INSANE.
A MATTER OF TIME BEFORE HE DESTROYS ME.
THE GODS!

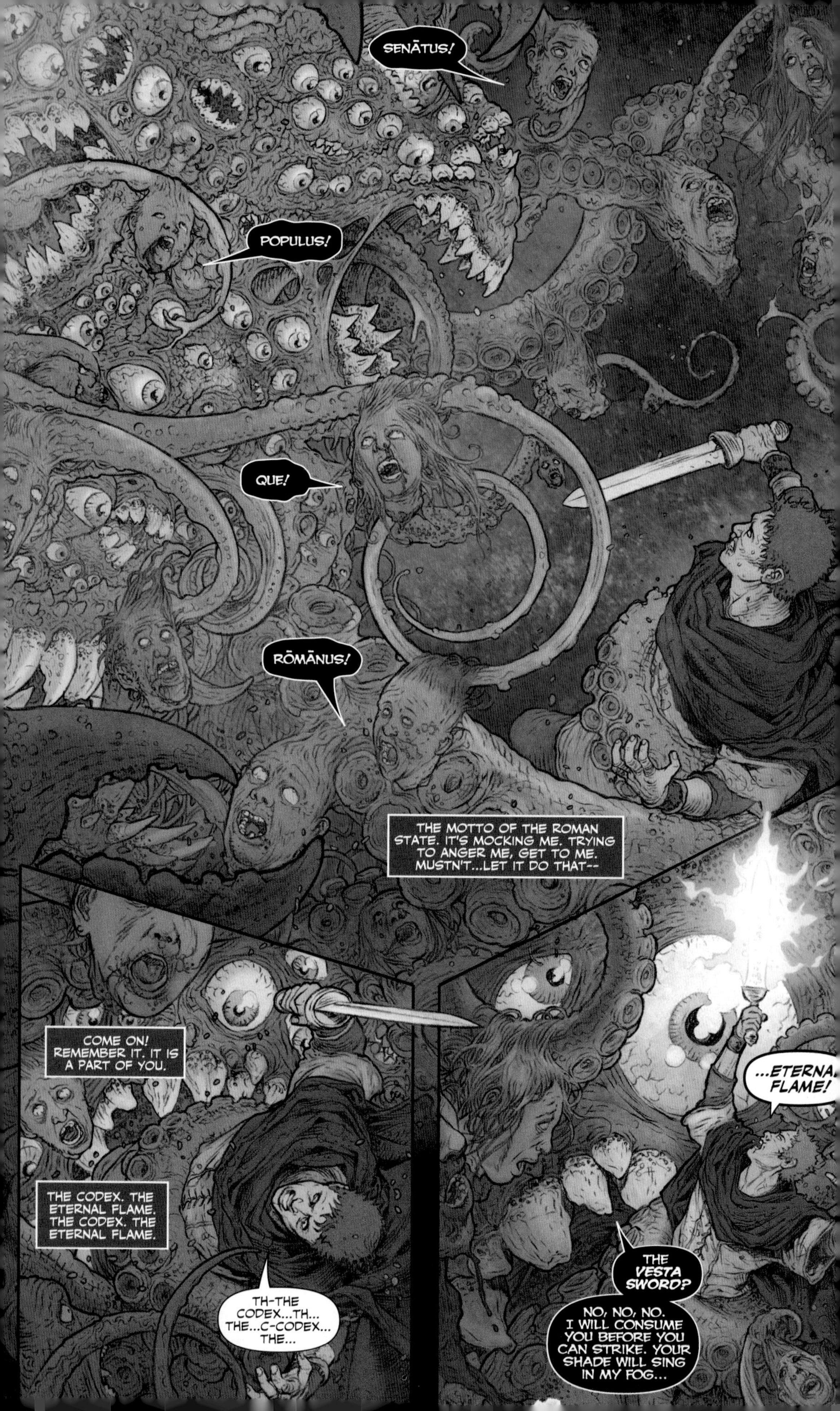
SENĀTUS!
POPULUS!
QUE!
RŌMĀNUS!
THE MOTTO OF THE ROMAN STATE. IT'S MOCKING ME. TRYING TO ANGER ME, GET TO ME. MUSTN'T...LET IT DO THAT--
COME ON! REMEMBER IT. IT IS A PART OF YOU.
THE CODEX. THE ETERNAL FLAME. THE CODEX. THE ETERNAL FLAME.
TH-THE CODEX...TH... THE...C-CODEX... THE...
...ETERNA FLAME!
THE *VESTA SWORD?*
NO, NO, NO. I WILL CONSUME YOU BEFORE YOU CAN STRIKE. YOUR SHADE WILL SING IN MY FOG...

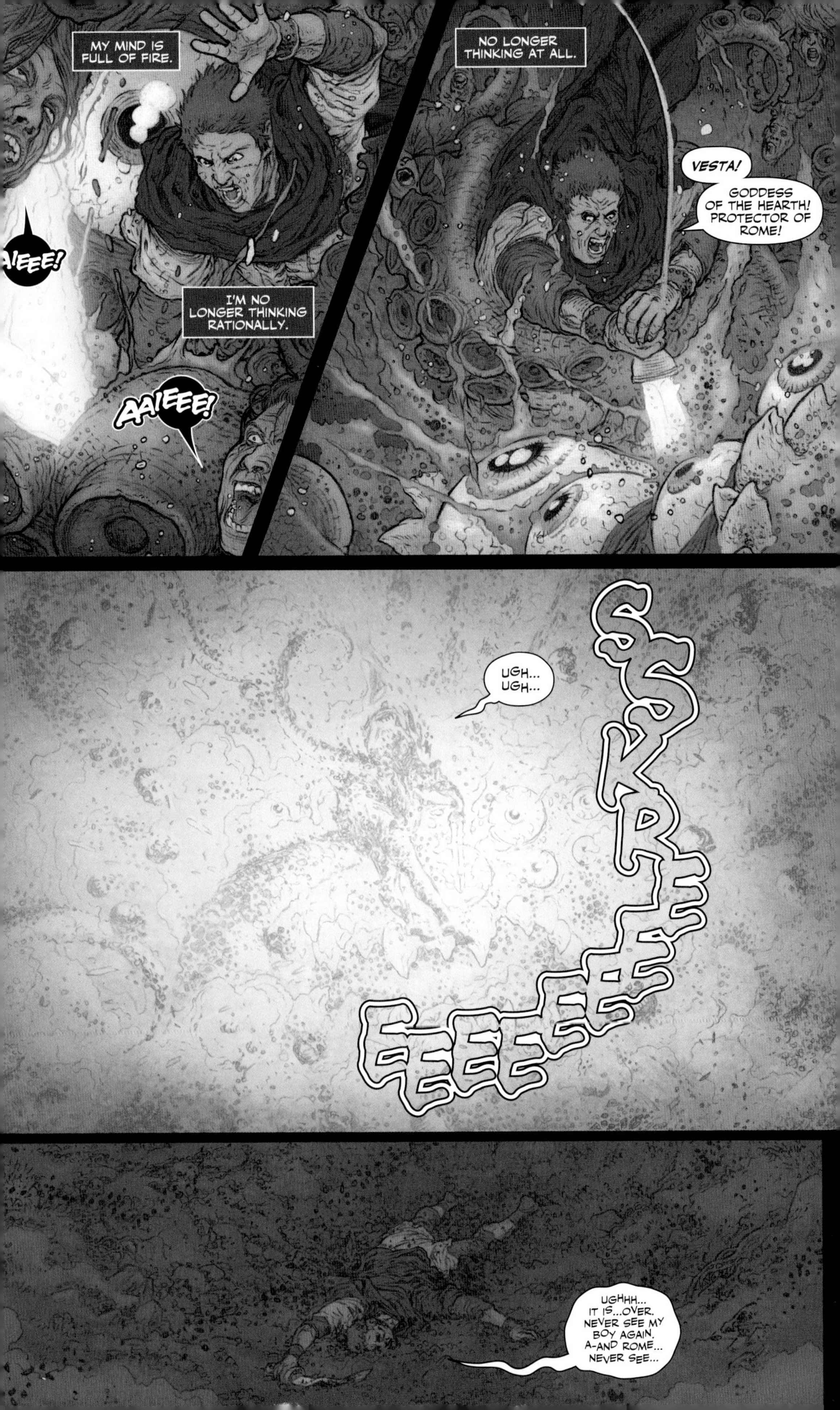
MY MIND IS FULL OF FIRE.
AIEEE!
I'M NO LONGER THINKING RATIONALLY.
AAIEEE!
NO LONGER THINKING AT ALL.
VESTA!
GODDESS OF THE HEARTH! PROTECTOR OF ROME!
UGH... UGH...
SSKREEEEEEEEE
UGHHH... IT IS...OVER. NEVER SEE MY BOY AGAIN. A-AND ROME... NEVER SEE...

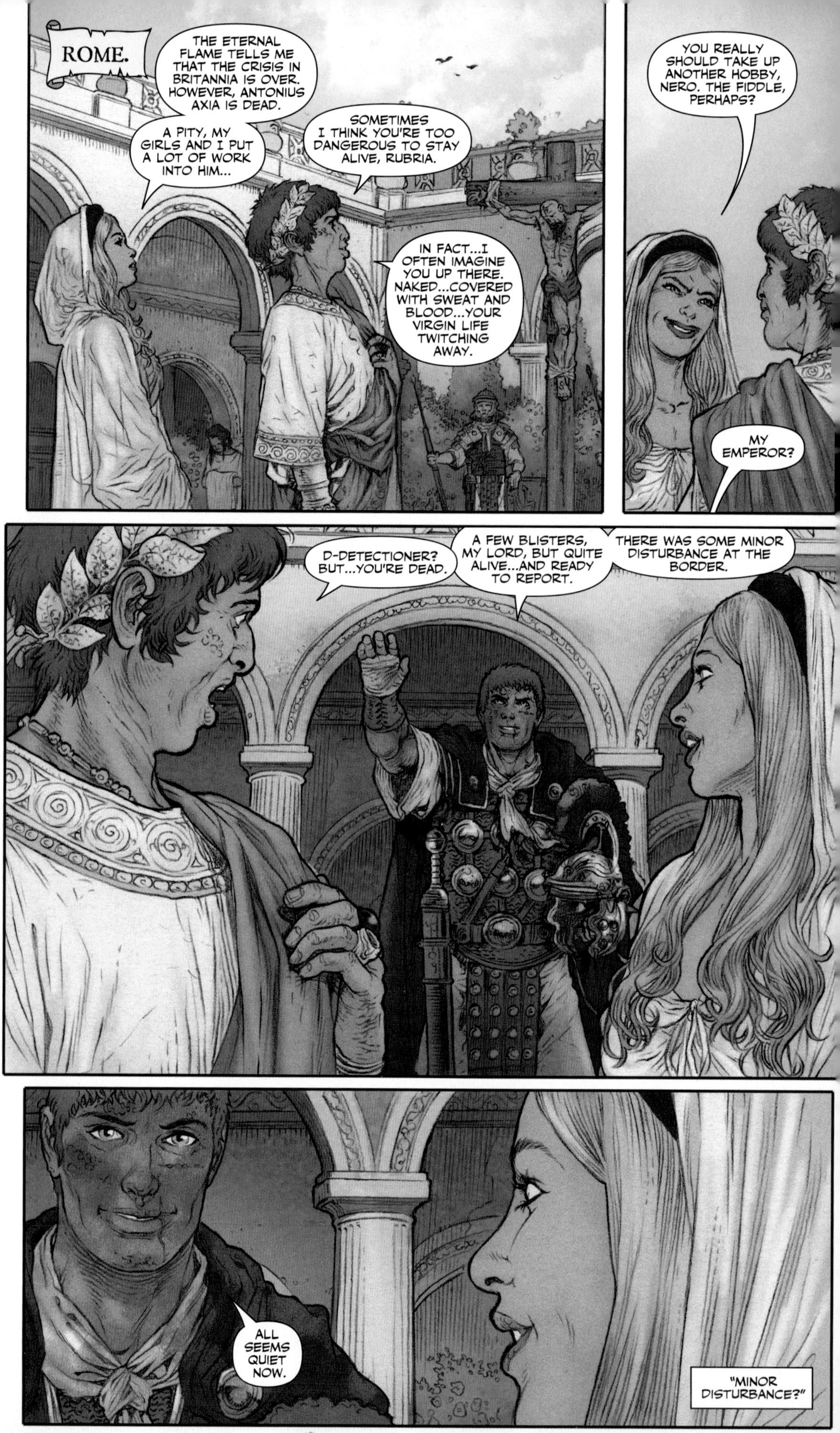
ROME.
THE ETERNAL FLAME TELLS ME THAT THE CRISIS IN BRITANNIA IS OVER. HOWEVER, ANTONIUS AXIA IS DEAD.
A PITY, MY GIRLS AND I PUT A LOT OF WORK INTO HIM...
SOMETIMES I THINK YOU'RE TOO DANGEROUS TO STAY ALIVE, RUBRIA.
IN FACT...I OFTEN IMAGINE YOU UP THERE. NAKED...COVERED WITH SWEAT AND BLOOD...YOUR VIRGIN LIFE TWITCHING AWAY.
YOU REALLY SHOULD TAKE UP ANOTHER HOBBY, NERO. THE FIDDLE, PERHAPS?
MY EMPEROR?
D-DETECTIONER? BUT...YOU'RE DEAD.
A FEW BLISTERS, MY LORD, BUT QUITE ALIVE...AND READY TO REPORT.
THERE WAS SOME MINOR DISTURBANCE AT THE BORDER.
ALL SEEMS QUIET NOW.
"MINOR DISTURBANCE?"

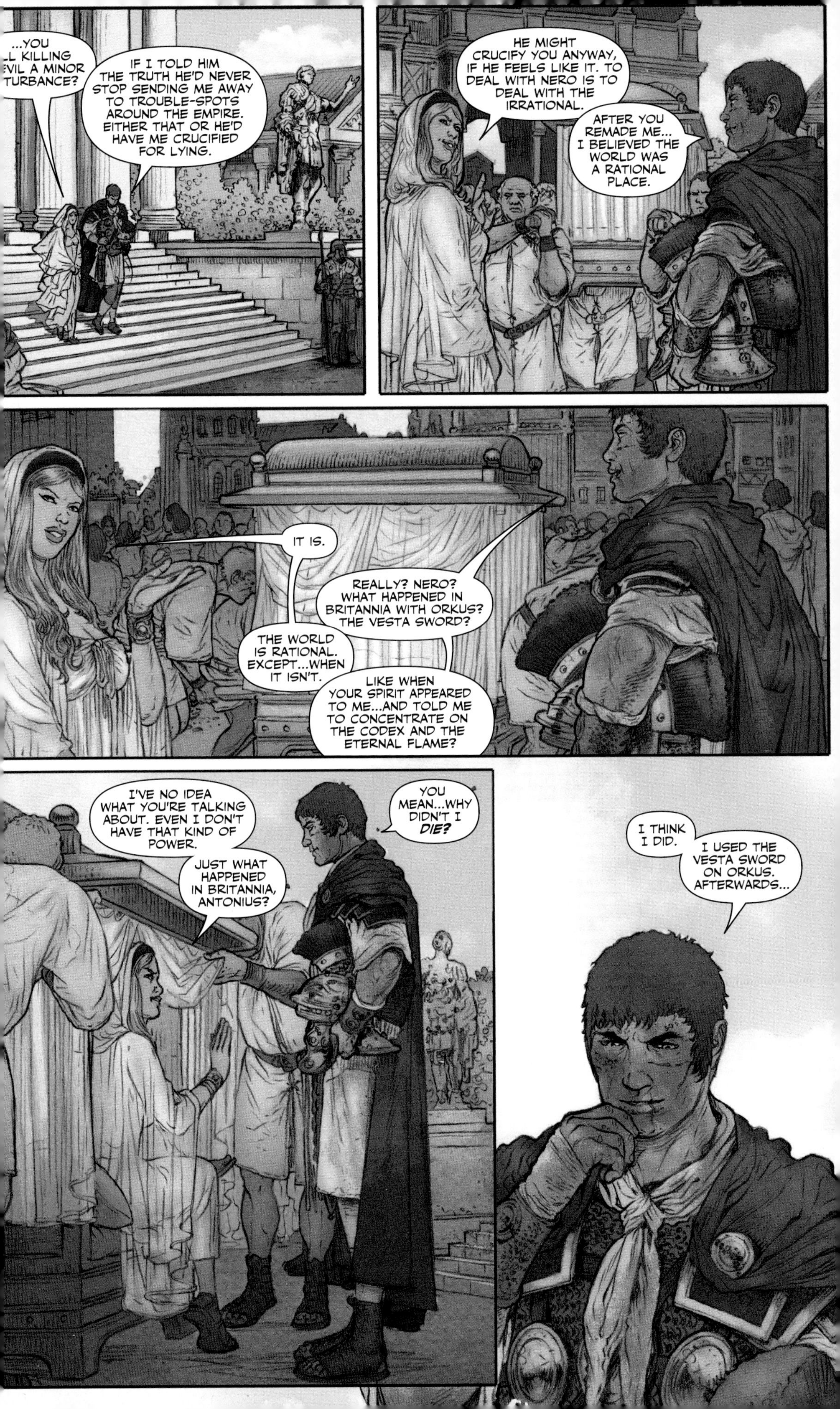
...YOU
L KILLING
EVIL A MINOR
TURBANCE?
IF I TOLD HIM THE TRUTH HE'D NEVER STOP SENDING ME AWAY TO TROUBLE-SPOTS AROUND THE EMPIRE. EITHER THAT OR HE'D HAVE ME CRUCIFIED FOR LYING.
HE MIGHT CRUCIFY YOU ANYWAY, IF HE FEELS LIKE IT. TO DEAL WITH NERO IS TO DEAL WITH THE IRRATIONAL.
AFTER YOU REMADE ME... I BELIEVED THE WORLD WAS A RATIONAL PLACE.
IT IS.
REALLY? NERO? WHAT HAPPENED IN BRITANNIA WITH ORKUS? THE VESTA SWORD?
THE WORLD IS RATIONAL. EXCEPT...WHEN IT ISN'T.
LIKE WHEN YOUR SPIRIT APPEARED TO ME...AND TOLD ME TO CONCENTRATE ON THE CODEX AND THE ETERNAL FLAME?
I'VE NO IDEA WHAT YOU'RE TALKING ABOUT. EVEN I DON'T HAVE THAT KIND OF POWER.
JUST WHAT HAPPENED IN BRITANNIA, ANTONIUS?
YOU MEAN...WHY DIDN'T I ***DIE?***
I THINK I DID.
I USED THE VESTA SWORD ON ORKUS. AFTERWARDS...

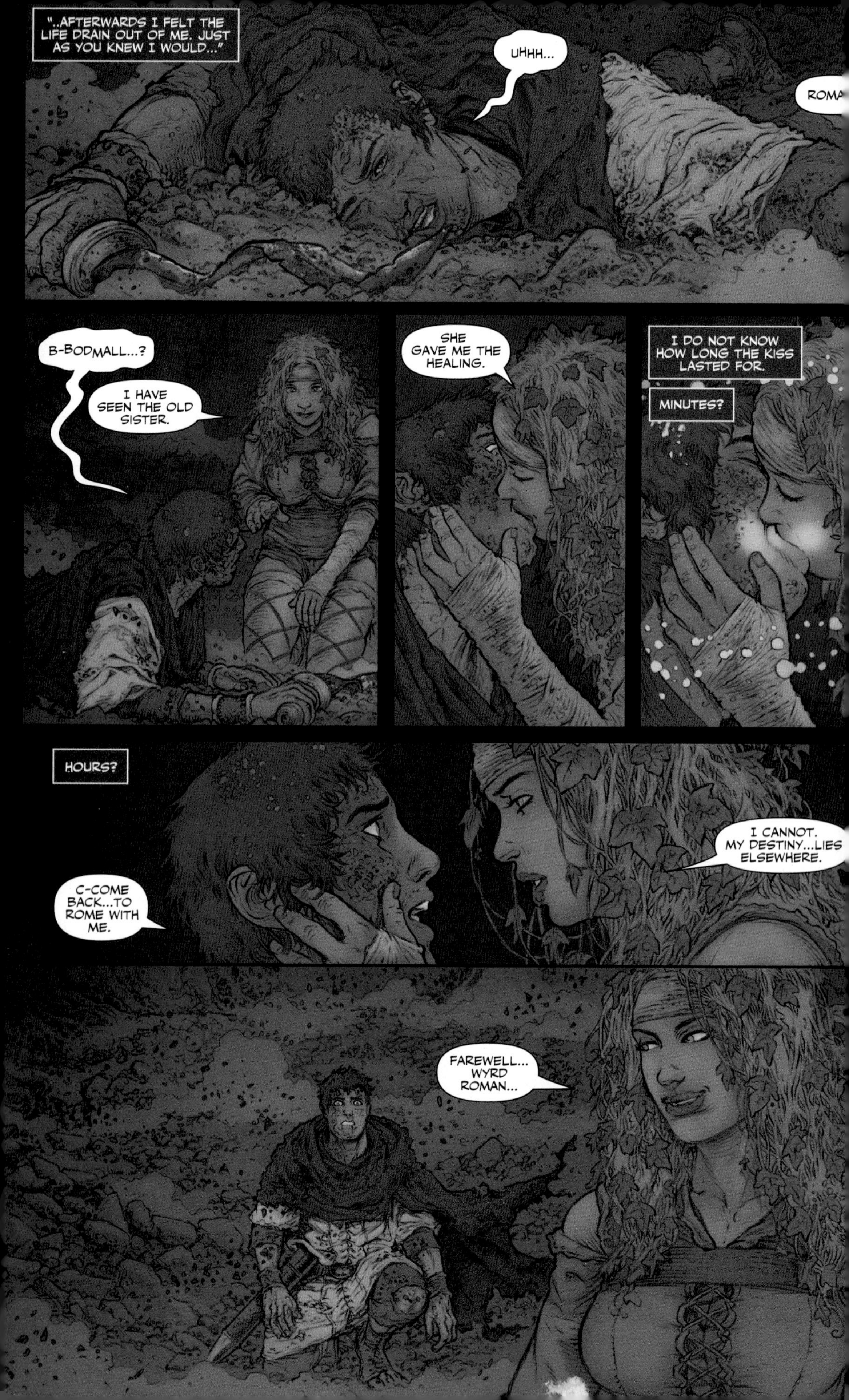
"..AFTERWARDS I FELT THE LIFE DRAIN OUT OF ME. JUST AS YOU KNEW I WOULD..."
UHHH...
B-BODMALL...?
I HAVE SEEN THE OLD SISTER.
SHE GAVE ME THE HEALING.
I DO NOT KNOW HOW LONG THE KISS LASTED FOR.
MINUTES?
HOURS?
C-COME BACK...TO ROME WITH ME.
I CANNOT. MY DESTINY...LIES ELSEWHERE.
FAREWELL... WYRD ROMAN...

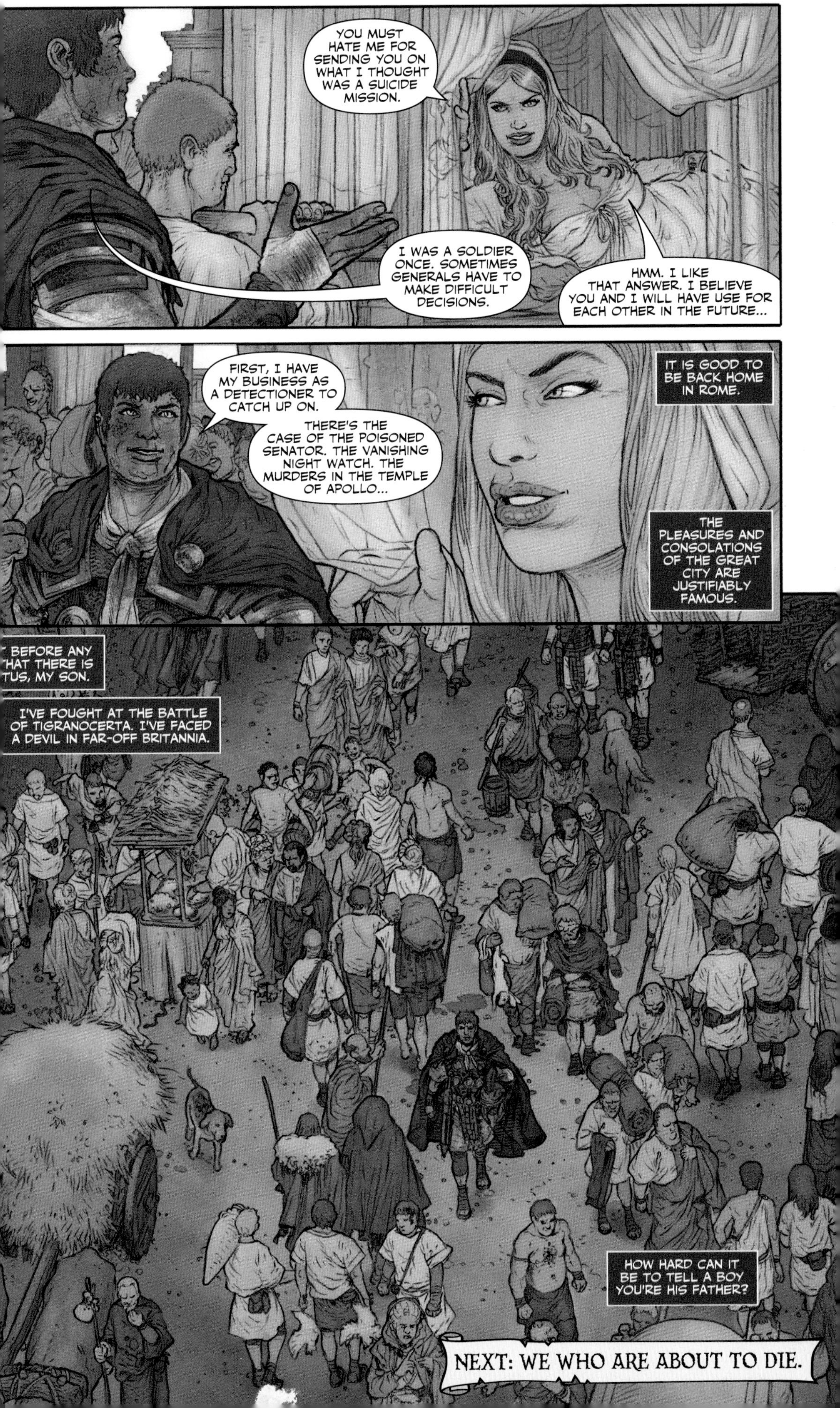
YOU MUST HATE ME FOR SENDING YOU ON WHAT I THOUGHT WAS A SUICIDE MISSION.
I WAS A SOLDIER ONCE. SOMETIMES GENERALS HAVE TO MAKE DIFFICULT DECISIONS.
HMM. I LIKE THAT ANSWER. I BELIEVE YOU AND I WILL HAVE USE FOR EACH OTHER IN THE FUTURE...
FIRST, I HAVE MY BUSINESS AS A DETECTIONER TO CATCH UP ON.
THERE'S THE CASE OF THE POISONED SENATOR. THE VANISHING NIGHT WATCH. THE MURDERS IN THE TEMPLE OF APOLLO...
IT IS GOOD TO BE BACK HOME IN ROME.
THE PLEASURES AND CONSOLATIONS OF THE GREAT CITY ARE JUSTIFIABLY FAMOUS.
BEFORE ANY
HAT THERE IS
TUS, MY SON.
I'VE FOUGHT AT THE BATTLE OF TIGRANOCERTA. I'VE FACED A DEVIL IN FAR-OFF BRITANNIA.
HOW HARD CAN IT BE TO TELL A BOY YOU'RE HIS FATHER?
NEXT: WE WHO ARE ABOUT TO DIE.

GALLERY

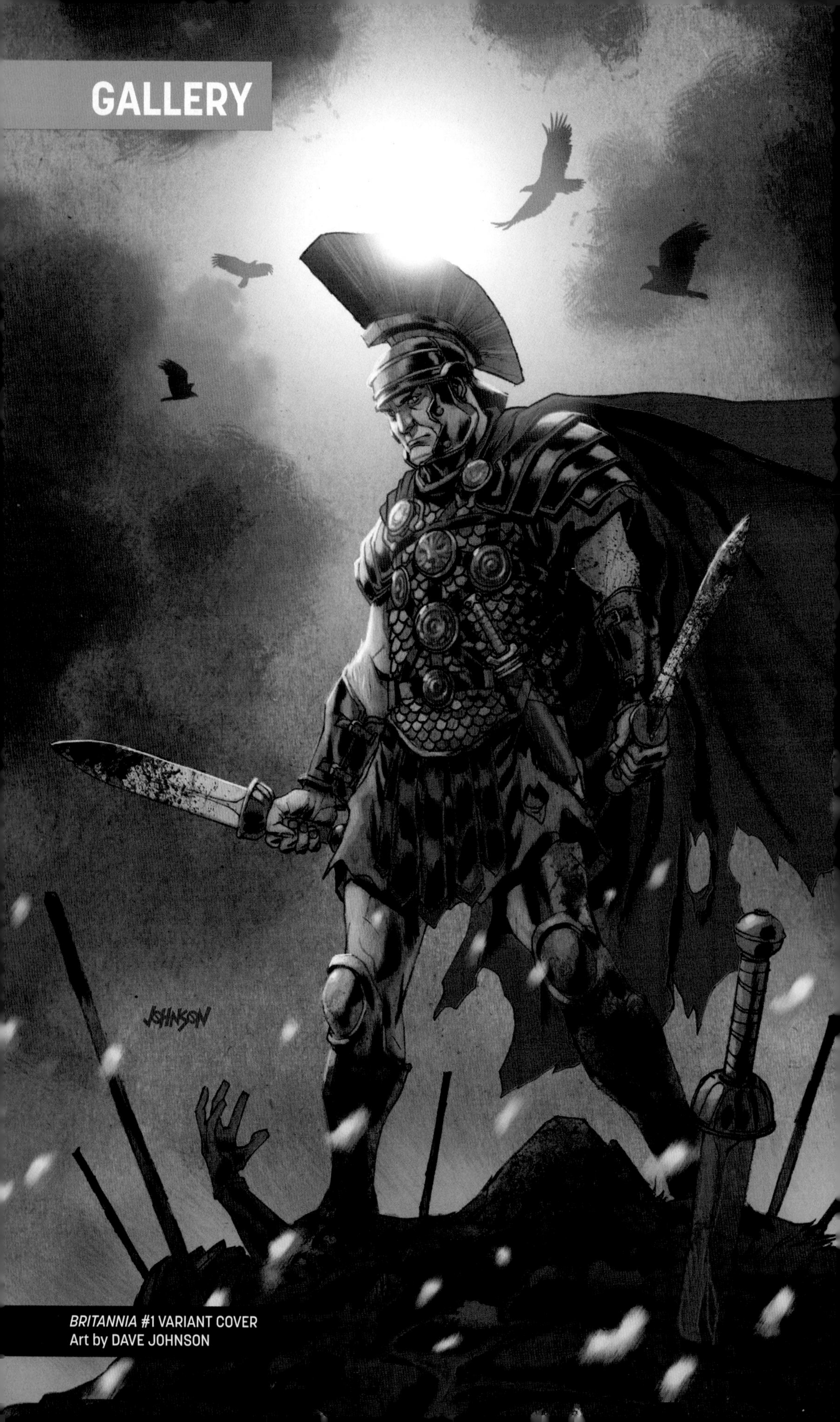
JOHNSON

BRITANNIA #1 VARIANT COVER
Art by DAVE JOHNSON

BRITANNIA #2 VARIANT COVER
Art by JUAN JOSÉ RYP with ANDREW DALHOUSE

BRITANNIA #3 VARIANT COVER
Art by KHARI EVANS with ULISES ARREOLA

BRITANNIA #4 COVER B
Art by ADAM GORHAM with MICHAEL SPICER

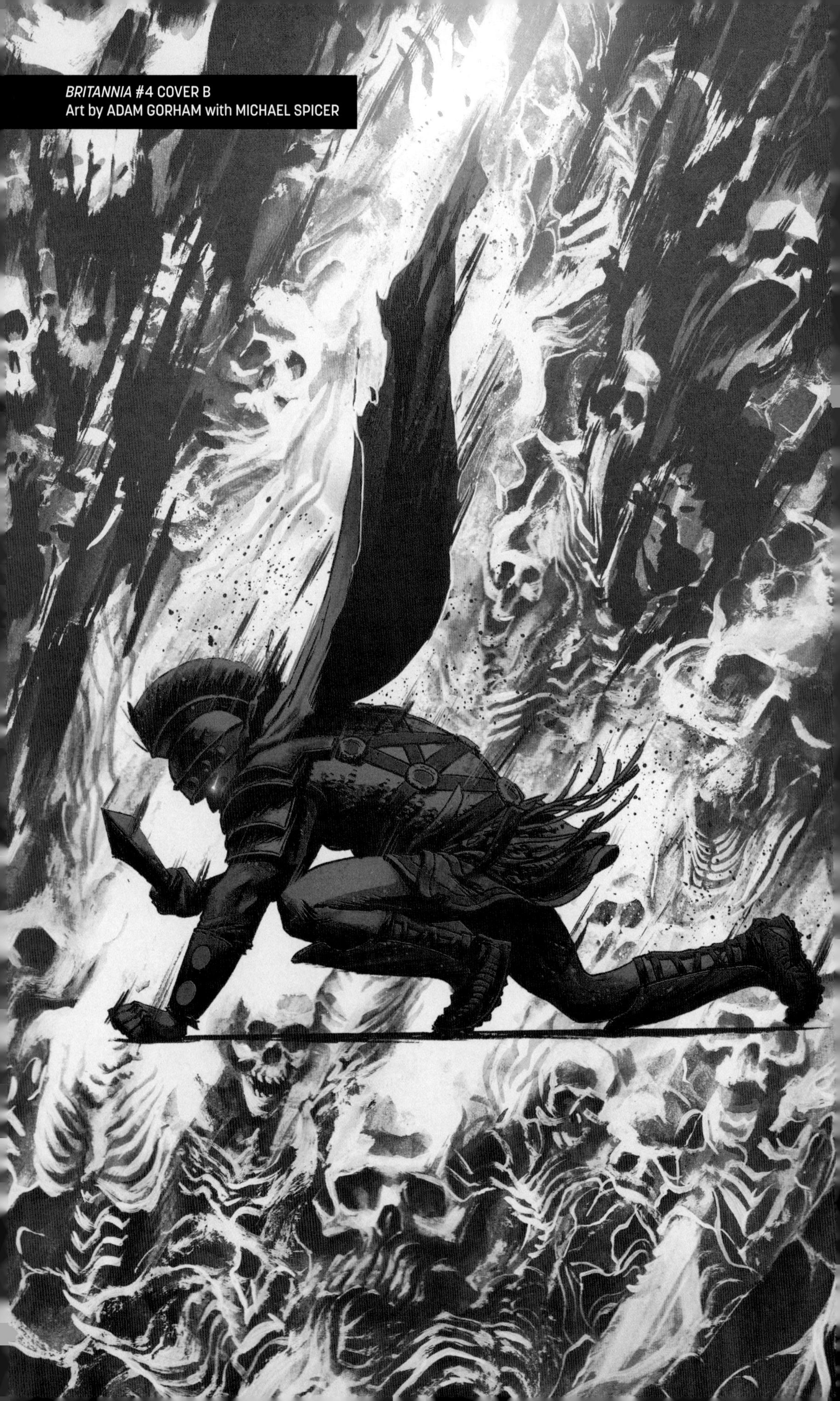

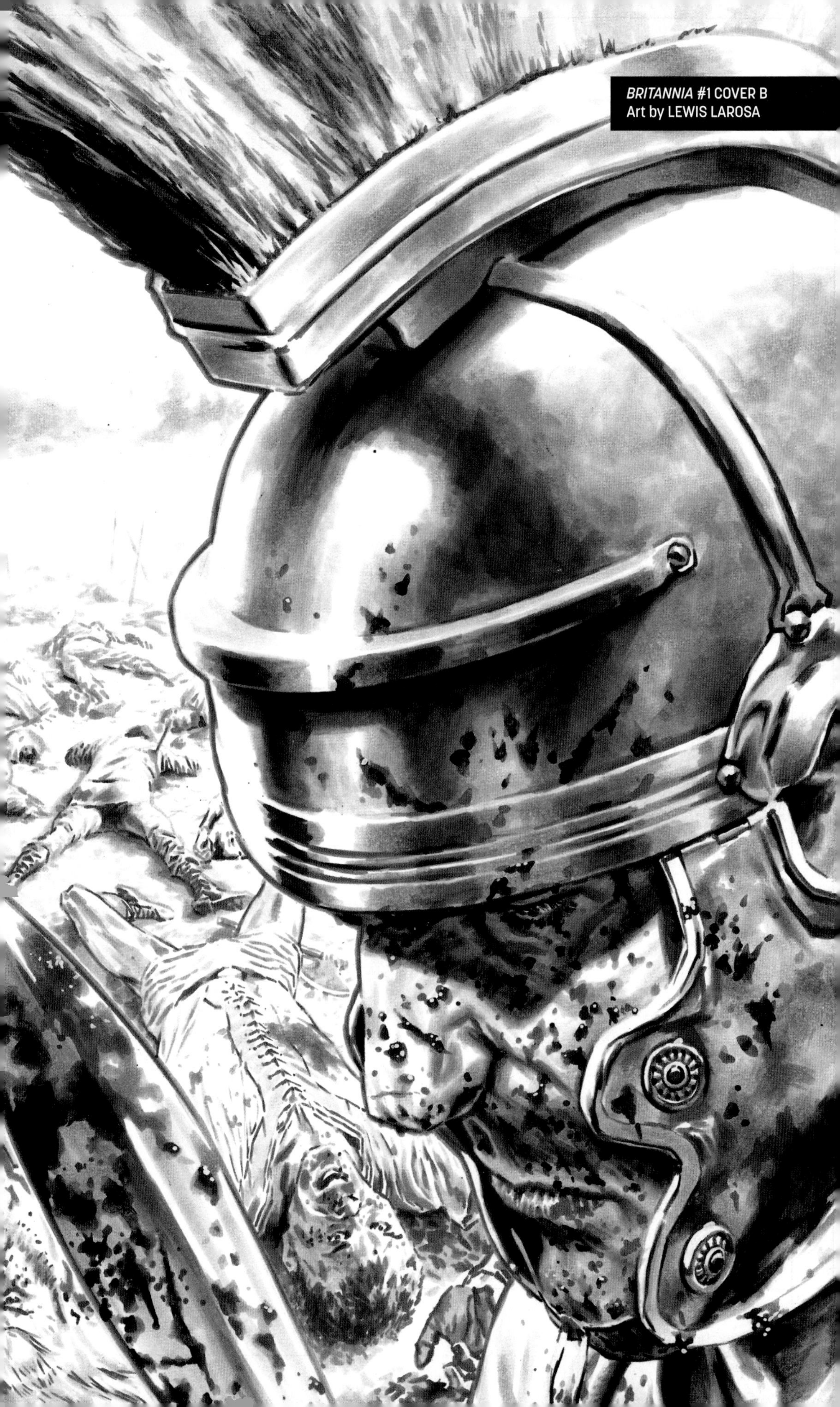

BRITANNIA #1 COVER B
Art by LEWIS LAROSA

BRITANNIA #1, pages 27-28
Art by JUAN JOSÉ RYP

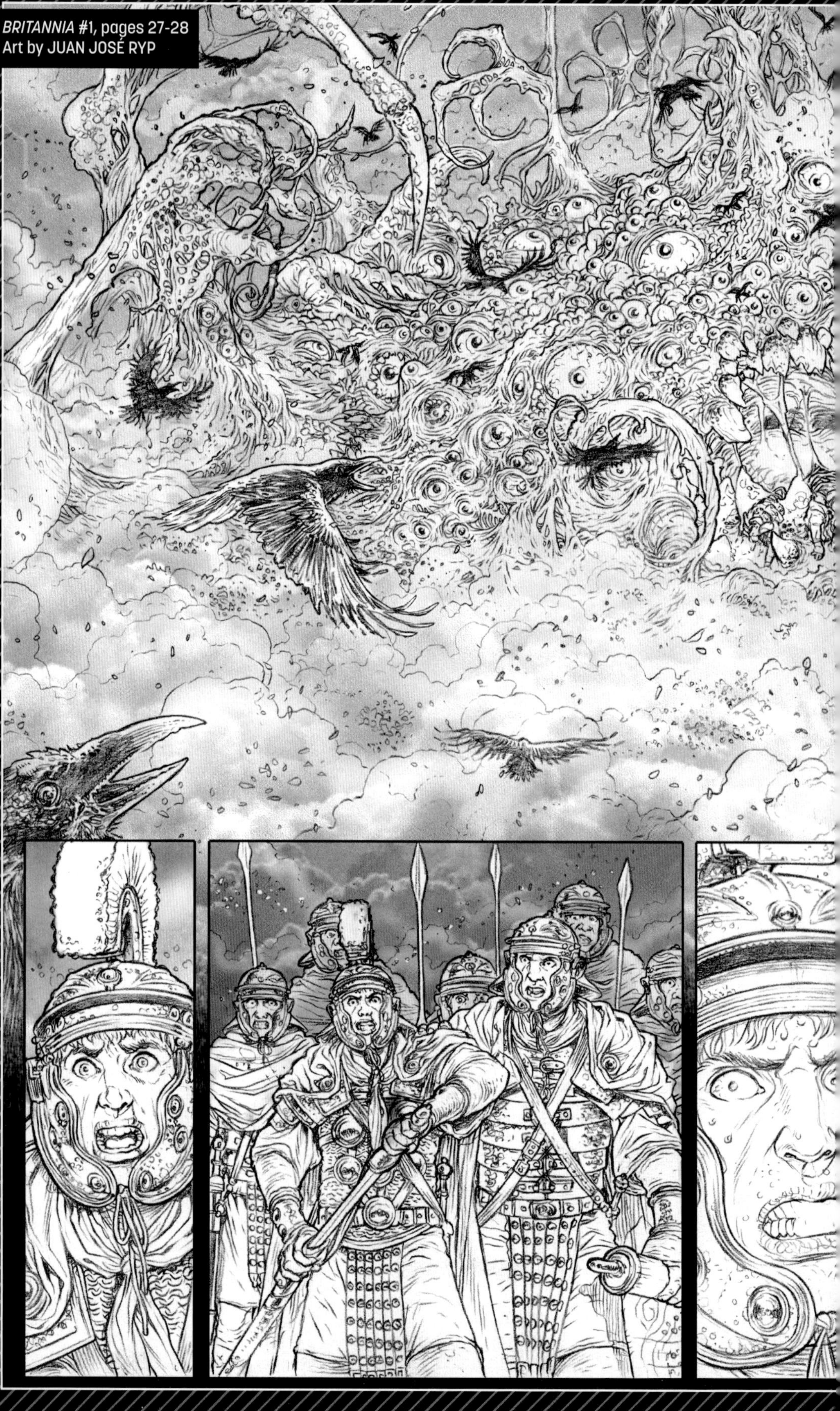

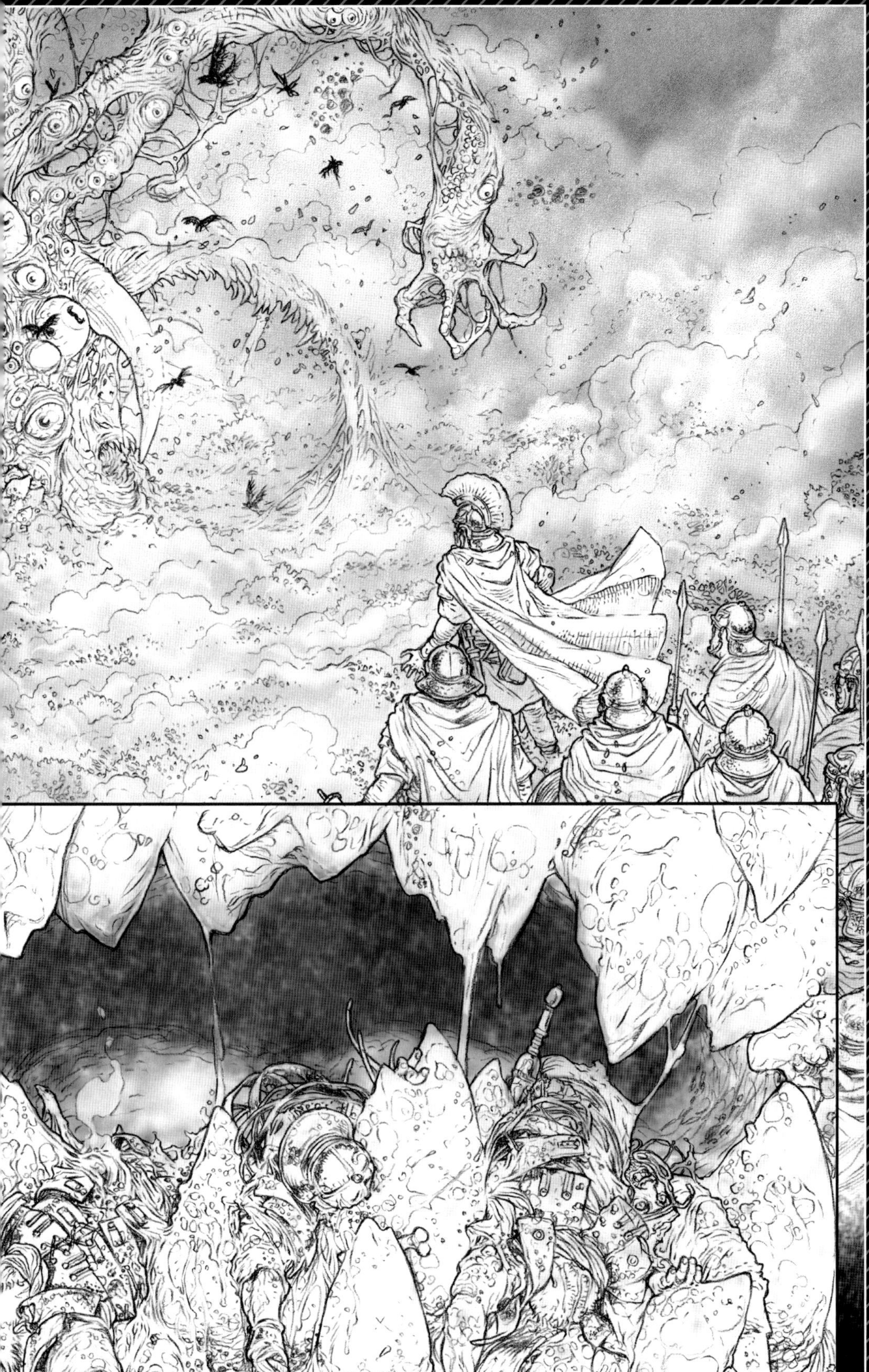

BRITANNIA #3, p. 3
Art by JUAN JOSÉ RYP

BRITANNIA #3, p. 17
Art by JUAN JOSÉ RYP

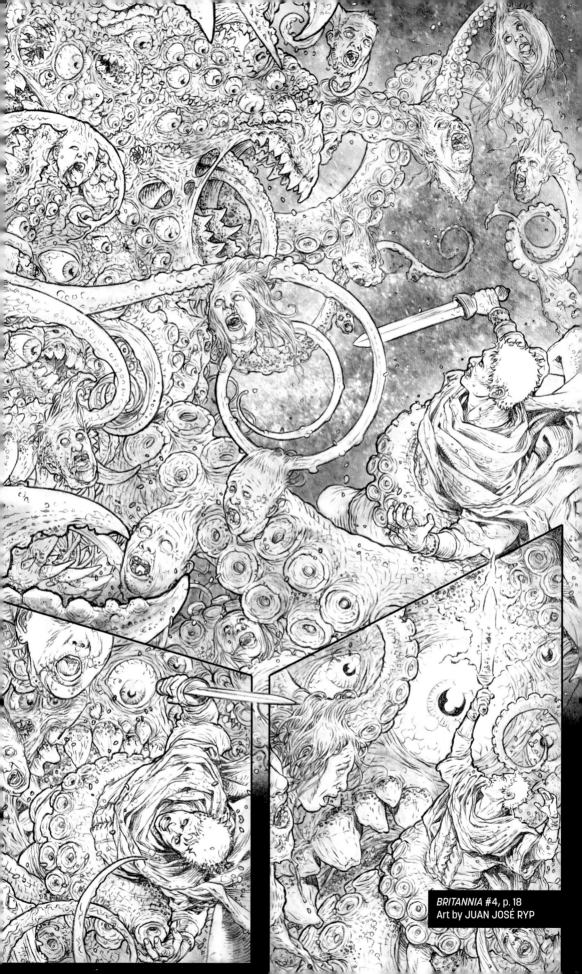

BRITANNIA #4, p. 18
Art by JUAN JOSÉ RYP

EXPLORE THE VALIANT UNIVERSE

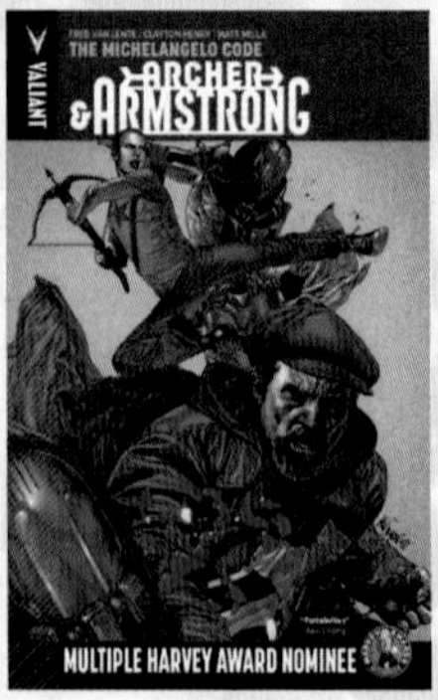
VALIANT
THE MICHELANGELO CODE
ARCHER & ARMSTRONG
MULTIPLE HARVEY AWARD NOMINEE

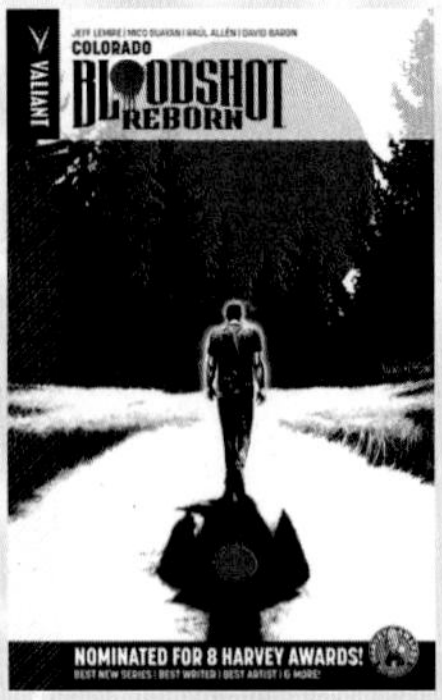
VALIANT
COLORADO
BLOODSHOT REBORN
NOMINATED FOR 8 HARVEY AWARDS!

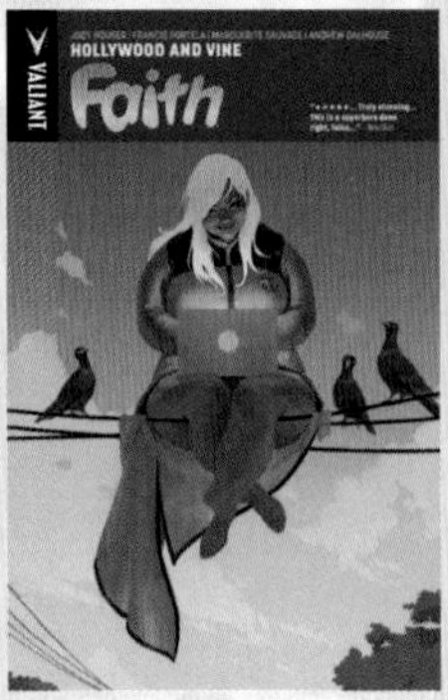
VALIANT
HOLLYWOOD AND VINE
Faith

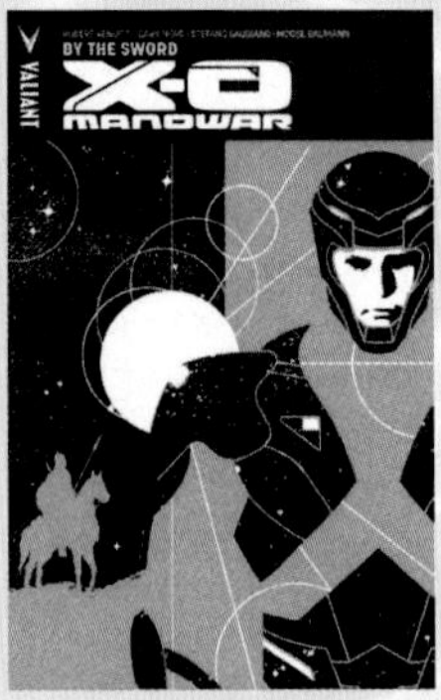
VALIANT
BY THE SWORD
X-O MANOWAR

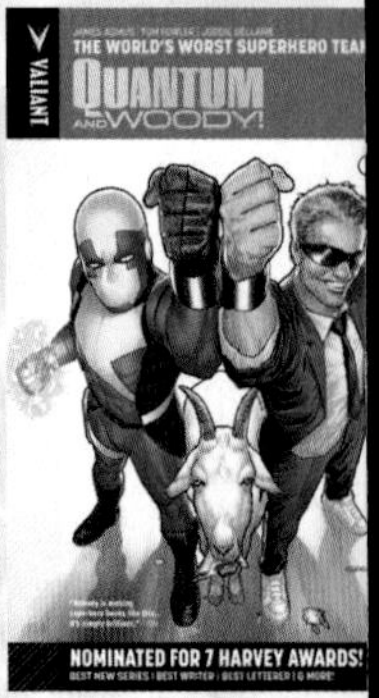
VALIANT
THE WORLD'S WORST SUPERHERO TEAM
QUANTUM AND WOODY!
NOMINATED FOR 7 HARVEY AWARDS!

4001 A.D.

4001 A.D.
ISBN: 9781682151433

4001 A.D.: Beyond New Japan
ISBN: 9781682151464

Rai Vol 4: 4001 A.D.
ISBN: 9781682151471

A&A: THE ADVENTURES OF ARCHER AND ARMSTRONG

Volume 1: In the Bag
ISBN: 9781682151495

Volume 2: Romance and Road Trips
ISBN: 9781682151716

ARCHER & ARMSTRONG

Volume 1: The Michelangelo Code
ISBN: 9780979640988

Volume 2: Wrath of the Eternal Warrior
ISBN: 9781939346049

Volume 3: Far Faraway
ISBN: 9781939346148

Volume 4: Sect Civil War
ISBN: 9781939346254

Volume 5: Mission: Improbable
ISBN: 9781939346353

Volume 6: American Wasteland
ISBN: 9781939346421

Volume 7: The One Percent and Other Tales
ISBN: 9781939346537

ARMOR HUNTERS

Armor Hunters
ISBN: 9781939346452

Armor Hunters: Bloodshot
ISBN: 9781939346469

Armor Hunters: Harbinger
ISBN: 9781939346506

Unity Vol. 3: Armor Hunters
ISBN: 9781939346445

X-O Manowar Vol. 7: Armor Hunters
ISBN: 9781939346476

BLOODSHOT

Volume 1: Setting the World on Fire
ISBN: 9780979640964

Volume 2: The Rise and the Fall
ISBN: 9781939346032

Volume 3: Harbinger Wars
ISBN: 9781939346124

Volume 4: H.A.R.D. Corps
ISBN: 9781939346193

Volume 5: Get Some!
ISBN: 9781939346315

Volume 6: The Glitch and Other Tales
ISBN: 9781939346711

BLOODSHOT REBORN

Volume 1: Colorado
ISBN: 9781939346674

Volume 2: The Hunt
ISBN: 9781939346827

Volume 3: The Analog Man
ISBN: 9781682151334

Volume 4: Bloodshot Island
ISBN: 9781682151952

BOOK OF DEATH

Book of Death
ISBN: 9781939346971

Book of Death: The Fall of the Valiant Universe
ISBN: 9781939346988

DEAD DROP

ISBN: 9781939346858

THE DEATH-DEFYING DOCTOR MIRAGE

Volume 1
ISBN: 9781939346490

Volume 2: Second Lives
ISBN: 9781682151297

THE DELINQUENTS

ISBN: 9781939346513

DIVINITY

Volume 1
ISBN: 9781939346766

Volume 2
ISBN: 9781682151518

ETERNAL WARRIOR

Volume 1: Sword of the Wild
ISBN: 9781939346209

Volume 2: Eternal Emperor
ISBN: 9781939346292

Volume 3: Days of Steel
ISBN: 9781939346742

WRATH OF THE ETERNAL WARRIOR

Volume 1: Risen
ISBN: 9781682151235

Volumel 2: Labyrinth
ISBN: 9781682151594

FAITH

Faith Vol 1: Hollywood and Vine
ISBN: 9781682151402

Faith Vol 2: California Scheming
ISBN: 9781682151631

HARBINGER

Volume 1: Omega Rising
ISBN: 9780979640957

Volume 2: Renegades
ISBN: 9781939346025

Volume 3: Harbinger Wars
ISBN: 9781939346117

Volume 4: Perfect Day
ISBN: 9781939346155

Volume 5: Death of a Renegade
ISBN: 9781939346339

Volume 6: Omegas
ISBN: 9781939346384

EXPLORE THE VALIANT UNIVERSE

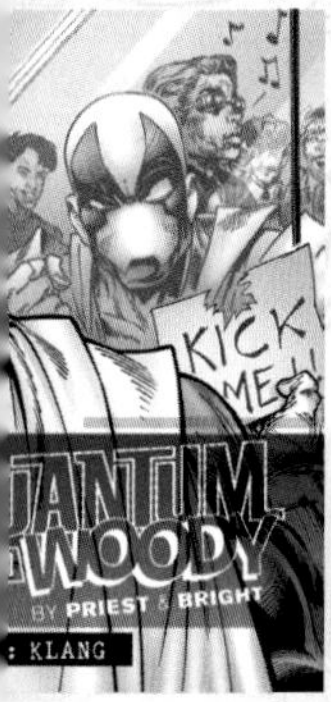
KICK ME!!
ANTUM
WOODY
BY PRIEST & BRIGHT
: KLANG

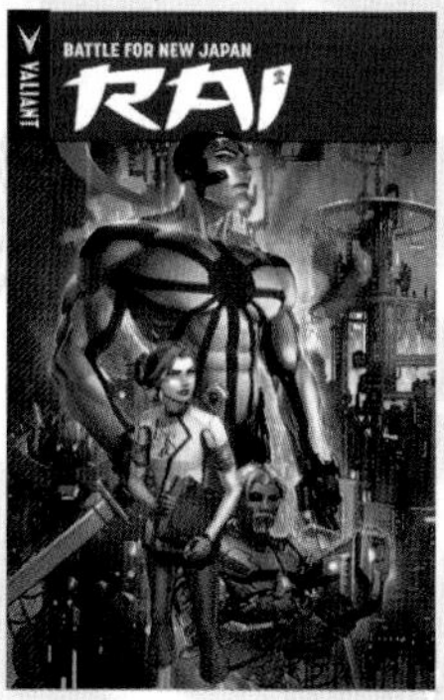
VALIANT
BATTLE FOR NEW JAPAN
RAI

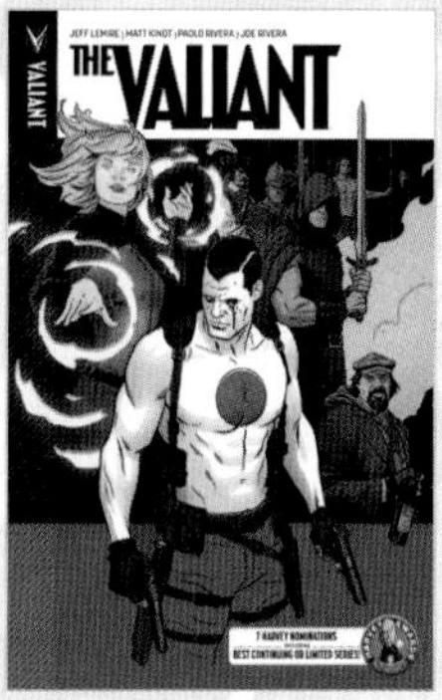
VALIANT
THE VALIANT

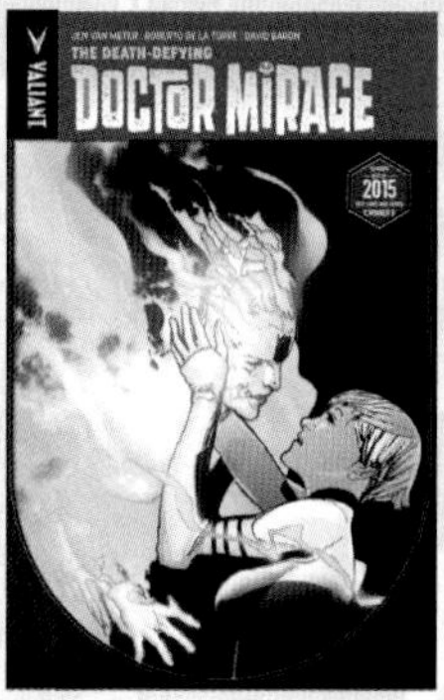
VALIANT
THE DEATH-DEFYING
DOCTOR MIRAGE

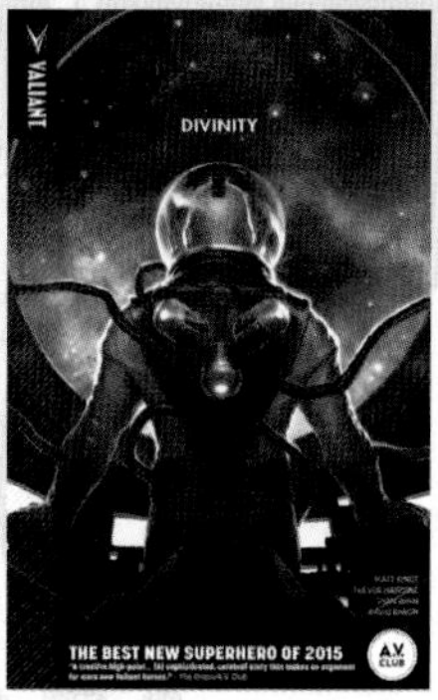
VALIANT
DIVINITY
THE BEST NEW SUPERHERO OF 2015

RBINGER WARS

ger Wars
781939346094

hot Vol. 3: Harbinger Wars
781939346124

ger Vol. 3: Harbinger Wars
781939346117

PERIUM

1: Collecting Monsters
781939346759

2: Broken Angels
781939346896

3: The Vine Imperative
781682151112

4: Stormbreak
781682151372

JAK

1: Weaponeer
781939346667

2: The Shadow Wars
781939346940

3: Operation: Deadside
781682151259

4: The Siege of King's Castle
781682151617

ANTUM AND WOODY

1: The World's Worst Superhero Team
781939346186

2: In Security
781939346230

3: Crooked Pasts, Present Tense
781939346391

4: Quantum and Woody Must Die!
781939346629

ANTUM AND WOODY PRIEST & BRIGHT

1: Klang
781939346780

2: Switch
781939346803

Volume 3: And So...
ISBN: 9781939346865

Volume 4: Q2 - The Return
ISBN: 9781682151099

RAI

Volume 1: Welcome to New Japan
ISBN: 9781939346414

Volume 2: Battle for New Japan
ISBN: 9781939346612

Volume 3: The Orphan
ISBN: 9781939346841

Rai Vol 4: 4001 A.D.
ISBN: 9781682151471

SHADOWMAN

Volume 1: Birth Rites
ISBN: 9781939346001

Volume 2: Darque Reckoning
ISBN: 9781939346056

Volume 3: Deadside Blues
ISBN: 9781939346162

Volume 4: Fear, Blood, And Shadows
ISBN: 9781939346278

Volume 5: End Times
ISBN: 9781939346377

SHADOWMAN BY ENNIS & WOOD

ISBN: 9781682151358

IVAR, TIMEWALKER

Volume 1: Making History
ISBN: 9781939346636

Volume 2: Breaking History
ISBN: 9781939346834

Volume 3: Ending History
ISBN: 9781939346995

UNITY

Volume 1: To Kill a King
ISBN: 9781939346261

Volume 2: Trapped by Webnet
ISBN: 9781939346346

Volume 3: Armor Hunters
ISBN: 9781939346445

Volume 4: The United
ISBN: 9781939346544

Volume 5: Homefront
ISBN: 9781939346797

Volume 6: The War-Monger
ISBN: 9781939346902

Volume 7: Revenge of the Armor Hunters
ISBN: 9781682151136

THE VALIANT

ISBN: 9781939346605

VALIANT ZEROES AND ORIGINS

ISBN: 9781939346582

X-O MANOWAR

Volume 1: By the Sword
ISBN: 9780979640940

Volume 2: Enter Ninjak
ISBN: 9780979640995

Volume 3: Planet Death
ISBN: 9781939346087

Volume 4: Homecoming
ISBN: 9781939346179

Volume 5: At War With Unity
ISBN: 9781939346247

Volume 6: Prelude to Armor Hunters
ISBN: 9781939346407

Volume 7: Armor Hunters
ISBN: 9781939346476

Volume 8: Enter: Armorines
ISBN: 9781939346551

Volume 9: Dead Hand
ISBN: 9781939346650

Volume 10: Exodus
ISBN: 9781939346933

Volume 11: The Kill List
ISBN: 9781682151273

Volume 12: Long Live the King
ISBN: 9781682151655

X-O Manowar Vol. 13: Succession and Other Tales
ISBN: 9781682151754

EXPLORE THE VALIANT UNIVERSE

VALIANT
HARBINGER
DELUXE EDITION 2

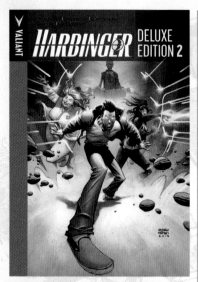

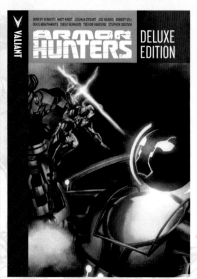

Omnibuses

Archer & Armstrong: The Complete Classic Omnibus
ISBN: 9781939346872
Collecting ARCHER & ARMSTRONG (1992) #0-26, ETERNAL WARRIOR (1992) #25 along with ARCHER & ARMSTRONG: THE FORMATION OF THE SECT.

Quantum and Woody: The Complete Classic Omnibus
ISBN: 9781939346360
Collecting QUANTUM AND WOODY (1997) #0, 1-21 and #32, THE GOAT: H.A.E.D.U.S. #1, and X-O MANOWAR (1996) #16

X-O Manowar Classic Omnibus Vol. 1
ISBN: 9781939346308
Collecting X-O MANOWAR (1992) #0-30, ARMORINES #0, X-O DATABASE #1, as well as material from SECRETS OF THE VALIANT UNIVERSE #1

Deluxe Editions

Archer & Armstrong Deluxe Edition Book 1
ISBN: 9781939346223
Collecting ARCHER & ARMSTRONG #0-13

Archer & Armstrong Deluxe Edition Book 2
ISBN: 9781939346957
Collecting ARCHER & ARMSTRONG #14-25, ARCHER & ARMSTRONG: ARCHER #0 and BLOODSHOT AND H.A.R.D. CORPS #20-21.

Armor Hunters Deluxe Edition
ISBN: 9781939346728
Collecting Armor Hunters #1-4, Armor Hunters: Aftermath #1, Armor Hunters: Bloodshot #1-3, Armor Hunters: Harbinger #1-3, Unity #8-11, and X-O MANOWAR #23-29

Bloodshot Deluxe Edition Book 1
ISBN: 9781939346216
Collecting BLOODSHOT #1-13

Bloodshot Deluxe Edition Book 2
ISBN: 9781939346810
Collecting BLOODSHOT AND H.A.R.D. CORPS #14-23, BLOODSHOT #24-25, BLOODSHOT #0, BLOODSHOT AND H.A.R.D. CORPS: H.A.R.D. CORPS #0, along with ARCHER & ARMSTRONG #18-19

Bloodshot Reborn Deluxe Edition Book 1
ISBN: 978-1-68215-155-6
Collecting BLOODSHOT REBORN #1-13

ROBERT VENDITTI | MATT KINDT | JOSHUA DYSART | JOE HARRIS | ROBERT GILL
DOUG BRAITHWAITE | DIEGO BERNARD | TREVOR HAIRSINE | STEPHEN SEGOVIA
VALIANT
ARMOR HUNTERS
DELUXE EDITION

Book of Death Deluxe Edition
ISBN: 9781682151150
Collecting BOOK OF DEATH #1-4, BOOK OF DEATH: THE FALL OF BLOODSHOT #1, BOOK OF DEATH: THE FALL OF NINJAK #1, BOOK OF DEATH: THE FALL OF HARBINGER #1, and BOOK OF DEATH: THE FALL OF X-O MANOWAR #1.

The Death-Defying Doctor Mirage Deluxe Edition
ISBN: 978-1-68215-153-2
Collecting THE DEATH-DEFYING DR. MIRAGE #1-5 and THE DEATH-DEFYING DR. MIRAGE: SECOND LIVES #1-4

Divinity Deluxe Edition
ISBN: 97819393460993
Collecting DIVNITY #1-4

Faith: Hollywood & Vine Deluxe Edition
ISBN: 978-1-68215-201-0
Collecting FAITH #1-4 and HARBINGER: FAITH #0

Harbinger Deluxe Edition Book 1
ISBN: 9781939346131
Collecting HARBINGER #0-14

Harbinger Deluxe Edition Book 2
ISBN: 9781939346773
Collecting HARBINGER #15-25, HARBINGER: OMEGAS #1-3, and HARBINGER: BLEEDING MONK #0

Harbinger Wars Deluxe Edition
ISBN: 9781939346322
Collecting HARBINGER WARS #1-4, HARBINGER #11-14, and BLOODSHOT #10-13

Ivar, Timewalker Deluxe Edition Book 1
ISBN: 9781682151198
Collecting IVAR, TIMEWALKER #1-12

Ninjak Deluxe Edition Book 1
ISBN: 978-1-68215-157-0
Collecting NINJAK #1-13

Quantum and Woody Deluxe Edition Book 1
ISBN: 9781939346681
Collecting QUANTUM AND WOODY #1-12 and QUANTUM AND WOODY: THE GOAT #0

Q2: The Return of Quantum and Woody Deluxe Edition
ISBN: 9781939346568
Collecting Q2: THE RETURN OF QUANTUM AND WOODY #1-5

JIM SHOOTER | DAVID LAPHAM
VALIANT
CHILDREN OF THE EIGHTH DAY
HARBINGER
VALIANT MASTERS

Rai Deluxe Edition Book 1
ISBN: 9781682151174
Collecting RAI #1-12, along with material fr
#1 PLUS EDITION and RAI #5 PLUS EDITION

Shadowman Deluxe Edition Book 1
ISBN: 9781939346438
Collecting SHADOWMAN #0-10

Shadowman Deluxe Edition Book 2
ISBN: 9781682151075
Collecting SHADOWMAN #11-16, SHADOWM
#13X, SHADOWMAN: END TIMES #1-3 and P
MAMBO #0

Unity Deluxe Edition Book 1
ISBN: 9781939346575
Collecting UNITY #0-14

The Valiant Deluxe Edition
ISBN: 97819393460986
Collecting THE VALIANT #1-4

X-O Manowar Deluxe Edition Book 1
ISBN: 9781939346100
Collecting X-O MANOWAR #1-14

X-O Manowar Deluxe Edition Book 2
ISBN: 9781939346520
Collecting X-O MANOWAR #15-22, and UNITY

X-O Manowar Deluxe Edition Book 3
ISBN: 9781682151310
Collecting X-O MANOWAR #23-29 and ARM
HUNTERS #1-4.

Valiant Masters

Bloodshot Vol. 1 - Blood of the Machine
ISBN: 9780979640933

H.A.R.D. Corps Vol. 1 - Search and Destroy
ISBN: 9781939346285

Harbinger Vol. 1 - Children of the Eighth Da
ISBN: 9781939346483

Ninjak Vol. 1 - Black Water
ISBN: 9780979640971

Rai Vol. 1 - From Honor to Strength
ISBN: 9781939346070

Shadowman Vol. 1 - Spirits Within
ISBN: 9781939346018

Ꝋ VALIANT | THE STORY STARTS HERE

THE DEATH-DEFYING
DOCTOR MIRAGE

A breathtaking, heartbreaking journey
into the realms of the unknown!
From Eisner Award-nominated writer

JEN VAN METER

And visionary artist

ROBERTO DE LA TORRE

"Stunning." – io9

DIVINITY

An all-new vision of 21st-century science fiction!
From New York Times best-selling writer

MATT KINDT

And blockbuster artist

TREVOR HAIRSINE

"High concept sci-fi executed perfectly..." – WIRED

THE VALIANT

A visionary adventure spotlighting a cast of heroes
and villains from across the Valiant Universe!
From New York Times best-selling writers

JEFF LEMIRE and MATT KINDT

And Eisner Award winning artist

PAOLO RIVERA

"A blockbuster that still feels personal... Don't miss it."
-Entertainment Weekly

VALIANT®

BRITANNIA®

VOLUME TWO: **WE WHO ARE ABOUT TO DIE**

VALIANT'S CRITICALLY ACCLAIMED, 10-TIME SOLD-OUT MAGNUM OPUS RETURNS WITH A BRAND-NEW JOURNEY INTO MYTH AND MYSTERY, FROM COMICS MASTER PETER MILLIGAN (*SHADE, THE CHANGING MAN*) AND INCENDIARY ARTIST JUAN JOSÉ RYP (BRITANNIA!)

PETER MILLIGAN | JUAN JOSÉ RYP
VALIANT
BRITANNIA

Fifty thousand Romans stand on their feet, watching from the rafters of the coliseum with captured breath as Achillia, a Gladiator unlike any that Rome has seen before, faces incredible odds - one lone warrior against five of Rome's greatest. Such is the tradition, when a female gladiator enters the fray. When the carnage is complete, the coliseum roars its approval as Achillia stands victorious. Now only one match away from winning her freedom, she has begun to gain renown. The women of Rome, suppressed by their husbands and fathers, have noticed. The men of Rome, husbands and fathers to a growing horde of women entertaining ideas of independence, have noticed as well.

On the other side of Rome, a strange mystery swirls through the Palatine Hill. In the dead of night, down winding alleys, Rome's elite swear that they see visions of a blood-soaked Apollo walking thecity...visions that are driving them mad. Even more are becoming sick with weird fever god-dreams. Panic ensues in the city. The Chief Vestal, Rubria, is arrested by Emperor Nero and threatened with crucifixion unless the deadly curse that's fallen on Rome is lifted. She asks Antonius Axia, hero of Britannia and Rome's only detective, for help. She offers only one clue...the gladiator Achillia.

Collecting BRITANNIA: WE WHO ARE ABOUT TO DIE #1-4.

TRADE PAPERBACK
ISBN: 978-1-68215-213-3